Board Games as Media

Board Games as Media

Paul Booth

BLOOMSBURY ACADEMIC
NEW YORK • LONDON • OXFORD • NEW DELHI • SYDNEY

BLOOMSBURY ACADEMIC
Bloomsbury Publishing Inc
1385 Broadway, New York, NY 10018, USA

BLOOMSBURY, BLOOMSBURY ACADEMIC and the Diana logo are trademarks of
Bloomsbury Publishing Plc

First published in the United States of America 2021

Cover design by Namkwan Cho
Cover image © Shutterstock.com

ISBN: HB: 978-1-5013-5716-9
PB: 978-1-5013-5717-6
ePDF: 978-1-5013-5719-0
eBook: 978-1-5013-5718-3

Typeset by Deanta Global Publishing Services, Chennai, India
Printed and bound in the United States of America

To find out more about our authors and books visit www.bloomsbury.com and
sign up for our newsletters.

To the good sports, the happy losers, the magnanimous victors;
To the laughers, the food orderers, the rules pedants;
To the play-my-turn-while-I-make-the-coffee'ers;
To the board gamers.

And to Brendan Riley, the best of them all.

Contents

Illustrations

Figures

All photos taken by the author, unless otherwise noted.

Tables

Acknowledgments

To say that this book wouldn't be possible without the following people would be an understatement. So much of what you are currently reading wouldn't be here if not for the incredible people with whom I've had the pleasure of talking, researching, and playing games. This book first came to life years ago in a conversation I had with Katie Gallof of Bloomsbury. Without her encouragement, it would never have seen the light of day. She is extraordinary.

Many of the ideas in this book were workshopped or discussed with a great number of people. Thanks to those that offered feedback on chapters: Emily Goldstein, Sam Illingworth, Kendra Knight, Andy Matthews, and Paul Wake; as well as some specific comments on individual points: Megen de Bruin-Molé, James Chapman, Pam Gardner, David Gunkel, Matt Hills, Jill Hopke, Cathy Johnson, Ken Krimstein, Nicolle Lamerichs, Alfred Martin, Asher Minix, Line Nybro Petersen, Brendan Riley, Katherine Tanski, Barbara Willard, and Jason Winslade. Thanks to the 2019 SCMS Seminar on Toys and Material Culture, organized by Jonathan Ray Lee and Meredith Bok, and attended by Ahmed Asi, Nick Bestor, Zach Horton, Reem Hilu, John Murray, Anastasia Salter, Evan Torner, and Benjamin Woo. Portions of this book have previously appeared as "Missing a Piece: (The Lack of) Board Game Scholarship in Media Studies," *Velvet Light Trap* 81 (2018): 57–60 and "Board Gamers as Fans," in *The Routledge Companion to Media Fandom*, edited by Suzanne Scott and Melissa Click, 428– 436. New York, NY: Routledge, 2018. I'm grateful to the editors for permission to use this material.

I'm lucky to live in Chicago, where a supportive network of board gamers thrives. Two game stores, Chicagoland Games (Dice Dojo) and Good Games, announced my survey and have been wonderful about chatting about games and recommending interesting ones to try. Bonus Round Café run by my friends Courtney Hartley and Drew Lovell is a wonderful place to enjoy a meal and a game, and I definitely recommend a visit to anyone coming to Chicago. There are a number of game groups around the city, but [toggle gaming] started by Andrew Smith and Kevin Zimmerman has been a great group to play with. I'm thankful to Andrew Smith, Rob Huber, and Brendan Riley, who have been instrumental within the group.

Thanks to everyone who played games with me to help in the research—Stephanie Ailor, Tony Bruno, Russell Ford, Alan Greenberg, Ashlyn Keefe, Wes Makin, Joann Martyn, Avery Riley, Brendan Riley, Finn Riley, Jenny Riley, Keisuke Sista, Ryan Valencia, Jenna Wolf, and Ryan Wolf. Special thanks to Ashlyn and Brendan for bridging multiple groups, to Russell for the title to Chapter 2, and to Ryan for some marathon Red Raven sessions.

To the 1,000 or so people who took my survey, a heartfelt thank you! And to the 65 who followed up by answering even more questions, I am eternally grateful. This book was made immensely richer by the kind participation of all the people whom I had the pleasure of interviewing. Space prevented me from printing as much of your answers as I would have liked (seriously, there was *so much* good material, I could write three more books worth!), but even if I didn't get to put it in this book specifically, know that your comments helped shape the content in both small and massive ways. Thank you to Kelly North Adams (kellynorthadams.com), Omari Akil (omariakil.com), Victor Aldridge, Tiffany Caires (@TheOneTAR), Victoria Caña (catquartetgames.com), Jay Carmichael (3 Minute Board Games), Isaac Childres (cephalofair.com), Christopher Chung (flashforwardgames.itch.io), Jonathan Cox (JonGetsGames.com), Rob Daviau (robdaviau.com), James Ernest (cheapass.com/), MaryMartha Ford (theultimateclapback.com), Jonathan Gilmour (@jongilmour), Paul Grogan (gaming-rules.com), Richard Ham (Rahdo Runs Through), Elizabeth Hargrave (elizhargrave.com), James Hudson (druidcitygames.com), Mandi Hutchinson (@boardgamerpinup), Christian Kang (@takeyourchits), Carla Kopp (weirdgiraffegames.com), Emma Larkins (emmalarkins.com), Ryan Lauket (redravengames.squarespace.com), Richard Launius, Sen-Foong Lim (bamboozlebrothers.com), Justin Lowe (@ggCoshade), Chaz Marler (Pair of Dice Paradise), Kathleen Mercury (kathleenmercury.com), Julio Nazario (@Junazaru), Juliana Patel (www.escaperoominabox.com/), Paul Peterson (paul-peterson.net), Danny Quach, Behrooz "Bez" Shahriari (stuffbybez.com/), Rodney Smith (@WatchItPlayed), Daniel Solis (danielsolisblog.blogspot.com), Janice Turner (wrengames.co.uk), Nikki Valens (@valens116), Martin Wallace, Sophie Williams (needycatgames.com), Calvin Wong (boardgamesdirect.com.au), Jonathan Ying (jonathan-ying.squarespace.com/work), and Eric Yurko (whatsericplaying.com/). And thanks to Jason Mittell for putting me in touch with Elizabeth Hargrave.

To my colleagues at DePaul University, I am thankful for your support in providing me time and resources for this project. Parts of this project were funded by a University Research Council grant. I'm also grateful for the chance to try out some of these ideas in classes, and I thank Luisela Alvaray, Samantha Close, Blair Davis, Michael DeAngelis, and Kelly Kessler for not batting an eye when I said I want to teach Board Games as Media. My thanks to the students in that course, whose thoughtful discussions helped make the book stronger and tighter. Special shout-outs to Rachel Fernandez, Katie Walsh, and Rebecca Woods for the fine editorial eyes.

Finally, and always, thanks to my favorite furry partner, Slinky. Even if you're knocking over meeples or stealing carrots from the table, there's no teammate I'd rather have by my side.

Introduction

Board Games as Media

In an April 07, 2018, *Saturday Night Live* (*SNL*) sketch, a group of friends are sitting around a table, playing the popular board game *Life* (1960, Hasbro). The group is multicultural, with a Black man, a white couple, and a Latinx woman all playing the game together. As with most *SNL* parody commercials, the sketch is spot-on: the camera zooms in on the characters having way too much fun with a relatively tame board game. They laugh uproariously as they pull cards at random like "I'm a Rock Star!" and "I'm going to law school!" The game—and the sketch—becomes more poignant, however, when the Latinx character (Melissa Villaseñor) draws a card that says, "I'm a dreamer . . . ." The announcer responds: "You bet! Introducing the *Game of Life*, DACA Edition!" Referencing both the Development, Relief, and Education for Alien Minors (DREAM) Act and the Deferred Action for Childhood Arrivals (DACA), the sketch overtly comments on the then-current Trump administration's claim that "DACA is Dead." Both the DREAM Act and DACA were US policies toward immigrants in the United States. The DREAM Act stated that some children brought to the United States illegally while underage were eligible to stay, while DACA stated that some undocumented immigrants brought to the United States as children were eligible to work.

The sketch continues, critiquing the bureaucracy, racism, and unfairness of the immigration system. "OK," says Villaseñor's character, "what are the rules?" Her friend responds, consulting the rulebook, "Says here you gotta get papers." "How do I get papers?" Villaseñor asks, more trepidatiously. The announcer comes back by saying, "It's fun! You'll wander aimlessly down the path to citizenship, but do it fast or you will get sent back to Honduras!" "Back to? I've never been to Honduras!" "Surprise! You were brought here as a baby." The sketch takes the lesson even further by unveiling the "Immigration court expansion pack," a huge board with flames, a warzone, barbed wire fences, and gravestones. "Now you'll need a lawyer card to get your papers! But you'll need a job card to get money for a lawyer card. Figure that out!"

Obviously, most of the board games that we play in our everyday life usually don't comment so pointedly on contemporary political issues, but the *SNL* sketch reveals a number of underlying issues that I hope to explore in this book. First, and perhaps stating the obvious, it's important that *the characters are playing a board game.* All the characters in this sketch are relatively young, representative of millennials and Gen Z. If we think about typical board gamers, the common image usually isn't one of young, hip people—we often think of rainy afternoons with grandparents playing endless games of *Scrabble* (1948, Hasbro) or *Monopoly* (1933, Hasbro). The sketch speaks to the rise in popularity of the board game as a cultural pastime for younger generations. Of course, board games are an ancient form of entertainment, and their popularity waxes and wanes over time. But as I will show, board games are an increasingly popular form of entertainment, especially among a crowd whose entertainment might more stereotypically be digital.

Second, and more importantly, the sketch reveals that *board games have important things to communicate about our culture.* Few of us that play board games think about the messages we might be getting from them. Whether it's because we view board games as an idle pastime, as an old-fashioned lark, or simply as disposable popular culture, we hardly stop to examine just what messages a board game might be communicating. Although I'm sure most board games aren't making particular comments about DACA, many either explicitly or implicitly reference and comment on contemporary cultural issues. They have meanings, they have messages, and they communicate to their players in a variety of ways.

This book is an attempt to start a conversation about the relevance of board games in contemporary culture, using methodologies drawn from media and cultural studies to help guide the conversation. It is intended to appeal to multiple audiences: academics drawn to the world of board games and media, board game players interested in the larger scope of their play, instructors and students drawn to board games as classroom experiences, and readers with a keen interest in changing paradigms of cultural pastimes. It's my hope that this book will serve as a "rules manual," as it were, for guiding future scholarship into board games. In her *Introduction to Game Analysis*, Clara Fernández-Vara notes that "the foundation to a more sophisticated discourse on games is to understand them as *texts.*"[1] Indeed, she notes, this means examining not only what games say, but also how games are played, the performance of them. And as Frans Mäyrä notes in his preface to *Game Research Methods*: "Game scholars need to be active in evaluating, adapting, and re-designing research methodologies so that the unique characteristics of games and play inform and shape the form research takes in this field."[2] We must use the unique elements of board games to form our critique and rely on new methodologies to focus our studies: "We need to remain receptive and inquisitive about methodologies that not only advance our understanding of games and their players, but also expand recognition of games as valuable tools, and objects of study, across other disciplines."[3]

Despite—and, perhaps, because of—their ubiquity, board games are given only a cursory glance in these methodological textbooks. As Fernández-Vara rightly notes, board games are texts; yet her book "focuses exclusively on preparing for the analysis of *digital* games. Non-digital games . . . pose a whole different set of problems."[4] The textbook *Game Research Methods* focuses only rarely on board games, with most of the chapters using video game imagery and examples to highlight different methodological approaches to studying digital games.[5] Yet, board games represent a unique textual entity: because game play consists of both the text and the player interaction with the text, in order to analyze the game we have to use critical discourses from other fields to make sense of the interaction between the two.* (For the purposes of this book, I am defining "game play" using Katie Salen and Eric Zimmerman's definition, "The experience of a game set into motion through the participation of the players."[6])

With something as ubiquitous and popular as a board game, it can be hard to take a step back and analyze the implications of our gaming. Even though board games are a mainstay in many households—from *Chess* to *Monopoly* to *(Settlers of) Catan* (1995, Mayfair)—they are a remarkably understudied phenomenon. A search of online academic databases for "board game" finds only a few articles, a couple of academic, historical, and popular books, and a surprisingly large number of articles about business (the pun forming from "board" room).[7] The articles that do exist often point to the relationship between board games and digital games, to issues of adaptation, or to board game use within education and pedagogy.[8] There are few articles that use cultural studies methodologies like ethnography, textual analysis, or industrial analysis to investigate board games as unique artifacts in and of themselves, as culturally significant, or as media

---

* Thanks to Reem Hilu, a participant at the Society for Cinema and Media Studies' (SCMS) 2019 Seminar on Toys and Games, for this insight. Throughout the book, footnotes are designated by symbols and comment on specific moments in the text; endnotes are designated by Arabic numerals and are purely citational.

entities. Yet, using these methodologies can reveal underexplored elements of games as well as approach underutilized elements of media and cultural studies.[*]

Board Games as Media attempts to correct this absence by, first, bringing attention to the underlying cultural shift that board games have helped to usher in and, second, offering a series of chapters that highlight different methodologies for studying and researching board games. Quite simply, this book is intended to develop board game scholarship and education by providing a foundation in new methodological perspectives on hobby board gaming.

As such, this book builds on research by analog games scholars like Stewart Woods and Marco Arnaudo, both of whom analyze aspects of contemporary culture through analog gaming.[†] As Woods notes, "games are not created in a cultural vacuum."[9] They reflect culture as much as they influence culture. At the same time, *Board Games as Media* differs from previous research in significant ways. First, I have endeavored to make this book unique by focusing not on any one particular genre or element of board gaming (Woods examines Eurogames—"accessible games that privilege the role of mechanics over theme in gameplay"[10]—while Arnaudo analyzes the narratological and historiographical import of board games, both methodologies that, because of his scholarship, I do not focus on in this book) but rather on hobby board gaming as a phenomenon in and of itself. I am interested in new ways that scholars can study board games, and the unique insights that studying board games as meaning-making entities might bring to our understanding of the importance of board games. Second, I have eschewed large theoretical discussions of theory in favor of more focused analyses of individual games. I draw this style from studies of popular culture which are grounded in the lived experiences of audiences and players. The effect I hope to achieve is a study with applicability across a range of arenas—academic scholarship, educational use, game player, and game designer.

In this book, I develop frameworks, articulate methodologies, and present case studies for how scholars, students, and teachers might study the board game in our digital age. Just as the film presents opportunities for artistic, cultural, and thematic analysis, just as television offers a space for critical commentary,

---

[*] As an example of using new methodologies for studying media texts, Andrew Reinhard's *Archaeogaming* uses methodologies from the field of archeology to uncover new insights into video gaming as well as revealing insights into archeology.

[†] A quick note on terminology. "Analog game" is a catch-all term for games that are not natively digital; "board game" more specifically refers to a type of analog game that usually features a board, a set of rules, and multiple pieces like cards and meeples. There are other types of analog games (card games, role-playing games, etc.), although there can be categorical overlap.

just as literature becomes a venue for symbolic analysis, so too the board game and its place in our society should be analyzed for its own unique viewpoint. In particular, I am interested in looking beyond mass-market games like *Monopoly* or *Scrabble*, which have been analyzed before and toward the rise in popularity of more complex hobby-based board games.[11]

After all, they have become very popular. As I've previously written, we are in the midst of a board game renaissance.[12] There has been a noted increase in the number of board games released each year: more than 3,500 new games are released annually, with that number increasing by 5.7 percent each year.[13] A recent online article shows that "over 5,000 new board games were introduced into the US market in 2016 alone."[14] This is not just a Western phenomenon: as Shephali Bhatt demonstrates, board game popularity has exploded in Eastern countries like India, and the global market for board games has reached $4.6 billion.[15] According *to Research and Markets*, the global board game market "is anticipated to reach values of more than $12 billion by 2023, growing at a [rate] of over 9% during 2017-2023."* Additionally, board games are one of the most popular categories for funding on crowdfunding sites like Kickstarter. According to Charlie Hall:

> Tabletop games . . . push[ed] the games category to an all-time high of more than $200 million. Data provided to Polygon by the crowdfunding platform show a nearly 20 percent increase in funds raised by successful tabletop projects over the previous year.[16]

It is not uncommon for big box stores like Target and Barnes and Noble to stock more complex and thematic games like *Ticket to Ride* (2004, Days of Wonder) and *Mansions of Madness 2e* (2016, Fantasy Flight). Venues for board game play are appearing in major cities around the world: board game cafes and hobby board game stores are becoming more common. Bars are hosting board game nights. Even games scholars are recognizing the increasing popularity and relevance of board games. In 2014, the scholarly journal *Analog Game Studies* premiered its first issue, and in 2017, *Game Studies*, one of the premiere scholarly journals about games, published an editorial by leading games scholar Espen Aarseth proclaiming that "from the next issue, *Game Studies* actively welcomes articles on games in general, and will not be limited to an empirical focus on digital games. It is time to recognize that the study of games cannot and should not be

---

* https://www.researchandmarkets.com/research/nc2qgm/global_board?w=5

segregated into digital and non-digital."[17] A renewed focus on board games is a welcome addition to scholarship, and follows a larger cultural trajectory of taking board gaming seriously.

As hobby board games become more common, it is important to take a step back and analyze what precisely they mean at this cultural moment. The messages that board games communicate help to shape our interpretation of the world around us. In a time of nearly infinite streaming television, film, and music, thousands of hours of original programming on Netflix, Hulu, and Amazon Prime, billion-dollar blockbuster movies, and an ever-increasing array of streaming options, why are everyday people flocking back to board games? Why board games, and why now?

This book cannot hope to answer all these questions, but it is an opportunity to explore the cultural messages communicated by board games. Beyond their ubiquity in our homes and stores, board games are an important artifact for reflecting on and analyzing cultural trends, historical antecedents, and thematic content in contemporary society. In *Game Play*, I described the board game as "part of, and also apart from, the media environment," but here I want to problematize this. What are board games, if not media themselves?[18] *Board Games as Media* attempts to begin a conversation about how board games—just like media texts—create and complicate messages, and how we—as scholars, as readers, as players—can investigate these messages. What does it mean to read a board game, and how can we go about doing so? Obviously, we read the rules and the text on cards. But to really *read* the act of game play—to understand what the game is trying to communicate—how do we make sense of this activity? Viewed through the lens of media studies, board games communicate a message between the creators and the players of the game. We play games for a variety of reasons: to have fun, to interact with our friends, to develop a deeper understanding of play. But how does the game play us? What do we learn when we play the game, and how do we understand the messages that the game is giving us?

I should note here that there have been many explorations of games as cultural objects before, but on the whole they have focused on *video* games and only tangentially (if at all) discuss board games. There is a lineage between the two; as Markku Eskelinen notes, video games are "remediated [analog] games."[19] And other scholars have discussed the importance of examining board games within the larger game studies field.[20] But as Woods points out, most games scholars "have typically discussed board games with a view to establishing connections and/or design features that relate to video games . . . [and] academic attention to the specific area of board games remains relatively sparse."[21] Board games *are* like video games in some useful ways, but they are also quite *unlike* video games in other respects: for example, they are tangible, emphasize face-to-face social interaction, are manipulable, and provide the opportunity to change the underlying state of the game. Board games offer unique insights into contemporary culture that a mere linkage to video games does not unpack.

In *Board Games as Media*, I am particularly interested in applying a specific *media studies* lens to the hobby of board gaming. The reasons for this methodological shift reflect the changing relevance of the board game in contemporary life. If board games are becoming more ubiquitous, are taking up more leisure time, and are becoming more thematically complex and rich, then it makes sense to examine them not simply as vacuous pastimes, but as meaningful (and meaning-full) moments of cultural resonance. For decades, scholars have used particular styles and methods of media analysis to understand the larger influences and cultural meanings of film, television, radio, digital media, video games, social media, and other "traditional" (re: screened) modes of entertainment. This mediated entertainment has a vocabulary, a scholarly tradition, and a set series of techniques for analysis. But what happens if we apply these media studies techniques to board games? What has to change in our understanding of media when we move from screens to boards? How do the tactile and social natures of board games affect the deeper themes and meanings of them? What new insights into contemporary culture can we understand if we shift our understanding of what "counts" as media in the age of the board game?

Not all scholars see the relevance of applying media studies techniques to board games. For example, Aarseth writes that applying terms from media studies, like *narrative*, is problematic: "Narrative terms in game studies . . . are usually brought in, like the cane toad to Australia, to solve some difficulty that at first glance seems easy to fix, but soon brings more trouble than the original problem."[22] Yet, the implications for this shift relate to more than just the board game. One of the key attributes of board gaming is the social activity of the participants: we don't just play games; we play games *with each other*. Focusing on social activity in games allows us to develop a stronger connection to other mediated social activities: mobile games on our portable devices, location-aware technology, social virtual reality (VR) interaction, second-screen viewing, even mobile dating. The board game renaissance is happening at the same time as an explosion in interactive digital entertainment, and both are related to similar cultural trends—a loss of face-to-face social interaction, a lack of social opportunities after high school or college, a changing work/life balance. Even while digital technology has made it easier than ever to develop networks of friends online and to keep in touch with those scattered around the globe, board games force us to participate in structured, in-person social activities. The board game renaissance seems to be a response to this changing digital environment. To this end, it is important to reflect on the particular opportunities that exist for studying contemporary media if we open the scope of media studies to examine board games.

Media studies, defined loosely, is the analysis and investigation of *that which mediates*—or, in other words, that which is a tool or outlet for storing and delivering information to others ("media" here is the plural of "medium," or something that lies between and links two other things).[23] This is a tautological definition, of course, so diving a bit deeper we can note that media studies is the analysis of a system of information transmission outside of interpersonal communication. Put very broadly, media studies investigates content in a variety of modes: the production of content (e.g., industry studies and political economy), the content itself (textual analysis), the delivery of content (technology studies), and the reception of content (ethnography and audience studies) within a cultural setting (cultural studies). Media has been historically defined rather loosely in the field: in an introductory textbook, Julian McDougall argues that media studies is "the study of everyday life."[24] Media studies, then, finds its objects of analysis within multiple realms. Toby Miller and Marwan Kraidy note that media have given rise to three related topics of scholarly inquiry:

- Technology, ownership, and control—their political economy;
- Textuality—their meaning; and
- Audiences—their public.[25]

As a bounded experience, board games can act like media texts by creating an alternate world for viewers/players to mindfully inhabit, what Arnaudo calls "an impression of reality."[26] Additionally, by virtue of their unique positioning as cocreating experiences between creators and players, board games bring interactivity and playfulness to the forefront of media analysis. For example, the game *Mansions of Madness 2e* is a Lovecraftian-themed game that allows players to choose different characters to attempt to solve a horrific mystery. The game makes use of an app to randomize the board and create new facts about the story in each play session (see Chapter 5). Thus, the game follows a specific, set narrative, but develops differently each time it is played, necessitating individualized analyses. Textual and cultural studies of interactive media allow a greater fluency with this form of player experience. And games like *Mansions of Madness 2e* also have dedicated audiences that continue purchase expansions, collectible decks, new games, and extra content, a phenomenon that can be analyzed by using methodologies drawn from ethnographic and economic analyses.

Of course, board games do not, at first, even appear as media. In fact, because media studies predominantly focus on *screens* (e.g., movies, television, and digital technology), other types of media tend to be elided. Take costuming for example, or theater, or graphic novels—none of these are "traditional" media studies texts; they probe the boundaries of media. In the same way, most board games do not have screens, and thus do not fit into the paradigm of "mediation." But focusing almost exclusively on screen studies is both limiting and reductive. Linking scholarly attention to a device or product, rather than the experiences or affect generated through interaction with the product, artificially delimits the results of the study. Board games allow scholars to open up media studies from the screen and focus instead on the activity of mediation, regardless of medium, as a guiding principle of media viewership. And by "studying games as activities," we create an important part of game *and* media studies, "on par with studying the game rules, aesthetics, experiences and interaction models."[27]

Developing media studies methodologies to investigate board games allows us to integrate the player more cohesively into the experience itself, and this book uses methodologies that draw from board game elements to structure its analyses. A board game experience is only partially relatable to the object that we can purchase in the store or pull off of a shelf. One must connect the different areas of media analysis—technology meets textuality meets audience studies, to see the game in full. As Jakko Stenros and Annika Waern note:

> In game studies, games are most often seen as *systems*. This has made the play *activity* an under-explored area of game studies.
>
> Games are always *second order design*; game designers create structures that guide player engagement and activity, but their experience is created by their activity with and within the game, and not primarily by the game itself. It can be argued that games are not complete until they are played.[28]

In other words, and put more specifically in terms of board gaming, the game itself, as a mutable, textual, tangible object, does not *come into being* without the addition of player agency. In literary terms, this connects with reader-response theory, the approach to studying literature that shows any text emerging from the interaction between reader and text. When I sit down to play *Pandemic* (2008, Z-Man Games), for example, the disease cubes are all in bags, the board is folded up in the box, and the player tokens are neatly stacked away; the game is at rest. One might be able to analyze the *contents* of the game (the rather interesting choice of which cities to include in *Pandemic* would make a fine intercultural study), but there is an inability to analyze *Pandemic* as a game system without the play session itself. The pieces, the cards, the board, the dice, the rules—these all exist in the box, but without the interactive element of the player, the game is only half complete. As Stenros and Waern go on to note, "what we experience is not 'the game' but a play session, and that session does not exist unless we actively create it."[29] Of course, this is true of digital games as well, but importantly, digital game systems are always contained by the programming: the "*facilitation of playing* is done by the system."[30] Digital games prescribe the gaming; board games reveal a more mutable interaction between game system and player.

This argument is, of course, the basis for the narratology/ludology debate in game studies, a paradigm now over a decade old. To summarize, a narratologist would identify the *narrative* of the game as the most influential component (largely drawing on literature and hypertext studies), whereas ludologists would identify the *ludic nature* of the game as the most crucial element (largely drawing on game studies). Rather than get bogged down in a decades-old debate (that never really resolved anyway), I find it's more productive to view any new methodology as an opportunity to reimagine the possibilities of study—to refresh our understanding and reinvigorate our research.

It's not my intention to turn this book into a polemic. I don't think getting mired in disciplinary issues is as productive as simply focusing on the games themselves and what they have to tell us about contemporary culture. Board games have a lot to offer scholars and viewers of media. Ultimately, however one chooses to examine or analyze a game determines the outcome of the study. In this, *Board Games as Media* can hopefully provide some new and alternate methods for studying, researching, learning about, and enjoying board games.

Chapter Outline

The first chapter uses a textual analysis of board games as a means to explore contemporary game ideology. I offer the term "ludo-textual" as a way of analyzing the interaction between players and material elements within board games. This chapter focuses particularly on the differences between a cooperative and a competitive play style as indicative of ideological concerns. I analyze two popular games, each with a different scope and focus, for the messages the elements communicate. As of the time of writing (December 2019), both of these games were in the top twenty on BoardGameGeek, the website ranking and social hub for board gamers around the world, and thus have hundreds of thousands of board game players and fans ranking them highly. I use the game *Scythe: Rise of Fenris* (2018, Stonemaier Games), a campaign-style game, to view issues of alternate history and decision making as indicative of an ideology of competition. Campaign-style games build a narrative over multiple play sessions by changing the rules and opening state of the game, although the game can be reset to an initial state. *Scythe* presents an alternate view of the period between world wars in which giant mechs are now common and different political entities vie for control of the continent. I also analyze *Pandemic Legacy: Season 1* (2015, Z-Man Games), a Legacy game that depicts an oncoming global plague and the people that fight it. A Legacy game is like a campaign-style game except one literally changes the board/cards/state of the game in order to progress the narrative (e.g., ripping up cards). Once completed, it cannot be replayed. *Pandemic Legacy* highlights both the interconnectedness of character and player, and I focus on the underlying development of the cooperative elements in the game.

The second chapter of the book explores what it means to have a rhetoric of board games. This chapter explores the underlying game structures of strategy and randomness as argumentative strategies. Rhetoric and videogames have been usefully connected in the past, most notably by Ian Bogost in his 2007 *Persuasive Games*. He describes the way videogames create a *procedural rhetoric*, or a rhetoric in which an algorithmic process creates a persuasive argument. In concert with this, and through the examination of two board games—*This War of Mine* (2017, Galakta), and *Holding On: The Troubling Life of Billy Kerr* (2018, Hub Games)—I develop a rhetoric that emphasizes the *interactive potentiality* of board games. This chapter considers board games through a rhetoric of possibility—that is, the rhetorical arguments that board games make are always tempered through the choices taken and not taken by players.

The third chapter analyzes the interplay between mechanics and theme by using a *ludic discourse analysis* of four games from 2016 to 2017 that each focus on a particular act: colonizing Mars. The games are *First Martians* (2017, Portal Games), *Martians: A Story of Civilization* (2016, RedImp Games), *Pocket*

Mars (2017, Board and Dice), and *Terraforming Mars* (2016, FryxGames). All together these games reveal the ways that board games can create implications that determine the way players understand the world around them through notions of colonization and capitalism.

The fourth chapter takes a wider view of the board game industry through an industrial analysis of board game authorship. I analyze the way that discourses of authorship are deployed by the industry to promote and sell games. I focus on three techniques of board game authorship: the *créateur*, a board game designer with a singular style; the *crafter*, a board game designer with a diverse and vast repertoire; and *branded aestheticism*, wherein the board game company takes on an author-function. This chapter explores the characteristics of game authors, Ryan Laukat (Red Raven Games), Vlaada Chvátil (CGE Games), and Fantasy Flight Games.

The fifth chapter explores the relationship between board gamers and fans, focusing on *ludic fandom* as a way of understanding how individual players emotionally engage with board games. The majority of work that concentrates on relating games and fans concentrates on video gamers as a type of fan audience. Video gamers are posited as the most active of audiences, as they must interact in a more obvious way with their media texts. The fan appellation arrives through the designation of video games as a type of media. Because board games have been relegated to the "closet" of the academy, they are less interpreted as media products than are video games; and thus board gamers are less likely to be considered "fans." In this chapter, I unpack this reading of gaming and the bifurcation of game players into board and video in order to demonstrate how the notion of fandom in fan studies can usefully be expanded in order to develop a greater framework for understanding the relationship between games and media. I will compare two case studies of board games based on video game properties— *XCOM: The Board Game* (2015, Fantasy Flight Games) and *BioShock Infinite: Siege of Columbia* (2013, Plaid Hat Games)—to uncover three ways that board game players can be interpreted as fans: first, through knowledge acquisition; second, through affective play; and third, through identification role-play. Ultimately, this chapter explores the boundaries of fan studies, asking fan scholars to see fandom as a continuum of experiences rather than a media-influenced identity.

In Chapter 6, I use ethnographic methodologies to report the results of a survey I conducted in April 2019 about hobby board gaming. Over 900 people responded to the survey, answering questions about the motivations and desires of hobby board gamers. The survey asked both qualitative (open-ended) and quantitative questions. Chapter 6 looks at the quantitative data to give a portrait of who is playing games, what types of games they are playing, and what they enjoy about playing games. The survey revealed a wide variety of answers, including a contemporary increase in complexity in games and a renewed focus on game play mechanics.

In Chapter 7, I report the qualitative results of the board game survey. I revisit the quantitative results from Chapter 6 in order to explicate players' motivations for playing board games, their ideal board gaming experiences, and their thoughts on the rise in popularity of board games. The results of the survey reveal a great variety of opinions about gaming, but a general appreciation for the socialization that board games engender, a focus on the intellectual challenges of games, and a tension between playing games to avoid digital technology yet needing digital technology to find new games.

In Chapter 8, I turn to a discussion of diversity and inclusion in the board gaming hobby and industry. Using interviews with board game designers, board game players, and intermediaries like online content creators, I focus on the power dynamics within board gaming. The stereotypical view of a board gamer is of a middle-aged, white, cis-gendered male, and while this is far from the entirety of the gaming community, it is also still the overwhelming identity of both gamers and creators.[31] The interviews reveal both some significant progress in diversifying the industry and hobby and some setbacks. Using two games— *Wingspan* (2019, Stonemaier Games) and the aborted *Scramble for Africa* (unpublished, GMT Games)—as counterexamples, I reveal why diversification is important and offer some industry tips on increasing diversity in the hobby.

The final chapter explores an autoethnographic analysis, focusing on my own history and play with the game *Gloomhaven* (2017, Cephalofair Games), a massive exploration and fighting game that involves multiple characters, narratives, and play styles. I use this method of self-reflection to analyze not only *Gloomhaven*, but also my own experience with the game as reflective of the cultures of which I am a part.

Finally, in the conclusion to the book, I use an ecological framework to interrogate the environmental impact of board games. Largely made up of cardboard, wood, and plastic, board games are not an ecologically sustainable product. What steps can we, as gamers and scholars, take to lessen the impact that board games have on our planet?

Despite their long history, board games have been little studied in the academy. They are hard to analyze because they are so personal—every play experience will necessarily be different each time. They offer an object missing a major component: the players themselves. But undertaking a board game analysis reveals so much more than just the mechanics of the game; it uncovers the player at the heart of all media. For without players—without audiences—what use is media studies at all?

Part One

Textual Analysis

Meeples, Miniatures, and Cubes

Ludo-Textual Analyses of Board Games

In the beginning of their authoritative *Characteristics of Games*, game designers/ academics George Skaff Elias, Richard Garfield, and K. Robert Gutschera note that little attention "has been paid to . . . games themselves, as games: what it is like to play them, what features differentiate one game from another, or what features make one game a more or less enjoyable experience for its players."[1] Their book goes on to offer a number of different characteristics by which game players, scholars, and students may define games, including things like the level of player interaction, the rules and system of game play, the amount of randomness or luck in a game, and the amount of effort players may need to put into winning a game. As a guide to a "high-level description" of games, *Characteristics of Games* does a thorough job of looking at game mechanics and how the concept of a game emerges from the construction of different characteristics.

But what about their statement: the game, *as a game*? For board games specifically, how can players, students, scholars, and hobbyists read the various material and immaterial elements of a board game as separate components that, in various combinations, create different meanings for the players? In this chapter, I use textual analysis (an examination of the actual material elements of games) and formal analysis (an examination of the structures that unite those elements) to demonstrate a deeper reading of the ideology of board games. In this analysis, I focus particularly on the differences between a cooperative and a competitive play style—using two of the most popular games on BoardGameGeek, *Scythe: Rise of Fenris* (2018, Stonemaier Games; as of December 2019, at position 9 and hereafter referred to as *Rise of Fenris*) and *Pandemic Legacy: Season 1* (2015, Z-Man Games; as of December 2019, at position 2 and hereafter referred to as *Pandemic: Season 1*) as indicative of ideological concerns. *Rise of Fenris* tells an alternate history of twentieth-century "Europa," where different factions vie for control over the continent. As a campaign-style game, the end of one play session of *Rise of Fenris* affects the next play session and the whole game is replayable. *Pandemic: Season 1* depicts an oncoming global plague and the people that cooperate to fight it. As a Legacy game, *Pandemic: Season 1* has a similar campaign style to *Rise of Fenris*, except the actual game components (board, cards, etc.) are physically altered throughout each session, making the game unreplayable as a campaign. Both of these board games use a similar set of textual elements (cards, cubes, miniatures, boards, and tokens) and different play styles to create compelling play sessions, from which players can glean different ideological meanings.

In this chapter of *Board Games as Media*, I use a traditional media studies analysis technique—textual analysis—to open up new facets of board game play. By articulating a particular tension within board game play, competitive versus cooperative play styles, I demonstrate how a *ludo-textual analysis* (a textual analysis that invokes participatory elements) takes into account both game textuality and player engagement. To do this, I examine how *Rise of Fenris* and *Pandemic: Season 1* invoke these different play styles to make different ideological statements about the human condition. In the original game *Scythe*, which *Rise of Fenris* builds on, players directly compete: or, to put it a bit more academically, they "struggle against each other within the artificial conflict of a game."[2] Winning the game means beating the other person, and the underlying situation is conflict based. Each person controls a different faction in this alternate history world, and each faction has different powers. The important element I want to concentrate on in this chapter is the "alternate" part of this history. In *Scythe*, this is most obviously represented by giant mechs—mechanical devices—that "assert force over the uncharted lands surrounding the Factory and . . . protect their workers and territories."[*] The mechs are representative of a counterfactual world where history pivoted (in this case, Nikola Tesla invented the giant machines); however, as I demonstrate, the game's underlying ideology both affirms and contradicts the diverse meanings of counterfactuality. Conversely, in the original *Pandemic*, which *Pandemic: Season 1* builds on presents another counterfactual, narrative-driven board game where players take on different roles (each with particular skills) and cooperate to save the world from an impending global pandemic. Throughout the game, players must combine their skills to complete a variety of tasks, some of which repeat each session and others of which change

---

[*] https://stonemaiergames.com/games/scythe/mechs/

depending on how far along in the Legacy game the players have progressed. To this end, cooperation is a key element of the game: there are always more tasks than players have actions, so careful consideration of each player's move and how it relates to other players' moves facilitates success. Analyzing the importance of characters' shared abilities and actions reveals an ideological focus on a reliance on connections with others as a key component of the digital age. Importantly, my arguments in this chapter are not to be taken as the "final word" on these games' ideologies: every text contains multitudes of ideological readings, and this analysis is just one out of many possibilities. Game analyses begin by examining how similar *textual* elements combined with differing *player interaction styles* can lead to a greater understanding of the underlying values and beliefs that are present within the board game. This ludo-textual analysis examines how player interactivity augments pure textuality.

Textual and Formal Analysis

Board games are both textual objects and systems of interaction. A ludo-textual analysis augments a pure textual analysis with an additive of interactive and participatory elements: it "depends on playing a game and forming an understanding [of] how the game system works."[3] It allows us to see board games as more than just a text, as more than simply constructed by the designers. They are instead complex systems that unite the designer, the author, the publisher, and the player as cocreators of meaning. We cannot simply open the box, look at the components, and read the rules to get an understanding of the game. We must look at how players themselves interact with the game's system, each other, and the on-the-board components to get a fuller reading of the game's text. Play is inseparable from text. As Mattia Thibault notes in his analysis of the narrative of board games:

> When the player accepts the rules and starts playing, he[/she] doesn't call into question the [game] rules anymore; they became a part of him[/her], of what he's[/she's] doing. In the same way, he[/she] accepts the result of a dice throw and makes it a part of him[/her] in his[/her] new self: the subject of the play.[4]

Simply put, the *text* is not enough for a *textual analysis* of board games.

Textual analysis is an examination of the elements within a particular text to determine what that text communicates. It is an interpretation of the components, wherein "an artifact and its specific elements are examined closely, and the relations of the elements are described in detail."⁵ Textual analysis can be used in a variety of forms, as Alan McKee describes: "Whenever we produce an *interpretation* of something's *meaning* . . . we treat it as a text. A text is something that we make meaning from."⁶ Thus, anything can be a text, because we can read meaning in any construct. When we perform a textual analysis, we're reading the human behind that construction. Textual analyses form the building blocks of many other forms of scholarly analyses, and the backbone for the analyses I conduct in the next four chapters.

If a textual analysis examines the elements themselves, a formal analysis examines "the role of each element in the composition as a whole"; that is, it seeks to understand how those elements work together.⁷ A formal analysis studies "how the text is constructed, the pieces that make it up."⁸ In Clara Fernández-Vara's textbook on game analysis—which is focused almost entirely on video games—she notes that a formal analysis examines structures, and that "games are often structured systems, in the form of rule sets, which are models that lend themselves to study of their form."⁹ A formal analysis of board games cannot take into account those algorithmic computer programs; thus, we need a different system to investigate both the textual and the formal elements of board games.

McKee's *Textual Analysis: A Beginner's Guide* offers a thoughtful exploration of what makes textual analysis a compelling methodology for researchers who want to understand how people make sense of the world around them. For McKee, textual analysis is about finding the meaning within objects that others have made meaning with. It can be conducted on any type of object that has meaning—most commonly, we tend to use it on media objects (e.g., books, films, and television programs), but we could conceivably conduct a textual analysis on any object that someone else has also found meaning in, whether it's human-created or not. The goal of a textual analysis is not to say whether something is *good* or *bad*—textual scholars try to avoid value judgments—but rather to identify the specific elements that comprise meaning and articulate how that meaning is exposed. Textual analysis is not the same thing as a review. As scholars, we don't watch a film and then offer a judgment on it; rather, we might watch a film and discuss what the images of femininity in it might mean, or how the representation of violence provides a novel version of war. The same text can produce different meanings, and the quality of the analysis thus depends on the arguments and examples provided by the analyzer.

This might make textual analysis seem subjective, and at times it can be. You and I might have different interpretations of a particular text. But subjectivity in textual analysis is not boundless; obviously, there are some interpretations that are beyond the limits of reasonability. If we were playing a game of *Monopoly* (1933, Hasbro) and I said that, actually, the game involved aliens kidnapping people and turning them into dogs, you would have a very good case for disagreeing with that interpretation. As McKee describes, "Ways of making sense of the world aren't completely arbitrary; they don't change from moment to moment. They're not infinite, and they're not completely individual."[10] The key to subjective methodologies like textual analysis is to base the analysis in specific examples and arguments. Can others follow your thought process and argumentation? Additionally, there are significant advantages to subjective methods like textual analysis. Subjectivity can be a powerful method of understanding how other people and cultures think: "We . . . understand our own cultures better because we can start to see the limitations and advantages of our own sense-making practices."[11] Subjectivity can make us more empathetic players and people because we catch a glimpse into someone else's mindset.

As I've noted earlier, a simple textual analysis details how all the elements in a text reveal an underlying meaning that can be interpreted. But board games offer a more complex negotiation of textual elements, because the game system itself cannot be fully understood without player involvement and participation. That is, board games are unique in the game/textual landscape for the way that these elements hinge on both the social interaction of the players and the physical interaction of the players with the game system. Marco Arnaudo notes that "nothing happens unless a player materiality does something" in a board game.[12] This "ludo-textual" element highlights the interactivity of a board game. A wooden block isn't a character until the player makes it so.

To begin a ludo-textual analysis, we must look at the textual elements first and then articulate how player interaction portends new readings. As Arnaudo describes, "The material nature of analog board games can contribute to make their content particularly vivid."[13] A textual analysis of a board game might start with components so common we may not even think of them as textual: for example, the actual board itself can be an object of analysis. How are spaces demarcated? What do the locations stand in for? The abstract representations on a board are all created and suggest meanings that go beyond the simple articulation of game play. For example, the playing pieces in *Monopoly* might be read to symbolize aspects of finance—the wheelbarrow to carry all the money, the boot could represent poverty—or perhaps they could just represent aspects of everyday life. The many hex pieces of *Catan* (1995, Mayfair Games) that can be laid in different patterns suggest a landscape that might produce a particular type of resource; yet at the same time, they also represent only the resources available *in that game* and preclude readings of resources (fish?) that don't exist in that world. A textual analysis could reveal what isn't there as much as it reveals what is. (Both official expansions to *Catan*, like the *Oil Springs* (2011, Mayfair Games) scenario and the fan-made "Global Warming" expansion (2018),* highlight how the textual elements in the game can symbolize larger cultural meanings of environmentalism, for instance.)

A ludo-textual analysis adds a participatory element to this traditional textual analysis: components of a board game include the pieces we use to mark various places on the board as meaning is actualized. Traditional games utilize wooden or plastic pieces to symbolize any number of characteristics: perhaps a red block is your character; or perhaps it symbolizes the amount of wealth you have; or perhaps it marks a level of damage on your character. But that wooden piece doesn't *come into being* as a meaning-making object until it has been placed on the board and its use assumed by the player. Does the block represent wealth or damage? That depends where the player places it and how it is manipulated. The same cubes can stand in for "poverty" in one game (*London*, 2010, Treefrog Games) and "wealth" in another (*Terraforming Mars*, 2016, FryxGames); they could mean "happiness" (*The Pursuit of Happiness*, 2015, Stronghold Games) or "sadness" (*Dungeon Petz*, 2011, Czech Games Edition). The same object takes on different meanings in different contexts, and different objects in that same context can take on that same meaning—if I were to replace the red damage cube with a green plastic disc, it would contextually mean the same thing even if the text itself was different.

Ludo-textual analysis also factors into games that utilize more thematic content. In the game *Dead of Winter* (2014, Plaid Hat Games), for instance, cartoonish character standees represent the survivors of a zombie outbreak. How players understand a character largely depends on *ludo*-textual attributes, beyond how each character looks like a person, with gendered, racial, age, and occupational attributes but also how each character is used in the game (main character, side character, etc.). For example, one goal of the game is to keep the

---

* See Paul Wake and Sam Illingworth's expansion: https://boardgamegeek.com/thread/1966742/global-warming-scenario-unofficialfan-made

morale of the characters above a certain level; if it drops below, the whole group loses. Usually, when a character is removed from the game (re: dies), morale will go down. Forest Plum, one of the characters in the game, is a creepy Mall Santa and can be removed from the game to raise morale instead. But keeping a character in play allows a player to have more control over the board. So, the choice to include Forest Plum is a ludo-textual one, built from both the textual attributes and the game play usage of the character.

The material elements "affect . . . the dynamics of identification between players and characters" in board games.[14] A ludo-textual analysis might look at each of these characters within a specific player's experiences with that character to determine the ideology of the game. And what we do with the pieces left in our inventory during down times—stack them? Build tiny towers?—reveals this interactivity in action. In addition, the different material elements of a board game have no inherent meaning without understanding their relationship both to each other and (importantly) to the players themselves.

To help develop a greater fluency with the elements of games, Aki Järvinen developed a formal analysis of games that focuses on four levels of the game system.[15] Järvinen's work highlights not just the *components* of the game, but also their *arrangement* (the environment) in the game as constitutive of meaning. Beyond the physical aspect of the game, Järvinen noted the *compound* elements of games: the rules, the mechanics, the information (i.e., the players' decision-making abilities), and the interface of the game. Finally, he noted two *behavioral* elements, the players themselves and the context in which the players sit, that can affect our understanding of games. Järvinen's analysis helps illustrate the many sites where player interaction affects the textuality of the game, from the physical, to the textual, to the experiential. To move from one level of the game to a different one requires understanding how games create meaning in the first place. Players can connect with the game through the materiality of the game, but only in specific contexts (space/time) of play. How I understand *Catan* now may differ from how I might understand it in twenty years, or twenty years ago.

Finally, developing a formal analysis of board games helps to unpack and determine an underlying ideology and reading of games. The definition of ideology is a complex one, and it has many different meanings across different academic fields; however, for the purposes of this chapter, we'll be looking at ideology as a *collection of beliefs about how the world operates*. Ideology makes the artificial appear natural. For example, some people might have a collection of beliefs about how a person's sex determines the way that person should act in the world—that women are submissive, or that men are violent. Alan McKee notes that "dominant discourses" can "appear to be 'common sense'—that's just how things are."[16] Ideology functions to make it seem as though those beliefs are "natural"—or, in other words, that they are universal and unquestioned, even if they are anything but. For video game scholar Ian Bogost, games "simplify . . . the real world in order to draw attention to relevant aspects of that world," and we can "learn to read games as deliberate expressions of particular perspectives."[17] In other words, we can read ideology through the game. By analyzing the formal elements of a text and developing arguments about how the textual elements work together to produce meaning, an analyst can start to unpack the ideologies that may have shaped the way the text was created; similarly, the ideologies that a text espouses become knowable through this type of textual analysis.

One of the most common ways to understand ideology through a board games analysis is via the game's theme. Theme is the structure that guides the relationships between textual elements within the game. It's a metaphor for what the game is trying to communicate. Theme is like a narrative, "related through a number of game elements, primarily the contextual backstory offered on the box and rules, and the graphic design of packaging and components."[18] For example, in *Dead of Winter*, the theme of zombie apocalypse becomes apparent through the iconography on the box and within the game itself, as well as with the mechanics that guide the actions of the player: with limited resources, how do you both fight zombies and help the survivors at camp? In *Catan*, the theme of "settling an island" is communicated both through the objects in the game— roadways, towns, and cities—and through the underlying mechanic of trading particular resources (Brick and Lumber) for a road; it makes sense to use these two resources to build a road as opposed to, say, Wool and Wheat. (I'll talk more about theme and mechanics in Chapter 3.)

Putting theme, formal elements, and player interaction together helps us understand the ideology created by the game. For example, Jonathan Ray Lee notes that *Catan* has an underlying capitalist ideology as it "plays out ethical dilemmas raised by the emergent and systemic inequalities generated by capitalist systems."[19] Using resources—which by necessity of the game are limited to what has been randomly generated—to build cities and roads means that there will always be the "haves" and the "have-nots" in the game. Ray's point is that the unequal distribution of resources, an underlying truth of capitalism, is reflected within the game's theme and mechanics. Similarly, Jonathan Walton describes how the game *Pay Day* (1975, Hasbro) relies on "a 1950s/Boomer 'economic common sense'" ideology that "trains players for a life of household budgetary management in which they are supposed to be cautious (but not too cautious!) with their money," encouraging players "to internalize a liberal or neoliberal attitude."[20] Beyond economics, other board game studies have noted how board games can reflect Orientalism and other racialized identity markers, gender, and sex characteristics within board games, among others.[21] But these analyses only read the game elements, ignoring the interaction of players with and within the game system. Only through a ludo-textual analysis of board games, one that fully captures both the material elements of the game and the individual experiences of play, can a full ideological reading emerge.

Scythe and *Pandemic*: Legacies of Conflict and Cooperation

It is a time of unrest in 1920s Europa. The ashes from the first great war still darken the snow. The capitalistic city-state known simply as "The Factory," which fueled the war with heavily armored mechs, has closed its doors, drawing the attention of several nearby countries.[*]

So begins *Scythe* (2016, Stonemaier Games), a board game set in an alternate version of Europe of the 1920s, the era between the world wars. During the game, players control factions within "Europa," each of which is trying to gain power. As the description of the game articulates, "players conquer territory, enlist new recruits, reap resources, gain villagers, build structures, and activate monstrous mechs," huge machines of war which have been repurposed for a variety of industrial or agricultural tasks. During the game, each faction vies for control of the continent. *Scythe* is an engine-building game where players slowly build up a system of repeated actions: one generates resources in order to complete tasks, which can help generate more resources to complete different tasks. On each turn, players take two actions. The choice of the second action depends on your choice of first action, and each player may have different combinations of actions they can take. The ultimate goal of the game is not necessarily to take over the most land—this is not strictly about conquest—but rather to have the greatest fortune at the end of the game. Players earn money by completing tasks, including upgrading and deploying the mechs, building

---

[*] https://stonemaiergames.com/games/scythe/

structures, enlisting recruits, occupying territory, winning combat, and earning popularity and power within the game. In the campaign version of the game, *Rise of Fenris*, players can upgrade their factions in a variety of ways as they play through eight repeatable game sessions that reveal Nikola Tesla's child and Rasputin vying for control of the continent.

A simple textual analysis of *Scythe* might reveal a number of different readings of the way the components of the game symbolize an alternate version of history. The game is designed by Jamey Stegmaier with "art and worldbuilding by Jakob Rozalski," and the art is eye-catching, as painted scenes of early-twentieth-century peasants in the field or soldiers on the road are thrown in contrast with humongous, anachronistic machines that dot the landscapes on the box top and cards within the game (Figure 1.1).

The effect of Rozalski's work in *Scythe* is to present an alternate version of the past, to reimagine history in different ways. For *Scythe*, the mechs are the most obvious anachronistic element of the game, as they are historically inaccurate, but can be used in the game to move troops and resources or engage in combat. Other moments of "alternate history" appear throughout—for instance, the factions are named not after real-world countries, but rather after suitably "alternate" versions—Saxony instead of Germany or Rusviet Union instead of Russia.

These mechs are also one of the first things we see when first opening the box: the colored plastic miniatures, arranged in near rows and encased in molded plastic holders, look like plastic battle pieces from *Warhammer 40K* (1993, Fantasy Flight Games). They offer a tactility to the game, as they look like

Figure 1.1 Mech in 1920s *Scythe*, art by Jakob Rozalski, *Scythe* game by Jamey Stegmaier. Used with permission.

Figure 1.2 Crimean mechs in *Scythe*.

toys, little mechanical soldiers in an epic sci-fi battle. Each design echoes and underlying narrative of the game—they are agricultural tools redesigned for war (Figure 1.2).

There are other plastic miniatures in the game as well: each faction is represented by a character; each character has a backstory, a unique design, and an accompanying symbolic animal. For example, the Saxony character, Gunter Von Duisburg, is accompanied by Nacht, a wolf, while the Celtic character, Connor of Clan Albion, is accompanied by a wild boar. Textually, the choice of character and animal symbolizes the area the character is supposedly from; the pseudo-Russian character, Olga Romanova, has a Siberian Tiger, native to Russiad; Bjorn, the Nordic character, is accompanied by Mox, a Muskox (Figure 1.3).

Another textual element of the game that resonates with this alternate version of history is the game board, which sees a landscape that vaguely resembles the European continent, but also conspicuously does not. Huge lakes populate the landscape, and the proportions and relative distances are significantly different from the real-world analogues.

From a formal standpoint, therefore, the textual elements all add up to depicting a situation that is close to, but not exactly like, the state of European

Figure 1.3 Characters from *Scythe*—l to r, Zehra and Kar (Crimean Khanate), Gunter von Duisburg with Nacht (Saxony Empire), Olga Romanova and Changa (Rusviet Union), Connor and Max (Clan Albion), Anna and Wojtek (Polania Republic), Akiko and Jiro (Togawa Shogunate), Bjorn and Mox (Nordic Kingdom).

history in the 1920s. In this, the game appears to be referencing a common genre of speculative fiction, the "counterfactual" or "alternate history" genre. Alternate histories show us two things: how our decisions have consequences, and how human decisions can create meaningful change in the world. According to Karen Hellekson, the basic model of an alternate history text revolves around the idea "that some event in the past did not occur as we know it did, and thus the present has changed."[22] The larger point of the alternate history is to ask, "how do particular moments in history shape who we are as a people?" Alternate history "rewrites history and reality, thus transforming the world and our understanding of reality"; they "make readers rethink their world" and "critique . . . the metaphors we use to discuss history."[23] For Matt Hills, these "counterfactual" histories actually disrupt our ideas about how we build our own histories; they create "ontological disruption and decentering" of rational thought, allowing audiences to see the real world in more critical ways.[24] In other words, we are forced to see our history as constructed rather than simply a "natural" state of affairs.

When we examine the textuality of *Scythe: Rise of Fenris* through a ludo-textual lens, however, this ideological connection to the alternate history is alternately reinforced and undermined via the underlying participation of the players in the game as well as the construction of player engagement. This becomes clear when the pieces are put on the board and the competition for control commences.* Every aspect of the game sets players in contrast with one another. A simple textual example, for instance, reveals this competition: each player has been given a Player Mat, from which they can choose their actions. But each Player Mat is arranged differently: first actions pair with different second actions on each Mat, and a different number of cubes may be placed on actions to make them easier or harder. One Mat is not inherently better than another, but the simple *textual* fact that they are different serves a *ludo-textual* purpose to differentiate each player from the others and to emphasize different play styles. For example, the Mat labeled *Agricultural* makes it easier to feed workers (which allows for more of them to enlist) and also gives more money at the start of the game. The *Industrial* Mat makes it easier to upgrade actions and, ultimately, to deploy the Mechs. While players don't have to follow the pathways charted on the Mat, the textual elements do help to articulate a particular way to play.

To end the game, players must complete objectives, but scoring money at the end depends on the number of territories a player controls (there are a limited number, which means players are naturally competing for advantage) and resources (there are not limited resources, but the more territories one controls, the more resources can be produced overall). From an ideological perspective, then, the theme of the counterfactual or alternate history is, on the one hand, reinforced by the way players complete the objectives. Alternate history texts attempt to show us that our decisions have consequences, and *Rise of Fenris* manifests this directly. *Rise of Fenris* quite overtly bills itself as a game that focuses on players' decisions. The website reads:

> *Scythe* gives players almost complete control over their fate. Other than each player's individual hidden objective cards, the only elements of luck are encounter cards that players will draw as they interact with the citizens of newly explored lands and combat cards that give you a temporary boost in combat. Combat is also driven by choices, not luck or randomness.[†]

---

* In *Scythe*, there is a solo mode, but even that is framed as a competitive one, where the player competes against an automated enemy. In *Rise of Fenris*, players can have a truce, but they are still working against each other to win the game.
† https://stonemaiergames.com/games/scythe/

Players win or lose depending on *their own decisions*; combat in the game can be kept to a minimum, and in fact, it is possible to play an entire game and never encounter the other player. This is *indirect competition*: both players are attempting to reach the same goal, and they do not necessarily have to interfere in the other players' options to do so. The game also allows *direct competition*, where one player can disrupt another player's plan. For example, in a game I was playing, I was just in the beginning of building my game engine. I needed to produce a particular resource (metal) to deploy more mechs, and I needed the mechs to help get a resource (wood) which would allow me to build buildings. I was set to collect the first set of resources when my opponent swooped in and stole the metal on a space I was occupying. This threw my engine in disarray—my next few turns were shot as I attempted to rebuild the resources I needed—and I was not able to fully recover as my opponent completed his engine to victory. While it didn't make much of a narrative difference to this strategy if it was an alternate history or not, the fact that it was alternate history reinforced the underlying ideology of decision making. History turns on decisions, according to the counterfactual, and demonstrated in *Scythe*.

On the other hand, *Rise of Fenris* simultaneously undermines the counterfactual ideology that we create our own histories—that history is not a natural consequence of one thing, but rather a confluence of many individual, human decisions. The competitive nature of *Rise of Fenris* contradicts this aspect of the alternate history when playing the campaign version. While the regular game of *Scythe* never directly details what caused the world to be different, the campaign *Rise of Fenris* articulates a specific moment, and inventor, that changed the course of history: Nikola Tesla. In 1901, Tesla invented the huge mechs that changed how war was waged, and thus created a "new world order"—an arms race between the nation states. In this history, the Great War began not through the assassination of Archduke Franz Ferdinand of Austria, but through the ever-escalating reliance on mechs and competition between nations. Upon witnessing the horrors his mechs brought to the people during wartime, Tesla goes mad and disappears. His (fictional) daughter, Vesna, attempts to use new mechs to prevent another war while Rasputin commandeers mechs and leads an army of evil soldiers called "Fenris" to take over the continent.

During the campaign game, players start with particular factions, but also control Vesna and Rasputin at times in a battle to control the future of the continent. Like the regular game, where the end goal of the game is not to change the landscape, to assert dominance, or to obliterate the other player, the goal in *Rise of Fenris* is also to amass a fortune. Many of the *decisions* that a player can take in the game lead to *individual* changes in a particular game session, but the larger narrative of the game has to fit into the already-created scenarios. Campaign games depend on narrative development, as Arnaudo notes: these games "take the idea of progressive revelation very seriously, to the point that they come with many game parts sealed in marked envelopes and boxes, and the players are expected to open each container and add the new components only when instructed by the game."[25] After the first session in the campaign game, for example, players have the option to attempt a truce or go to war: this decision affects whether the second scenario will be "war" (Scenario 2A) or "peace" (Scenario 2B), but regardless of which scenario is played, the third scenario ("A Plea from Vesna") will always be the same. Our decision here had no consequences on the narrative of the game; the only consequence was that the penultimate scenario included slightly different components. Similarly, each scenario is won in the same way—whoever can earn the most money wins (different scenarios may set up the conditions for earning money differently). In order to fit the eight scenarios in one campaign, competition must be tempered; factions cannot, for instance, destroy other factions, and characters cannot die. The narrative of *Rise of Fenris* is predetermined and players have no option but to follow the path set out by Stegmaier. The point of a campaign game is to develop game stories over time, and while a *textual* analysis might reveal that the counterfactual theme matches the games' ideology, a *ludo-textual* analysis shows that the narrative preempts meaningful narrative (re: historical) decisions.

If *Rise of Fenris* articulates a competitive game mechanic within the campaign format, *Pandemic Legacy: Season 1* illustrates what happens when a cooperative game is played over in a Legacy style, with multiple, connected game sessions. The original *Pandemic* (2008, Z-Man Games) is, perhaps, one of the best known cooperative games.[26] As described on the publisher's website, "As skilled members of a disease-fighting team, you and the other players work together to keep the world safe from outbreaks and epidemics. Only through teamwork will you have a chance to find a cure."* Cooperation is the key mechanic in this game, as players must work together to complete different actions to both eradicate diseases and save cities from plagues. Like *Scythe*, the game has multiple textual elements that connect it to its underlying ideology, but a ludo-textual analysis

---

* https://www.zmangames.com/en/games/pandemic/

reveals connections within the Legacy game to different ideologies, including those about the cooperation and connectivity.

Board games are traditionally competitive—that is, games consist of multiple players vying for control and, ultimately, victory over the others in the game. Competition is the most common style of game play, and we can observe it in many of the games we see and play in our everyday lives: sports are generally competitive, most mass-market games are competitive, and with some minor exceptions, most popular multiplayer video games are competitive. Competition—or, *agon*, as games scholar Roger Caillois calls it in his influential 1961 *Man, Play and Games*—is seemingly a fundamental part of game play, as we assume that most games must have a single winner and, therefore, one or more losers. Competition is not necessarily a bad thing in games, and competitive games can offer meaningful experiences.[27] Indeed, as Katie Salen and Eric Zimmerman assert, at a certain level, all games are competitive, even solo games and games played cooperatively, as in each of those cases players are working against (competing with) a game system. Yet, even despite the ubiquity of competition, there is a fundamentally different feeling when playing a board game competitively against or cooperatively with other people. Playing competitively puts players on opposite sides of the board; while they can still talk and share as much as they might want to, there is less of a feeling of "being in it together." The social dynamics reward secrecy and individualism. The most engaging cooperative sessions, in contrast, often find a form of groupthink, where players work in sync to problem solve. Unlike a competitive game, where players are working against each other, cooperative games can enhance group dynamics as players work together to defeat a challenging system.[28] The designer of *Pandemic*, Matt Leacock, describes them as offering a "feeling of togetherness."[29] One dynamic is not better than the other, but they do each provide different affective journeys. A ludo-textual analysis can reveal that, when playing competitively against other players, the actual experience of the game can be significantly different than compared with playing cooperatively.

A simple textual analysis of *Pandemic* reveals similar components to *Scythe*: we may not have plastic miniature mechs or characters, but there are cubes of various colors, a board with a map on it, markers of various sizes, and cards that depict countries. Analyzing these texts shows us a clear picture of a connected world. Cities on the board are connected by thick, colored lines and are color-coded depending on the region. Thus, textually, the elements in the game point to the interconnectedness of the globe—no city is an island (not even Sydney, the only city on the Australian island continent).

The game uses a Hand Management mechanic along with Action Point Allowance—all players have a certain number of actions and they can do any of those actions on their turn, and they can only hold seven cards in their hand at a time. Players must collect sets of cards in order to "cure" diseases (as represented by cubes on the board), but a random mechanism in the game—cards drawn every turn—adds more diseases to the board. However, every-so-often, an "Epidemic" card will be drawn, which accelerates and intensifies the diseases by adding a new city to the spread of diseases, and reinfecting cities that have been infected recently. Thus, there is a random element in drawing some cities, but after a few rounds, players will also know which cities are more likely to come up when drawing cards. These mechanics necessitate careful planning, as there are always more actions available than there are characters to take them.

Characters are key to *Pandemic* and its Legacy version, *Pandemic: Season 1*. Unlike a campaign-style game, which can be reset and played again, a Legacy-style game embodies consequential change. Moments in the game can affect textual elements, as the board can be altered with stickers, cards can be destroyed, and attributes added to characters. Like many story-driven games, the experience "comes to life" when players begin to know their characters, "making it possible to establish a deep connection with the theme and the characters in the game."[30] In traditional *Pandemic*, each character has a special ability that can be advantageous in a variety of situations. These

> individualized characters . . . don't have inventories or goals, but they do have special powers that are some of the best in the cooperative field because they make a constant difference in the game on a turn-by-turn basis. . . . Each turn, players think about how their power can affect the game as a whole—which is a great goal for adventure-style powers.[31]

For instance, the Dispatcher can move another player's pawn instead of their own (e.g., they can dispatch someone somewhere on the board). A simple textual analysis thus reveals that the ideology of connection seen on the board and the cards is mirrored in the characters; each character can help the group in different ways, using their special abilities.

A ludo-textual analysis demonstrates how the Legacy version of *Pandemic: Season 1* takes this ideology further. As Christopher Allen and Shannon Appelcline note, "individual characters with special powers" are "at the forefront of cooperative gaming," as it is crucial to use these special abilities to complete the game.[32] And as with the ideology of the original *Pandemic*, when *players* feel connected to their characters, and characters are connected to one another via their special abilities, the group can win the game. In the Legacy game, which takes place over one year's time frame within the world, a number of diseases appear across the world. Yet, rather than curing them at the end of the game, at the end of the first scenario ("January"), players learn that one disease is *incurable*. The disease eventually mutates and cubes that represent the disease are replaced with green, infected people (while that city becomes "faded").

The characters that players control also develop over time. When they first start playing, players not only take on a particular role (with requisite attributes—a Dispatcher, for instance, can still move others around the board), but also get to name the character and can continue to play as them throughout the game's campaign. Additionally, at the end of every session, players have the option of adding additional characteristics to the characters they represent. Positive abilities can be added to enhance each character. For instance, Jonathan Schwartz, the Medic character I controlled, had not only the ability to cure more diseases per action, but additional abilities, like "Forecaster: At the start of your turn, look at the first two Infection cards," which helped him identify when new cities would appear. Characters could also have more specific relationships with one another; my Medic was a rival with Riley Adams, which meant he could discard two cards to pick up a card that this other player played. He was also a coworker of Demarius Martin, meaning they could pass cards back and forth. Ending a turn in a city with a disease outbreak resulted in a scar, a negative characteristic. For instance, a character might find themselves *Germaphobic*, meaning they have to discard cards to enter a research station. My Medic was *Indecisive*, meaning that he could not build a roadblock (Figure 1.4). The point here is that characters change over time, and the way they change is player-directed, augmenting play with character identification. Although players have a limited number of options of abilities to add (twenty-one negative attributes; four relationships, sixteen positive attributes), the great variety of combinations can result in different players having wildly different experiences.

Through player customization of the characters, the textual elements change; a ludo-textual analysis takes this player interactivity into consideration. From an ideological perspective, a ludo-textual analysis reveals how the connectivity highlighted by the original game continues in the *Legacy* version. Not only are cities connected, but players can make characters connected as well. They may

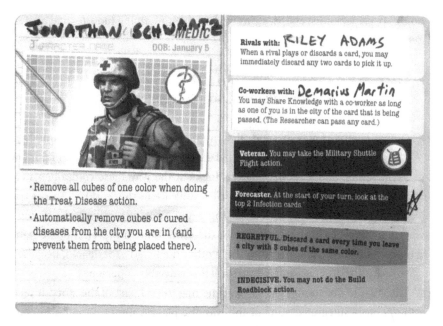

Figure 1.4 Jonathan Schwartz, the hardest-working Medic in *Pandemic Legacy: Season 1*.

not start that way, but through player investment the characters become more real, and also change throughout the game as more abilities are added. The game requires us to see each character as important and unique, and yet no character is separate from the others.

In many ways, this ideology of cooperation and connectivity reflects the changing world outside of *Pandemic: Season 1*. While digital networks and social media may be facilitating greater *communication*, individuals can still feel disassociated from their immediate social networks. People develop more weak ties through digital communication, and fewer strong ties in the physical world. In other words, we are in contact with more people than ever before (or at least have the possibility to be) but we don't feel as close to as many people as we might have in the past. One palliative to this spread of weak ties is, as *Pandemic: Season 1* both ideologically and practically illustrates, the board game. Unless we play solo (see Chapter 9), we always play board games with others, in social spaces, and build those strong social ties (see Chapters 6 and 7). *Pandemic's* ideological focus on community and connection is not just about the ways characters must work together; it's always about the way board games themselves create stronger bonds. In the game, characters must work together to save the world, and in doing so, players must cooperate as well, as the underlying ludo-textual analysis demonstrates.

Conclusion: Meeples Together

All games have components, and all components can be read for the underlying meanings that they represent. A textual analysis reveals how these components make meaning; and a formal analysis looks at the way these components can come together to "make deliberate expressions about the world."[33] This is true of all media, whether we are unboxing a toy, watching a film, examining a television show, or playing a game. At the same time, however, a board game is also significantly different from these other mediated experiences, because it necessarily doesn't come into being until it is played by a person.

Thus, while the components of a game may reveal part of the story, it takes a much more integrated view of the way the players use those parts to come to a fuller conclusion. Rather than a representational look at cubes, meeples, cards, or boards, a ludo-textual analysis takes into account the meaning of a player's contributions in concert with those physical items. The characters in *Pandemic: Season 1* can represent a profession, but in the right hands, they could also become connected to other characters, representing lived experiences in a way that deepens the experience of the players and coheres the ideological message of the game.

There are, of course, limitations to a textual analysis: first and foremost, like the other qualitative methodologies examined within this book, textual analysis doesn't rely on numbers or quantifiable data to reach conclusions. More empirically minded scholars may view such methodologies as weaker and inherently subjective. Textual analysis depends on the ideas and connections made by the researcher; ludo-textual analysis adds in the additional component of understanding player action as well.

Yet, subjectivity can be a strength rather than a weakness. As I described earlier in the chapter, subjectivity allows us to try to understand someone else's viewpoint. By observing the choices that a player makes, we can understand their way of thinking. Further, empirical studies are hard to generalize in terms of human behavior, of which board game play is composed. Human beings are imperfect, inconsistent creatures: how one person reacts at one time may be wildly different from how they react at a later time. *Pandemic: Season 1* may be a very different game if one plays it from the relative safety of a twenty-first-century American suburb, but it becomes a wholly different story if one were to play during, say, the COVID-19 epidemic that hit the world in 2020 (during that actual pandemic, Matt Leacock, the creator of the game *Pandemic*, penned an op-ed for the *New York Times* that detailed why cooperation is important for solving a real-world disease). The context matters.

A textual or even ludo-textual analysis does not have to be the end of a board game analysis. As my discussion of *Scythe: Rise of Fenris* and *Pandemic Legacy: Season 1* has illustrated, many games (especially modern, thematic games) have ideological meanings that can be further understood and developed. An examination of the pieces coupled with a discussion of the competitive or cooperative play styles reveals these underlying ideologies. One doesn't have to look at the play styles particularly, and I could imagine a ludo-textual analysis that examined mechanics more fully, or detailed player dialogue. The point is that a ludo-textual analysis opens up the game components and game play elements to find further cultural relevance. And in doing so, game scholars reveal how board games make comments about the world we live in.

A Depressing Choose-Your-Own Adventure

The Interactive Potentiality of Board Games

At first glance, scrounging for food in a decimated city's war zone or helping a terminally ill person come to terms with the mistakes he made in his life does not appear to be traditional narrative fodder for board games, a medium more associated with cute animals or play money than dramatic and depressing subject matter like death, mortality, and war. Who would want to sit down for two hours to play a game where the end is the literal death of the main character? Or where there is a very real chance you might get emotionally attached to a character only to see them shot by a sniper? Yet, all of these serious topics, and scores more just like them, have been featured in games that appeal not just because of their play mechanics, not just because of the cooperative or competitive styles, but also because of the arguments and underlying themes they're creating with the difficult subject matter of the game. These are games about serious topics, and they reflect a serious agenda. In playing through them, players are encouraged to see the world in a new way, to experience a mental shift in their understanding of morality, virtue, social interaction, and other serious aspects of the world.

In this chapter, I am interested in the way board games can make arguments by emphasizing *strategy* or *randomness* in game play, to persuade players to see the world differently. In order to investigate these modes of meaning-making, I undertake a rhetorical analysis of two games, *This War of Mine* (2017, Galakta), and *Holding On: The Troubled Life of Billy Kerr* (2018, Hub Games), to uncover a variety of ways that board games can persuade their players. Persuasion is not new to games. As games scholar Ian Bogost notes, all games encourage players to "understand, evaluate, and deliberate" the world around them, and the games described in this chapter are focused on creating expressions about survival, life and death, and love.[1] Unlike the previous chapter, which examined games' ludo-textual attributes to arrive at an underlying ideology, this chapter uses rhetorical analysis to understand how games themselves create a convincing point of view. How do board games persuade their players? And what are the consequences when they do? Of course, while the two games I'm focusing on in this chapter are well suited to the type of rhetorical criticism I'll be conducting, it should not be inferred that *only* board games about "depressing" topics can create arguments. All games can create arguments; all games can shape the way players interpret their own lives. Through a rhetorical analysis, board game scholars can dig down into the underlying structures of the game that illustrate these arguments, and can develop their own ways of interpreting what games are telling them.

I argue that a rhetoric of board games emphasizes *possibilities* rather than *procedures* at play, what I'm calling an *interactive potentiality*. In *Game Play*, I described interactive potentiality as when "players must negotiate their own activity within the larger boundaries encompassing the game."[2] In other words, players of board games make choices that are guided, not controlled, by the game rules. Ultimately, the rhetorical argumentation games make must be facilitated by the players' own interactions with the game. I examine the way that the arguments of a board game can be filtered through an emphasis on players' decisions: in the case of the games in this chapter, through the tension between strategy and randomness in game play. All games usually contain aspects of both strategy (making plans and decisions) and luck (something beyond the players' control). Specifically, this chapter examines *This War of Mine* as using *player strategy* to emphasize a rhetorical argument about how the choices we make affect the lives of others (extrapolating that to a larger geopolitical sense as well) while *Holding On* uses *game randomness* to create a rhetorical argument about the unpredictability of our life's events (extending that within a personal storyline). Thus, in analyzing the way different games emphasize strategy or randomness, board game players can recognize the rhetorical arguments games generate, and the meanings games create.

Rhetorical Analysis and Board Games

Any rhetorical analysis examines and critiques the particular strategies a communicator uses to persuade their audience to see the world in a distinctive

---

* This contrasts with video games, where unless players actually hack the system, they must abide by the algorithmic rules that structure the game world.

way. Traditional rhetorical scholars, for instance, might look at how claims are supported by logos (reason), pathos (emotion), and ethos (character). We might think about a politician who quotes statistics about gun violence to make a case for gun control (logos), a commercial that tugs at the heart strings to encourage us to purchase a particular brand of soup (pathos), or a celebrity using their history of social activism to promote a socially conscious film (ethos). Board games might also use logos, pathos, and ethos to create arguments: a game about managing resources effectively plays on logical/mathematical models, a game that asks us to care about characters is relying on pathos, and a game that we purchase because we like the designer relies on ethos. Rhetorical analysis is often used to examine "the intended effect of the object of criticism on its readers": that is, analysts are concerned not just with *how* the arguments are made, but also *what effect* those arguments have on the audience.[3]

Thus, rhetorical analysis can be applied to any situation where an audience might be persuaded to believe something, or to think a particular way, including traditional speeches, mass media communication, electronic communication, and—importantly—in board games. Applying a rhetorical critique to a board game takes some massaging of traditional rhetorical methods; rhetoric is often discussed in terms of deliberate speech rather than interactive play actions.[4] For instance, exploring how a particular speaker forms an argument requires seeing a distinction between the act of speaking and the act of hearing—although both participants play a role in constructing the *meaning* of the speech, the underlying focus of this type of traditional rhetorical structure sees the speaker as central to the speech itself (of course, other forms of rhetorical analysis emphasize the audience's role in understanding the speech through different contexts too). Yet, board games pose a unique challenge in understanding this act, because so much of a game is based on the interaction between player and game.[5]

The term "rhetoric" is often applied today in a pejorative way (e.g., "This politician is nothing but empty rhetoric!"), and partially this can be attributed to the fact that early rhetoricians focused on two different ways of applying rhetorical techniques. Traditional rhetoricians would focus on the strength of the argument, while the sophists—a kind of wandering instructor in ancient Greece who would teach techniques of performance—focused more on the style of presentation. In contemporary argumentation, both content and style are important for communicating an argument to an audience; and in board games, this can be applied to the way the game's theme/narrative and the representation of that theme/narrative both contribute to a player's understanding of the game (see Chapter 3). A key shift in the history of rhetorical criticism was the "new rhetoric" of the early twenty-first century. Scholars such as Kenneth Burke articulated the importance of relationships for persuasion. Burke's focus on a speaker's "consubstantiation" with his/her audience (that is, finding points in common between them) presented wholly new ways that persuasion could occur.[6] Persuasion occurs not because of a didactic relationship of the speaker to the audience, but rather through the mutual feelings of identification shared by participants in the communication process. Burke's method of dramatism, for instance, highlighted "the importance of rhetoric in constructing and mediating human society," by focusing on how language itself helps to construct reality.[7] Again, to connect this to board games, we can see how the features of communication within the game—the images on the cards, the actions taken by the players, even the elements that structure game play itself—can impact players' persuasion through their identification with the game and the game designers. While a traditional rhetorical analysis of board games might look at the representations within the game, and how the game integrates that representation into the style of play demonstrated by the players, a new *interactive potentiality* rhetorical analysis might examine how individual players are encouraged to use those representations as foundational for persuasion.

Games have not traditionally been the focus of rhetorical criticism. Partly, this is because games are a leisure pastime: they are played, not taken seriously. We associate games with lazy days, children's play, or holidays, the exact opposite of more "serious" (or, "refined") activities that "should be" culturally valued. Board games are therefore unremarked-upon as meaning-making entities. In the realm of video games, however, Ian Bogost has articulated a striking rationale for why games should be understood in precisely these valuable terms:

> Video games are not just stages that facilitate cultural, social, or political practices; they are also media where cultural values themselves can be represented—for critique, satire, education, or commentary. When understood in this way, we can learn to read games as deliberate expressions of particular perspectives.[8]

My focus on rhetorical analysis of board games has precedent: Bogost's groundbreaking *Persuasive Games* argues that a new type of rhetorical structure, a procedural rhetoric, reflects a "persuasive and expressive practice" at work in video games.[9] Because video games are an algorithmic system—that is, they are governed and controlled by a set of rules that outline what players can do and how players can act within the game system—they also function *persuasively* "for making arguments with computational systems and for unpacking computational arguments others have created."[10] As he writes, "A game's procedural rhetoric influences the player's relationship with it by constraining the strategies that yield failure or success."[11] For players of video games, the arguments made through the rules of game play can articulate particular ways of perceiving the world: Bogost gives the example of Molleindustria's *McDonald's Videogame*, which forces players to either make unethical business decisions or lose the game, creating a critique of the fast-food industry through the application of procedures within the game itself.

Bogost, however, reflects that procedural rhetoric may not apply in the cases of board games where "human-enacted processes[,] the people playing the game[,] execute its rules."[12] Board games, unlike the video games he studies, use rules merely to set the stage and run the game, instead of completely delimiting players' actions through algorithmic manipulation. Board games cannot, by definition, control the interaction that players have with the game system. Just to give a relevant example—if a video game creator decides to lock the "camera" in a particular position, it is impossible (without hacking, and therefore changing the game state) to alter the view the player has of the game field. But a board game designer cannot artificially limit the perspective of a player who can, if she wishes, move her head or squint her eyes to gain an alternate viewpoint. Player agency trumps creator control. Or, if I decide to cheat and break a rule in a board game, nothing (except cultural mores) can stop me. A video game can delimit actions in a way board games cannot.

So while Bogost argues persuasively that rules are a defining feature of procedural rhetoric, I'd like to make a complementary proposition: because the board game only exists within the actions of the player, it by necessity must invoke player agency. Players of board games must have a consubstantial identification—that is, as Burke describes, "attributes of a common ground or substance"—with aspects of the game in order for the rhetorical argument to take hold.[13] For game players, the "thesis" of the game becomes articulated through interactive potentiality, a sense that that all board games' argumentation requires player investment. This investment occurs through the interaction between the material components of the game combined with the actual game play. The game system engenders multiple possibilities constrained only by the input of the players because of the interaction between the players and the materials of the game. Tom Grimwood (2018) describes how a rhetorical approach to argumentation "insists on the materiality of communication,"[14] and here I take this literally: the materiality of the game engenders argumentation.

One commonly cited example of a socially relevant game that has used interactive potentiality through materiality to create argumentation is Brenda Romero's *Train* (2009). In *Train*, players have to load yellow pegs (representing people) onto trains efficiently, while being given instructions via a typewriter. At some point during the game, players learn that the destination of the trains they are populating is Auschwitz, and they have become complicit in the representation of Jews being loaded onto a box car and led to the gas chamber during the Second World War. The game's emotional/pathos punch is palpable, and it may seem obvious what message the game is sending. As Dean Takahashi notes in his review, "Train is not so much a game as a system" designed to communicate "complicity."[15] Yet, *how Train* communicates this argument is uniquely articulated through the board game's interactive potentiality. Because players follow the game system, they are consubstantial with the game's flow and structure: their actions within the game help the game to progress. Romero defines these as "procedural gaps" where players have to stop and identify with the game in order to continue.[16] They become part of the system. Interactive potentiality reveals the rhetorical message: that blindly following orders (or rules in a game) makes one complicit with those orders/rules.

Mary Flanagan's *Critical Play: Radical Game Design* further articulates the way games can "engage in . . . social issue[s]."[17] Flanagan gives numerous examples of these types of rhetorical games throughout history, including *The Landlord's Game* (1904), the first game granted a US patent, and which eventually was purloined into *Monopoly* (1933, Hasbro). Originally, *The Landlord's Game* critiqued the capitalist system through economic lessons, making the players complicit in the exploitation of the working class. These types of games, of which *Train* is one, "represent one or more questions about aspects of human life," what Evan Torner, Aaron Trammell, and Emma Waldron in the first issue of *Analog Games\ Studies* say "can offer an insight into the ways that games work to produce social change."[18] For Flanagan, as well as Romero, making board games isn't just about creating systems where players can interact; it's about how these games create arguments.

Strategy and Randomness in *This War of Mine* and *Holding On*

The interactive potentiality of board games to create rhetorical meaning can be observed through two examples of serious games, each of which uses player interaction in different ways. Two guiding elements of all board games are strategy and randomness. Both drive the progression of a game play session, although each works differently. Looking back through the history of game studies, early game scholars often characterized games based on this dichotomy: as we saw in the previous chapter, Roger Caillois's delineation of games referred to some as based in *agon*, or games of competition and skill; or those based in *alea*, or games of chance.[19] Strategy is the sense that a game's progression can be foreseen and enacted through the decision-making abilities of the players; or, as game scholar Stewart Woods writes, "the devising and implementation of longer-term plans in the pursuit of a given goal."[20] Randomness, or "uncertainty in outcome," is the sense that a game progresses because of factors outside the control of the players, which renders "the game less susceptible to any conclusive analysis" by players.[21] Randomness is not the same as having random elements—for instance, while a die roll is a random element, having the fate of the player depend on the outcome of multiple die rolls would increase the randomness in the game—and it is not the same thing as luck, which is a level of unknowability within a game system (e.g., whether your opponent has a particular aptitude for a game is luck).[22]

Most games invoke both elements, albeit in different amounts, and many "games can strike a remarkable balance between randomness and structure."[23] Luck and skill are not opposites, but complementary.[24] Take a common game like *Scrabble* (1948, Hasbro)—there are both strategic elements that are controlled by the players (deciding which letters to play in which order, knowing obscure words, counting tiles to know which letters might appear next) and random elements that the players have little control over (which tiles are chosen from the bag). Some games have much more strategy than randomness: Chess is a good example of an almost entirely strategic game, as player decisions about piece movement almost completely overshadow any random elements, like who one is playing against.[25] Some games are almost entirely luck-based: for instance, the game of *Candyland* (1949, Hasbro) is almost entirely random, given that players simply draw cards and move to the color on that card. Assuming a shuffled deck, there is no strategy to the game. In fact, one could argue that as soon as the deck is shuffled, the winner has been determined; revealing the cards simply manifests something that is already set.[26]

Both elements of game play produce different effects. Randomness in a game can add exciting moments of happenstance that can work well in a player's favor, or moments of tragedy when a player's advantage can be cut short by the cruel roll of the die. (All gamers have a story about that time they *could have won if only they'd rolled a six!*) In this way, luck can mirror the vagaries of fate, with all the religious connotations one wants to insert here—god is punishing or rewarding a good player; blowing on the dice helps create luck, and so on. Randomness can also shift players' attention from "the ludic functions of the [game] design to the enjoyment of the flow of the story."[27] Luck can be deliberately deployed in games to mirror a sense of uncertainty in our everyday lives, as Torner notes: "If what we call 'culture' is based on knowledge, ignorance, and practices that delineate the known from the unknown, then a designer's deliberate use of uncertainty becomes a decisively cultural act."[28] As we'll see, randomness can emulate a sense of *loss of control* that can be meaningful for the underlying structure of a game. Strategy can have the opposite effect: it rewards players that can plan, scheme, and outthink their opponents. There is nothing more satisfying than seeing one's best-laid plans play out exactly as intended—the right order of cards played, the correct spell cast to counter an enemy's attack, and so on. In this way, strategy emulates planning and effective choice in life, a reliance on our free will. As I'll demonstrate, strategy also mirrors the *sense of control* that can articulate a particular meaning within a game as well.

Contemporary board games' uses of both strategic and random elements help construct arguments about the thematic and representational content of the game. For the purposes of this chapter, I'll illustrate this using *This War of Mine*, a game based on the video game of the same title, about a group of survivors in a devastated war zone, and *Holding On: The Troubled Life of Billy Kerr*, a game in which an elderly Irish man has a heart attack on an airplane and is brought into a London hospital, where nurses have to keep him alive and help him come to terms with his own past trauma. Both of these games use both random and strategic elements; they are, as Woods describes, "relatively complex systems [created] from a variety of sub-mechanics."[29] At the same time, both games are heavily laden with theme; the actual random elements of each game are relatively simplistic, often no more than rolling a die or drawing a card. But when put in the contexts of what Woods calls the *thematic model* of each game—"the world into which the player is transported"—and the *thematic goal* of each game—the fictional motivation to pursue the goals of the game"—both games create rhetorically meaningful scenarios through interactive potentiality.[30]

This War of Mine

This War of Mine uses players' strategic decisions within play to create arguments about the brutality of war, the effects of posttraumatic stress disorder (PTSD), and the ethics of warfare in general. It accomplishes this argumentation by using strategy and the interactive potentiality of the players. In the game, players collectively take on the roles of three civilians living in a ramshackle, broken-down structure, trying to survive in a besieged city during a war. Additional characters can join the group, and collectively the players must all make decisions for the good of the group. The game is won when at least one of the three starting survivors makes it to the end of the game—that is, in a depressing reflection of wartime reality, two or more characters can die in the game and the players still succeed. The board game is based on a video game of the same name, and uses many of the same thematic elements, although there are specific differences that make board game analysis useful here: the video game is a solo experience, while the board game deliberately uses multiple players to collectively make decisions, highlighting the social aspects of the game; additionally, the tangible immersion in the game via the detailed components, the thousands of script elements, and the act of physically moving pieces around the board contributes to the interactive potentiality of the game play.

The characters in the game have multiple attributes that change depending on player decisions: hunger, wounds, illness, misery, and fatigue. As each attribute level increases, the character becomes unable to complete different tasks. If any characters' attribute reaches level four in the game, they die—four hunger means they starve; four illness means they succumb to their sickness; four misery means they can't take survival anymore and commit suicide. A typical game play session of *This War of Mine* can take a couple of hours, as there are many decisions to make and ways the game can progress. The game is split into a number of days, and each day is divided into seven phases: morning, day, dusk, evening, scavenging, night raid, and dawn. During each of these phases, players will have particular decisions to make regarding their characters and the strategic use of resources to survive. For example, during the dusk phase, all characters need to have one water token, and any players who do not eat food will have their "hunger" attribute raised by one. During the scavenging phase, players can decide to send characters to locations in the city to try to find supplies like water or parts to repair the structure, or trade with other survivors, but they might also meet residents, soldiers, or gangs who will possibly steal their supplies or kill them. During the night raid phase, raiders from outside the structure will attempt to invade the house and can steal food and supplies, as well as wound characters left there. And there is always the threat of snipers arbitrarily (e.g., randomly) taking out a character. At various times within the game, players will be asked to read a section of an enormous script (over a thousand sections with material for tens of thousands of different possibilities), which often outlines a number of difficult choices they have to take. Not knowing the outcome of the choices forces players to decide whether to risk their continued survival for the chance of success. For example, one script moment found our characters stumbling across a mound of freshly packed dirt in the ground. We had to decide whether to spend the time digging it up in case someone had buried food or supplies there. Spending more time meant we were exposed to gangs and had less time to explore a location, but we had the chance of finding something worth digging for. The interactive potentiality could have led in many directions, and our choices had real consequences. In the end, we decided to dig, hoping to find food, but found only corpses. We earned nothing except misery for our experience.

As the description of the game reflects, *This War of Mine* does not tackle a traditional "fun" subject for gaming like battling mechs across Europa or curing pandemics. Instead, it focuses on the horrors of war and the struggles of civilian characters to survive in a situation they themselves did not create. Unlike traditional wargaming in the tabletop hobby, which takes a command-centric view of war and players are generals controlling armies facing off on simulated landscapes, this "war game" shows the on-the-ground civilian consequences of war.[31] The characters in *This War of Mine* are everyday people—teachers, lawyers, athletes—and represent aspects of war often ignored or elided in traditional news reports or wargames.

This War of Mine is similar in many respects to *The Grizzled* (2015, Sweet Games), a game about soldiers in the trenches in the First World War. Like *This War of Mine*, *The Grizzled*

> encourages its players to feel things other than the joy, challenge, and pleasure people often seek from games. It sets itself apart from many cooperative games by insisting that injuries and traumas to one's character are unavoidable, and by centering its core game mechanics on facing the effects of trauma, rather than attempting to escape or evade its causes.[32]

Yet, there are some significant differences between these two games that reveal the horrors of war. In *The Grizzled*, for instance, each player takes control of a particular character—the identification with these soldiers affects players because of "unavoidable consequences accrue directly to the players' characters"[33]—but the trauma of *This War of Mine* emerges because all the players control all the civilian characters, characters who didn't even sign up for battle. In *The Grizzled*, each character can take on "limiting conditions" as the game goes on, which affect the players as well—for instance, characters might receive "Mute: You can no longer speak or communicate with other players in any way. You may not use a Speech," which applies to the *player* playing the characters. In Greg Loring-Albright's analysis, these conditions "shift the player focus toward the effect of trauma, rather than its cause." Yet, in contrast, *This War of Mine* features fewer specific player-character connections. All players play all characters, make decisions for all characters, and experience sadness when all characters dies. The horrors are made more explicit through this representational construct, as this dispersal of player connection focuses more on the cause of trauma than on the effect.

All attributes in *This War of Mine* have the same effect: the higher the level, the fewer actions the character has. This makes sense from a narrative perspective because it means that character is too weak to do anything, and from a game perspective it means that one has to be careful with balancing their characters' decisions. But it also makes it that much harder to get anything done, which actually constrains the actions players can take during the "day" phase. The interactive potentiality of the game means that meting out wounds, hunger, and other attributes is strategic and meaningful. Playing the game leads to cruel decisions about which characters to kill (who has less value than others). In our group, uncomfortable discussions followed these decisions, as we had come to see these figures as mimetic characters through the extended interaction we had with them.

For example, players have to decide collectively how to divvy up two units of food for four characters; how many characters get to take a weapon when scavenging, which characters to heal and which to leave ill. Do we continue to let one character starve, effectively killing her, so that the others might eat? We were encouraged by the game to identify with the characters through the many details of the characters' lives in the script, and as Arnaudo describes, this is so we "care about our character . . . attachment encourages us to take the events that involve her more seriously."[34] During my group's play session, we had a number of strategic decisions to make about the use of supplies, but we had to turn off our emotional connection to the characters and base these decisions on logic instead of emotion if we wanted to win the game (and made use reconsider what "winning" even meant). For example, we had to heal wounds on our characters, and our decision was based on whether or not we would be wasting bandages (the only tool to heal wounds) in future rounds—if the character was already close to death because of hunger, for instance, it didn't make sense to heal their wounds as the bandages could be better used to heal a character with greater chances of survival. In other words, we focused on one character's survival (the win condition), which meant reducing the amount of time that we spent doing anything other than what was absolutely necessary.

In *This War of Mine*, strategic choice and random elements imbricate to advance the interactive potentiality of the game. Other choices that players make in the game are also meaningful but random. For example, when exploring a location in the scavenging phase, we have to decide to take a shovel with us in case we encounter rubble (only a shovel can move rubble). It's a random draw from a deck of cards if we encounter the rubble, but the presence of the shovel can change the game (characters can only carry a set amount of weight, and a shovel adds to that). How much food to stockpile requires understanding whether or not a night raid will take that particular resource (night raids are drawn from a deck of cards, and knowing how many list "food" on them becomes a percentage game). Deciding which location to visit in and of itself (there are three at any time on the board) is strategic, as visiting a hospital, for example, will increase the likelihood of finding medicine or bandages, while visiting a police station will increase the likelihood of finding weapons. Supplies are found by rolling a die while at these locations, which juxtaposes the strategic understanding of the underlying mathematics of the game with the randomness that a particular die roll can engender (see Figure 2.1).

Using strategy and skills coheres the player to the characters because it forces the players to think about what they might do in these circumstances. I've previously called this a form of "pathos" in the game, where players' "affective actions happening to a character in a media text" creates a "feeling of connection between character and player."[35] The more players can learn about the characters and the world that the characters inhabit—in other words, the more players "increase . . . knowledge within a community," the more they "can either increase or decrease the skill[s]" used in the game.[36] Strategy becomes an important component of interactive potentiality, as the choices that players make, especially with the weight that each choice can bring, further cements the underlying argument of the game. In *This War of Mine*, players quickly learn

Figure 2.1 Three characters in *This War of Mine* scavenge to find medicine.

that there are never enough supplies to support all the characters. The strategy of which supplies to divvy up becomes linked to the underlying rhetorical act of the game, to force players to see the civilians and survivors of war as individuals at the mercy of larger forces. No matter how hard players/characters struggle, some will perish and others will emerge scarred for life. At the end of the game, the script offers surviving characters stories that depend on the level of misery they've suffered throughout the game: The more the misery, the more sad the story. In our game, even though he survived, Pavle's story was unhappy. Even after surviving the war, he lost his family. Other stories detail survivors of the war suffering from PTSD or physical ailments. The argumentation of the game relies on players having been invested in the characters, in the possibilities generated by the many choices made in the game.

At the same time, the randomness of the game highlights the fact that within war, there are also elements out of our control. My group actually played this game twice. The first time we had very different characters and some pretty dire circumstances right off the bat, so lost after the first day. Two of our characters, in a search for food, were shot and killed, and our third character, Anton, became emotionally scarred on one of his scavenging missions because he encountered a gang. Of course, narratively, the way this occurred was exciting. Because he had no weapons when he encountered the gang (a poor strategic choice on our part), Anton had to beat a gang member to death with his bare hands (mechanically, rolling a gray die and coming up with "fists"). In the process, though, Anton felt miserable about the death, and his guilt about this murder eventually drove him to kill himself. At the end of the second game, in which we barely eked out a victory, only one of our original characters survived (Pavle the soccer player) while one original character survived with misery at 3 (Bruno the chef). We left parts of the house unexplored simply because our characters didn't have enough energy (too much fatigue). We ended the game with a score of -17, revealing that even though we won, we did not succeed—a great metaphor for war itself.

But there is a further extension of this game's rhetorical argument—that if the choices we make as *players* affect the narrative of the *game*, then the choices we make as *citizens* can affect the narrative of the *world*. In other words, war is always a choice. There's no shame in this game. There's no shame in characters drinking moonshine to forget their misery for an evening or smoking to ignore their hunger, or in killing someone, or in leaving someone to die. There's no room for shame when you're just trying to survive. Making use of interactive potentiality, the lessons of *This War of Mine* rely on the careful deployment of strategic choice to cohere players to the characters and random elements to mimic the uncertainty of war.

Holding On

In contrast to *This War of Mine*, the game *Holding On: The Troubled Life of Billy Kerr* uses random elements within the game to simulate events that are simply out of the players'—or characters'—control. The game presents arguments about memory and dementia, about the ethics of medical care, and about the effect a traumatic past can have on someone in the present. In the game, players take on the role of nurses working in a hospital to which Billy Kerr, an elderly

Irish man, is admitted after he has a heart attack on an airplane. Played out over ten different scenarios, each of which narratively builds on the ones that came before, the game is ultimately won or lost not by Billy's survival (players are clued in at the start that he will eventually die) but by whether or not the nurses can provide enough palliative care while he is hospitalized so that he can recall memories from the past and come to terms with his and his Father's own culpability in the Troubles in Northern Ireland. Throughout the game, the interactive potentiality of the game creates an argument about the place of randomness in life. Ultimately, *Holding On* argues that no matter how hard we work, some elements of the world are completely out of our control. In other words, randomness is used rhetorically in the game to emphasize the role of fate rather than action. This finds a companion with the underlying narrative of the Troubles, which, for Billy, is out of his control: as a child he has no control over his father's actions, as a teen, he has no control over his friend's. He didn't want to get involved and his actions in many ways had consequences he didn't intend. In addition, the game uses randomness to mirror the vacuities of dementia, as the particular uncertainty of drawing a particular card or revealing a particular memory reflects the way patients with dementia can flit between memories, time periods, and experiences without conscious thought.

The consequences of this concentration on the game's randomness are twofold. First, the game feels unfair and unwinnable. It is extremely hard to make it through a game session without losing (the session is lost in a number of ways: if Billy dies before he reveals his lost memories, if the nurses become too stressed to work, if the hospital gets two warnings for not giving Billy enough medical care, etc.). But this is a deliberate strategy on the part of the game designers to reflect the world that we live in. As Greg Costikyan notes, "The world is in fact filled with terrifying uncertainty, and it is a tribute to the dauntless and objectively insane optimism of the human species that we, most of the time, are fairly cheerful about it."[37] Like the earlier example of *The Grizzled*, *Holding On* creates an affective connection between players and Billy, although unlike *The Grizzled*, Billy is a nonplayable character. The nurse characters that players actually play in the game are the definition of abstract: no names, no backstories, and nothing to differentiate them from each other except the color of the meeple. The subject of *Holding On* is undoubtedly Billy, and players encounter him not through *playing* him but through the perspective of a nurse, watching and talking with him. *Holding On* makes players identify with Billy by helping him uncover his memories through the mechanics of card reveals.

The game system is fairly simple. The game is split into days, with each day delineated into morning, afternoon, and night shifts. During each of these shifts, a card is revealed which details Billy's condition—it can be "stable," "declining," or "medical emergency." On most shifts, players have an option whether to perform medical care (which would stabilize Billy or even heal him) or perform palliative care (which can reveal some partial and clear memories). Players cannot do both in the same shift. However, there are always fewer nurses than there are needs for medical or palliative care: judicious use of the nurse resource must be maintained so that no nurse becomes so stressed out that they must spend the day at home resting (meaning they are unavailable to help the next day). The strategy of this part of the game reveals the importance of medical versus palliative care. The randomness of the cards drawn creates uncertainty about what, for instance, will happen to Billy in the night shift, so players must carefully plan how many nurses to use in an earlier shift. This sort of "uncertainty is necessary," as Costikyan notes, for "if our expectation is of predictability, we are unlikely to enjoy the game."[38]

Such reflections of card uncertainty also appear in the way Billy's memories come back to him. Cards are the only mechanism of uncertainty in the game, the only feature "that cause[s] the game to move from one state to another in an unpredictable (to the players) way."[39] There are multiple decks of cards in the game, and this exponentially increases the feeling of luck: "The randomness of a shuffled deck, the sequential way in which cards can enter play, and the self-contained nature of each card's content, tend to give these games a temporal rather than a spatial structure."[40] In order to have Billy reveal a memory during palliative care, players deal "partial memory" cards from the bottom of a shuffled deck. Each memory belongs in one of five rows, representing different connections between Billy's memories. The cards are dealt until a card from one particular row is revealed (usually, the player articulates which row they are seeking). Often during the game, specific memories will be requested (e.g., in scenario 4, memories only of Billy's daughter Sarah are required). It is possible that only two of the six cards in, say, Row 1 will be of Sarah, so players may not even have the right card once they've drawn it. Once partial memories are played into the grid, they can be filled in with more palliative care and an assemblage of clear memories (see Figure 2.2). It takes an enormous amount of luck in order to be able to draw the correct cards, at the correct time, without hitting an event (that can cause Billy to regress) or finding irrelevant memories. The randomness of the cards every time they are shuffled means that each new draw will depend

Figure 2.2 Clear and partial memory of Billy Kerr.

on luck. As Costikyan argues, "many games harness randomness as a means of creating moment-to-moment uncertainty, but reduce the overall effectiveness of randomness by performing many random tests, each of small weight."[41] Because the deck is shuffled, as well, players cannot necessarily "memorize" where cards are located in the deck, increasing the randomness—and this shuffling mirrors the way that Billy's dementia jumbles up his memories as well.˙

˙ In a thread on BoardGameGeek which postulated different fan-created variants to change the game, Michael Fox, the creator of *Holding On*, argued:

> The shuffling in the game is to emulate the turmoil going round in Billy's mind during his final days, as well as his reluctance (and sometimes inability) to speak to people about his regrets. It's an integral part of the story as well as the game. Removing it removes the human element of the game—you're not dealing with a machine, you're dealing with a man who is dying. Both this and your proposed "Competitive Variant"—neither of which are variants,

When playing *Holding On*, players are met with a great deal of frustration because a particular card may not appear. This is the challenge with randomness, as George Elias, Richard Garfield, and K. Robert Gutschera argue: "Players, especially more serious or expert players, will often object to random elements in a game. . . . *Players may wish to feel they are masters of their own fate.*"[42] Randomness can make it seem as though players' choices don't matter. *Holding On* deliberately utilizes randomness to echo this feeling, to create a situation where the interactive potentiality of player action can be offset by a poor draw of the cards, or an unlucky run of memories. Elias, Garfield, and Gutschera note that adding luck to a game can have many benefits, although adding to the thematic argument of the game is not one they mention.[43] Rhetorically, *Holding On* uses randomness to argue about the difficulty of working with patients suffering from dementia, and the sadness and frustration of trying to understand their lived histories.

At the same time, *Holding On* is a balancing act between trying to save a person's life and trying to help a person come to terms with the trauma of their own life. In Billy's case, players learn throughout the ten scenarios about Billy's experiences in the Troubles in Northern Ireland, how they contributed to the breakdown of his family, the loss of his wife, and an estrangement from his daughter. During the game, players are encouraged to look up aspects of the Troubles online to deepen their understanding of the historical event; this narrative thickening doesn't affect the game play, however. The actual play mechanic, the one that rhetorically works on the player, forces the player to either act to save Billy's life or further the narrative unpacking and get closer to the win condition. During my many play sessions of the game (most of which I undertook as a solo player playing multiple roles because my game group grew tired of the randomness in the game), I learned that in order to beat the game—to unveil more and more of Billy's memories—I had to atrophy Billy's condition. Strategically, this made the most sense: the less medical care Billy received, the more I could uncover his memories. But every instinct as a caring human being urged me to be more considerate of his life.* He literally had to suffer, and my

---

only suggestions—go against the spirit of what we're trying to do with *Holding On*. If you're looking for a cut-throat, full-on competitive euro with no luck, *Holding On* just isn't the right game for you. (https://www.boardgamegeek.com/thread/2115743/less-luck-variant).

Here we have a situation where the créateur (see Chapter 4) is attempting to force his particular reading of the games' argument onto the players.

* As one of my friends commented after playing, the idea that the nurses were supposed to balance making him comfortable with the talking to him felt a bit like some sort of ghoulish spectating, like

actions put them in that condition, in order to complete the objectives. The game forced me, though interactive potentiality, to cause a character's suffering to increase.

Ultimately, while the deployment of strategy and randomness in *Holding On* differed in specifics from *This War of Mine*, both games created rhetorical arguments using these attributes. Strategy cohered players to the characters, or forced players to make decisions that had specific consequences. Randomness became that unguided hand of fate, revealing the vicissitudes of a capricious god in terms of character survival or memory retrieval. In the games, these rhetorical arguments only worked because of the player's investment in the system. The interactive potentiality of the game revealed how player's actions determined the arguments being constructed.

Conclusion

Many board games use game elements like strategy and randomness to mirror real-life experiences. How players might deal with those experiences during play moves beyond issues like representation, and integrates unique board game elements (player interaction and investment) into the game system. In this chapter, I've focused on *interactive potentiality* as a unique board game characteristic that draws on rhetorical strategies for games to make arguments. Board games do make rhetorical arguments. They do try to convince players to believe a certain way or to take a certain position on an issue. Strategy and randomness are just two elements of games that help create interactive potentiality. Other rhetorical analyses might find different elements—player effort, for instance, or cooperation versus competition—as another source of interactive potentiality.

Regardless of the form it takes, a rhetorical analysis of board games must rely on the players to provide an element of the argument. In ancient Greek rhetorical theory, arguments are their strongest when audiences have to supply a missing element, what Aristotle called the "enthymeme." Enthymemes are unstated elements within an argument that are "assumed by rhetor when inventing and by audience when understanding the argument."[44] For board games, players

---

the nurses—whom we were playing as!—were more interested in prying into his life than making him comfortable.

themselves are the enthymematic element. By supplying their own strategies and reactions to luck, players complete the rhetorical argument. As Barry Atkins and Tanya Krzywinska suggest, "it is only in the act of playing a game, becoming subject to those formal regimes that act to interpolate the player and shape their experience, that we are able to understand at a deeper level the experience of playing."[45] Board games are always systems in flux; they only come into being with players. A rhetorical criticism of board games must take into account how the game utilizes the player, how the player utilizes the game, and all the multiple possibilities between the two.

— By use the investment and assumption of the players to make effective rhetorical arguments

Colonizing Mars

Ludic Discourse Analysis

The Red Planet. It has beckoned explorers, creators, and dreamers for centuries, from the first discussion of its canals, to the *War of the Worlds*, to the last dying cries of Martian Rover Curiosity in 2019. Mars has always held an appeal for those who have looked up to the heavens—a planet that is relatively close to Earth, that may have held life at one point, and onto whose surface we may one day send human beings in our endless quest for exploration. Mars has also been a favorite of storytellers—its dusty, red surface hiding (perhaps) little green men or untold scientific discoveries. Of all the planets, Mars fascinates us; Mars summons us; Mars dominates our astral thinking.

In addition to NASA's exploration, a raft of Mars-focused literature and film emerged in the 2010s including Andy Weir's *The Martian* (2011) and its 2015 cinematic adaptation and Mary Roach's nonfiction 2010 *Packing for Mars*. With this historical and literary attraction to the Red Planet, it is, perhaps, unsurprising that Mars is also a popular topic for contemporary board games. Scores of modern games are set on Mars, and there have been no fewer than four mainstream games set specifically within a universe of Martian *colonization* released between 2016 and 2017. That so many games have been released in such a short amount of time that all focus on the same general conceit makes for a remarkable chance to explore how board games can use different *mechanics* to approach the same *theme*. It is, in other words, an opportunity to satisfy our own curiosity about the relationship between theme and mechanics in the way board games communicate meaning.

In this chapter, I introduce ludic discourse analysis (LDA) as a methodology for investigating the different meanings determined by particular game texts. Specifically, I interrogate the messages that different game play mechanics communicate in relationship to the themes of the games. The games that I will explore in this chapter are (in alphabetical order):

- *First Martians: Adventures on the Red Planet* (2017, Portal Games)
- *Martians: A Story of Civilization* (2016, RedImp Games)
- *Pocket Mars* (2017, Board and Dice)
- *Terraforming Mars* (2016, FryxGames)*

While the theme of all four games is the colonization of Mars, each game emphasizes different ways this colonization might occur using specific mechanics to create a contention about colonization itself. This is, as I argue, the *discourse* of the game. By augmenting this discourse analysis with a discussion at how changing player choice and investment can shift the meaning of that discourse, we create a ludic discourse. Ultimately, analyzing the way the mechanics interact with the theme of these games illustrates that recent Mars colonization games' discourses emphasize the colonialist and neoliberal aspects of the activity.

Traditionally, discourse analysis has examined the way language can shape a listener's version of the world. Arthur Asa Berger has defined discourse analysis as a methodology that "deals with our use of language and the way our language shapes our identities, our social relationships, and our social and political world."[1] For example, a discourse analyst might examine the style, expression, and content of and about a particular phenomenon, like the release of a blockbuster film or the visit of a president to another country. What people are saying about these events, and how they frame them using language, becomes fodder for the analysis. Discourse analysts often look at language *about* a particular object outside of looking at the object itself. Thus, discourse analysis looks beyond an object to argue that the way that object is framed by language has meaning, intention, and consequence.

The interaction between a game's discourse and its players' choices creates a board game's ludic discourse. I abstract the concept of *discourse* here from being strictly about language to being more generally about activities. There is some precedent for using discourse analysis in this manner. Teun van Dijk has noted how discourse analysis can apply to the written word as well as language, while Berger goes on to describe how it can apply to the meanings created via images.[2] David Machin and Andrea Mayr have shown a multimodal approach to

---

* *On Mars*, a Kickstarter-backed game, was due for release in October 2019 but was pushed back to December and was thus unable to be included in this analysis. There are other Mars-themed games as well, but I'm focused on these four, which all were released within about a year of each other.

discourse analysis in which "the same kind of precision and . . . systematic kinds of description that characterized the approach to language" in discourse analysis can be applied to "visual analysis" and "other modes of communication such as toys, monuments, films, sounds, etc."[3] And in his introductory book about discourse analysis, James Paul Gee actually uses the rules of a game (*Yu-Gi-Oh!* [1999, Upper Deck]) to illustrate discursive work.[4] Thus, a *ludic discourse analysis* presents further ways of studying board games, as with the previous two chapters, as meaning-making objects. Games, as we have seen, necessitate the participatory processes of an engaged player; thus, the meanings that are created via game play must function in combination between the game system (which sets up the theme and rules of the game) and the player engagement (which determines how those rules are enacted and that theme understood).

For this chapter, a board game's LDA forms from the way a board game's mechanics interplay with the game's theme. An LDA could be performed via other characteristics of games—the play styles (cooperative/competitive), a thematic analysis, and so on. A *theme* is the overarching narrative, setting, or scenario that describes the story or subject matter of the game. Themes can be abstract (e.g., "shapes") or they can be complex and specific (e.g., "escape from a locked room"). For the purposes of this chapter, the overarching theme of all the games that I examine is "colonization of Mars." A game's *mechanics*, alternately, are the mechanisms and procedures by which players enact the game play, the constructs of roles that define how the game is played. As designer Matt Forbeck describes, mechanics are "the stuff you work with as you play the game."[5] There are scores of mechanics that apply to board games. Some of the most common include Worker Placement (where players are allocated a limited number of actions across multiple stations) or Deck Building (where players gradually add cards from a limited pool to their hand). In the next section, I give a more thorough breakdown of some of the most common mechanics in these Mars colonization games.

Articulating the interaction between theme and mechanics through an LDA can reveal the game's underlying ideology. For example, using a Worker Placement mechanic prescribes the types of actions that one might do in a game; uniting that with a matching theme (or, say, making a car in a factory) creates a *discourse* where players are encouraged to see the two as natural, common sense, and connected. (In contrast, imagine the same theme but matched instead with a Bidding mechanic, where players bid on which car will be made better; the game means something different because we read the juxtaposition of the mechanic and the theme in different ways.) How do game mechanics constrain or prescribe the way that individuals read the game? An LDA looks at the power inherent in a game's design to prescribe particular readings onto the game. In the four games discussed in this chapter, notions of colonization and capitalism frame this thematic discussion.

Discourse Analysis and Board Game Mechanics

At its most basic, discourse analysis tries to "understand or interpret social reality as it exists": that is, it examines

> how language constructs phenomena, how it reflects and reveals it. In other words, discourse analysis views discourse as constitutive of the social world—not a route to it—and assumes the world cannot be known separately from discourse.[6]

What we say can mean very different things depending on any number of discursive contexts: who we are speaking to, the tone we use to speak, the social situation we are in. If I say "that's rubbish," it can be interpreted in a variety of ways depending on whether I'm talking about an item I'm throwing away, an episode of television, or a piece of student writing. According to Margaret Adolphus, "the very ethos of discourse analysis is that language and discourse (in the sense of a speech communication) is not a fixed, immutable reality, but one that is moulded by a social context, and can in turn build up a picture of the world which is unique to the author of the discourse."[7] But written/spoken language is not the only thing that discourse analysis can analyze. The reason discourse analysis looks at language is that, as Gee points out, "language allows us to do things . . . to engage in actions and activities."[8] But we can apply the effects of discourse on any action or activity, whether it is lingual, verbal, or ludic. As Rodney Jones, Alice Chik, and Chrisoph A. Hafner explain, "the production of multimodal texts, for example, call into question analytical paradigms that focus only on written or spoken language."[9] Indeed, "new [d]iscourses emerge and old ones die all the time," and it is not surprising that new media can alter how we conceive of discourse analysis.[10]

But what would a discourse analysis look like in terms of board games? I'm using the term "ludic discourse analysis" to describe how the specific semiotics of a board game—meaning the structure, the rules, the actions, the mechanics, and so on—help to shape the way players of the game interpret the theme of the game. I'm not the first person to use this term; in her PhD dissertation studying role-playing games, Sonia Fizek uses LDA to describe the performative function of player/character dialogue on the choices made within the game.[11] Fizek's use of the term falls more in line with traditional discourse analysis (e.g., of spoken language) than of the ludic properties of games, however. Similarly, Hans-Joachim Backe used their own LDA to examine ecological messages in video games, but again focused on language use rather than the game itself.[12] LDA is also different from what Pieter Wouters, et al. have termed "Game Discourse Analysis (GDA)," which the researchers applied to serious video games to examine how the flow of information in game affects the effectiveness of the game at communicating its social messages.[13] Here, GDA is a way of understanding video game communication; a digital engagement that influences how gamers understand the messages in a game.[14]

Ultimately, the mechanics of any game force a particular discursive viewpoint on the players because of the way players themselves enact those mechanics into being. An LDA takes into account the players' own complicity in co-constructing the mechanics that govern the underlying rules/structure of the game. As players of board games, we decide how to deploy the mechanics in the game in various ways that might or might not connect with the theme of the game. For example, as I discussed in the previous chapter, *This War of Mine* (2017, Galakta) engages players with many different choices. I could use the mechanics of the game to starve a character to save others, or I could choose *not* to do that, to distribute food evenly and hope for a quiet night. The way a game might encourage me to make a particular decision over another is discursive. Different mechanics will lead to different discursive patterns; if we are playing a game with a hidden traitor, we will "naturally" be suspicious of everyone else in the game. One leads to the other. In a board game, we become part of the game's theme through player enactment.

In many ways, an LDA builds on the work of theorist Michel Foucault, who illustrates how discourse moves beyond language to reveal the societal power that determines "a sort of general recipe for the exercise of power over men: the 'mind' as a surface of inscription for power . . . the submission of bodies through control of ideas."[15] In this sense, discourse is a specific set of beliefs that are organized to convince others to think a particular way, or as Mel Stanfill describes it, "the set of socially possible ways of thinking about a concept, practice, or population. It delimits the framework of common sense. . . . Discourse creates reality."[16] Applying discourse analysis in this way allows the researcher to see the influence that a set of texts can have on others.

So how does one perform an LDA? For traditional discourse analysis, James Paul Gee argues that asking specific questions allows the analyst to interrogate the objectives of a text. He provides twenty-eight "Tools" to help shape the type of questions one might ask of a text; for example, and relevant to this chapter, Tool #4, *The Subject Tool*, provokes analysts to ask,

> why speakers have chosen the subject/topics they have and what they are saying about the subject. Ask if and how they could have made another choice of subject and why they did not. Why are they organizing information the way they are in terms of subjects and predicates?[17]

Other relevant tools are #14, *The Significance Building Tool*: "ask how words and grammatical devices are being used to build up or lessen significance (importance, relevance) for certain things and not others"; and #15: *The Activities Building Tool*: "ask what activity (practice) or activities (practices) this communication is building or enacting."[18]

For an LDA, we must ask certain questions of the text to determine what the text's answers might be. It is interpretative and argumentative, meaning that different people may come up with different discursive readings. This chapter asks one particular question (although many different questions are possible): "How do the mechanics prescribed by the game lead the players to interpret certain things about the theme, and not others?" And the way that I will answer that question is by investigating the relationship between mechanics and theme in four games of Mars colonization.

The tension between theme and mechanics in board games is a long-standing and central one; it has been the subject of discussion among board game players and creators for years.[19] Do the actions of a game reflect the thematic content of the game? Do they contradict it? Or is there no relation at all? Forbeck notes that in "the best games, the mechanics and the metaphor [his term for 'theme'] inform each other."[20] As Stewart Woods articulates, when the mechanics and the theme of a game match, it "serves not only to make the game more readily understandable, but also provides the player with a role around which their actions within the game can be contextualized."[21] Greg Aleknevicus notes that the best games connect their theme and mechanic: "The wholesale grafting of a theme onto a set of mechanics is dishonest if those mechanics have no real world connection to that theme."[22] As I've previously written, the tie between theme and mechanics is crucial to understand the way players connect to games.[23]

In terms of theme, we might consider the story or representation the game is trying to communicate, In *Characteristics of Games*, George Elias, Richard Garfield, and K. Robert Gutschera use the term "conceit" instead of theme, defining it as "the sense of an extended metaphor."[24] Conceit/theme is *about* something, and while some games "might have a very light" conceit—"chess," they claim, "is vaguely about medieval warfare"—other games might have "a more elaborate conceit"—"*Tomb Raider* is about swashbuckling archeology."[25] They offer a ten-point "scale of intensity" for conceit, which runs from "Purely abstract" games like tic-tac-toe to "full-on simulation" games like *Squad Leader* (1977, Avalon Hill).[26] In contrast, mechanics are the actions within the game that determine player engagement, the activities that players engage in. Katie Salen and Eric Zimmerman argue that the "core mechanic" of a game "contains the experiential building blocks of player interactivity"; how players actually interact with the game, what they physically do.[27]

There are infinite numbers of themes and scores of mechanics that can be applied to games; new themes are introduced every year and some of the most avant-garde game designers work to create new mechanics in games. For instance, Deck Construction is a common mechanic in which players have a large deck of cards and gradually (and randomly) add cards to their hand—they know what cards may be in the large deck, but not necessarily which ones will come up in their hand. Traditionally, Deck Construction has been used when players have control over their larger deck: in *Arkham Horror: The Card Game* (2016, Fantasy Flight Games), for example, players can "purchase" cards from sets to add to their deck, controlling the type of deck (e.g., more strength vs. more magic) they create. A recent adjustment to Deck Construction has created a refashioned mechanic, however. The Unique Deck game from Fantasy Flight gives players just one unique deck and no ability to change it (the contents of each deck are computer generated, and no two decks are alike). By removing the deck building capacity of the game, the mechanic changes, which changes the way people interact with the game.

The Mechanics of Mars

Although all of these games focus on the colonization of Mars, each of them emphasizes the *way* that colonization will happen via different mechanics (and slightly different thematic elements). In this section, I conduct an LDA on each of these games to examine the mechanics used and argue that each game constructs, influences, and shapes how players think about colonization through the actions they are encouraged to take to succeed in the game. I ask the question, "How do the mechanics prescribed by the game lead the players to interpret certain things about the theme, and not others?" I also then analyze the LDA on the four games as a whole to interrogate the underlying ludic message that the colonial imperative to "conquer" Mars is natural, inevitable, and ultimately corporate.

First Martians: The Initial Landing Party

First Martians: Adventures on the Red Planet is a complex game (taking two or so hours to play) that focuses on the specific issues that accompany the first colony and colonists on Mars. The characters are the first humans on the planet and are charged with building the first colony habitat. The game reflects a *personal theme* about colonization: each player takes on the role of one person within a fledgling colony, while the game as a whole is controlled by an app that randomizes the disasters that befall the colony. Played cooperatively, the game details a narratively driven adventure wherein various buildings in the colony have to be set up, building materials must be obtained, gardens must be planted, probes must be found, communication with Earth must be established, and more colonists eventually must be welcomed to the planet. The theme of the game thus focuses on *specific issues and dangers with building a colony on Mars*. Through its various components, the game emphasizes the physical location of the colony, highlights the elements necessary to support life in the harsh planetary environment, and details everything that could go wrong. To that end, the game board focuses on two distinct elements: a small map of just the section of Mars in which the colony (called the Hub) sits (Figure 3.1); and the parts of the Hub, including the Oxygen Generators, the Solar Panels, the Greenhouses, the Crew Quarters, the Med Lab, the Control Center, the Garage Hall (in which sit the two rovers), the Probe Bay (wherein players can gather samples from the Martian surface), the Lab, and the Working Bay (where one can enact repairs or upgrade the aforementioned facilities).

The mechanics of the game reflect the specific shape in which this narrative develops. There are five main mechanics within *First Martians*: Cooperative Play, Dice Rolling, Storytelling, Variable Player Powers, and Worker Placement.

Figure 3.1 The Hub, *First Martians.*

When viewed collectively, the five mechanics form a *collaborative* discourse—
namely, that it necessitates player collaboration that combines strategic planning
and a certain amount of luck, but although it can be accomplished in many ways,
it will happen regardless of the decisions players make.

First, and importantly, the major game mechanic of *First Martians* is Worker
Placement, a mechanic in which players choose to place one of their (limited
number of) workers onto one of a (limited number of) actions. Each choice
then reduces the options for other players on that turn. In competitive games,
as we will see in the analysis of *Martians* below, Worker Placement can be a
way of blocking other players, but in cooperative games like *First Martians*, it
can emphasize a groups' ability to distribute workers in meaningful ways. Also,
in the game, because each player has a Variable Power, discussion between

players articulates the best way to deploy that action (we saw the same type of mechanic in Chapter 1 with *Pandemic Legacy: Season 1* [2015, Z-Man Games]). Thus, combining Worker Placement and Variable Power means that "individual players have distinctive roles within a game," and thus the mechanics determine the notion that certain people are better (or better suited) for certain activities.[28] In *First Martians*, this is represented by each character's ability to reroll one colored die. The die is matched to the expertise of the character: the scientist can reroll dice in the Lab while the Mechanic can reroll dice in the Working Bay. The power matches the vocation of the character, emphasizing the *work* over any other identity characteristic of the character (like, say, their relationship to one another). The ability to reroll dice is important, as the dice determine whether a particular activity in the game will be successful or not: one could assign a "worker" to a particular activity and a roll of the die may see the activity fail. At the same time, Dice Rolling remains one of the only truly "luck" based mechanics in the game.

Thus, it is important for players to communicate and cooperate within their interaction in the Hub and with all the activities. The game mechanic discourse encourages players to fulfill their roles: to use the scientist more often in the Lab, or to use the Geologist more often in the Probe Bay. (The fourth character, the Medic, has the ability to remove extra damage from characters.) The game is thus entirely cooperative—there is no "competitive" mode of game play wherein players can sabotage each other or the colony. As a discourse, cooperative games tend to emphasize collective decision making and interaction, and *First Martians* encourages dialogue throughout.

First Martians follows a clear storyline, which is largely dictated by the required digital app in the game and the two campaigns in the box (each campaign tells one particular overarching story). As a mechanic, storytelling can deepen the immersion in the game world, but can also linearize game play. Although players may feel freedom to do any action they want in the game, only certain actions progress the story. For example, if the story is (as the introductory mission states) to build a greenhouse and plant a seed, then the "explore Mars" action isn't called for. Discursively, the story prescribes the actions that must be taken.

Furthermore, the app controls a number of aspects of the game. Each game session is called a "Mission," and each mission is made up for a number of rounds. At the start of each round, the app details a different piece of the Hub malfunctioning, while the ongoing story for each mission gets more complicated.

For example, the first mission of the first campaign, *The Labyrinth of the Night*, depicts communication disruptions between Earth and the Martian colony. The objective for the mission is to construct a radio tower far enough from the Hub that messages can reach Earth. There are seven rounds to complete this task, but each round sees new difficulties in the procedure that must be dealt with (e.g., the rover breaks, or the weather strands an astronaut outside the Hub). Later missions complicate things: Mission 2 requires testing of the antenna while Mission 3 sees a storm approaching.

The storytelling aspect of *First Martians*, combined with the other mechanics of Worker Placement, Cooperation, Dice Rolling, and Variable Player Power, emphasizes the inevitability of colonization and the importance of assigning the right people to the right tasks to make sure it goes right. An LDA reveals that players' decisions about these actions become prescribed. The game is more cohesive because everyone has to work together, but also everyone also has particular skills that they are best suited for. Building the first colony takes a bit of luck, some strategy, and everyone working together, but because the story will always continue, it seems like a conclusive end is not only possible but inevitable, if only the prescribed path may be followed.

Martians: Developing the Colonies

Another complex game, *Martians: A Story of Civilization*, discursively constructs the activity of colonizing Mars by laying out missions and scenarios for a colony with multiple cities on the Red Planet. There are four Hubs on Mars, each one with its own health, food, and oxygen needs. Each Hub is controlled by different corporations, which have funded these missions to Mars. The game takes a less personal, more community-oriented view of colonization; each player controls a single corporation in charge of one Hub rather than a single character. It can be played cooperatively (everyone shares resources), competitively (each player/corporation competes for a limited number of resources), or semi-cooperatively (resources are shared, but the player with the "happiest" Hub ultimately wins). During the game, which is largely directed by player actions rather than the game's overarching narrative, players must maintain their own Hubs by producing oxygen and food, and healing their sick. The survival of the colony is of the utmost importance—one cannot win without a surviving Hub—although ultimately the game is also won or lost depending on the outcome of various mission scenarios. The theme of the game thus focuses on *maintaining colony health and happiness* through corporate capitalism.

There are four mechanics that players use to enact the theme, including Worker Placement and Storytelling. Each player has a limited number of workers who can be placed out in and around the colony to produce different effects; some of these include excavating resources from the Martian surface, building greenhouses to produce food, treating "dirty ice" to create water, or using a powerplant to create energy. The other two mechanics help differentiate the game from other Worker Placement games: the play style (cooperative/semi-cooperative/competitive), and the Action Point Allowance System. Looking at all four mechanics together through the lens of the theme reveals the ludic discourse *Martians: A Story of Civilization* is communicating: namely, that control over a colony depends on equal access to unequal resources, so whether a community is united or not, there will always be economic incentives to undercut others. Ideologically, this neoliberal discourse also fits with the emphasis on corporations in the theme. Neoliberalism is a political philosophy that favors free-market capitalism and laissez-faire economic politics. One of the major tenets of neoliberalism is that the free market will solve or prevent many problems from occurring (it lies in opposition to socialism, which sees governmental, not corporate, control as central). While the creators of *Martians* could have used any thematic rationale for how Mars was settled (different international space agencies? Hubs with different leaders? Governments?), the choice to use corporations in the theme and innate competition over limited resources in the mechanics echoes with a discourse of contemporary neoliberal capitalism (as we'll see with *Terraforming Mars* as well).

Martians is determined by the unusual combination of Worker Placement with the Action Point Allowance System. As we've seen, Worker Placement creates a discourse of competition, even in cooperative games: there are fewer slots on some activities on the board than there are workers, so there is an innate sense of opposition. For example, the first player in *Martians* has the option to place a worker on any of nine slots; the next player may also have nine slots open (if the first player chose one that had two available slots) or may only have eight (if the first player chose one that only had one slot available). The next player has even fewer options. In Figure 3.2, there is only one slot available for the "heal" action, meaning only one player can go there in. Even if players are cooperating and discussing all their options, there are still fewer slots for the later players to decide on, meaning each decision has story and play consequences.

In addition, the Action Point Allowance System complicates matters, as players have three actions (in the game, they're called "time units"—e.g., the time it takes to complete an action) with their workers. Some of the slots for Worker Placement take more "time" than others, so not everyone will play all their workers in one round, and it costs one time to bring all your workers back to the colony. The frenetic scheduling (or overscheduling) of workers discursively constructs a meaning of limited time and resources, again reinforcing the capitalist impulses of the game. Workers can also become exhausted and unusable for a time, a natural outgrowth of economic exploitation.

The last mechanic in *Martians*, the storytelling aspect, differs significantly from *First Martians*. In *Martians*, each scenario has a different story that shapes the theme of the game; however, the practical outcome of the story is either opening up a new action slot or forcing the use of an already-existing action slot— that is, whatever the *narrative* tells, the end result is another Worker Placement option. Ultimately, all narratives lead to worker exhaustion. The narrative is won if the conditions on the new Worker Placement slot are fulfilled—for example, in the Force Field story, players have to build force field generators for the colony

Figure 3.2 Health actions slot in *Martians*.

using resources and an additional action slot. In "Face on Mars," players use a separate board to race to the top of a mountain on Mars, using one "time unit" to move a marker up and down. Unlike *First Martians*, which used its narrative to propel the actions players were taking, *Martians* highlights the storytelling mechanic simply to provide additional requirements for the players. The effect of this, when viewed through an LDA, is to again emphasize the artificial scarcity of time and workers in a corporate environment.

Pocket Mars: Technology Leads the Way

Pocket Mars is a short game that details the building of an infrastructure to house the rapidly growing colonies on Mars. The game is much smaller and shorter than the others described in this chapter; it only takes fifteen to thirty minutes to play and does not use the same mechanics that the others do. The theme of the game focuses on how a colony on Mars might develop with more people and more supplies sent over time, creating a discourse of a *reliance on technology*. Combined with the mechanics of the game, Area Control and Hand Management, an LDA reveals the politics of exclusion that undergird the experience of *Pocket Mars*.

In order to grow, the colony needs more technologies and buildings. Each player has a ship that transports colonists to the Martian colony. Each ship can hold colonists in the hold and a "prep module" in the cargo bay. In addition, players have a hand of cards that represents all the technological projects they could build on Mars to enable different activities. For instance, they could build a satellite dish that would allow them to take an additional colonist from Earth. On the Martian colony, there are five buildings that allow different activities to happen: the energy building provides additional energy, the communications building allows more colonists to arrive, the greenhouse gives a player room to grow their colony, the water treatment planet allows players to move cards around, and the construction building allows players to place colonists on Mars.

The two mechanics used in this game, Area Control and Hand Management, reflect a sense of competition among the players. An Area Control mechanic is defined as a way for a player to earn the most influence over a particular area through various means. In *Pocket Mars*, this is done by deploying various technologies into buildings. The higher number the technology, the more of your colonists that can move into the building. At the same time, a Hand

Management mechanic tends to reward players for playing cards in certain ways. Each card lists two different things it can accomplish; one of them occurs if it is played from the hand to the discard pile, the other if it is played from your ship's "prep module" to a building. Players take turns building technologies, moving colonists from Earth to the ship and then from the ship to the colony, and swapping colonists on Mars from one building to another.

The relative simplicity of the game makes an LDA a bit more difficult, as there is less theme to reflect on in comparison to the other games discussed in this chapter. However, there are some important points to make about the way *Pocket Mars* determines our understanding of the colonization process. First, colonization is here seen as intimately tied to technology. Colonists cannot be placed without technology leading the way; in fact, the mere fact of playing a piece of technology can trigger colonists landing on Mars or even moving from Earth to the ship. In this, *Pocket Mars* reflects an LDA of *control of technology means control over colonization.* The player with a better understanding of technology (as symbolized by the type of cards or the number on them) will be able to move more colonists.

Second, colonization is seen as an act of limited space, determined by privilege. On each building, players earn more points if they have a colonist in one of the sectors as opposed to the other. Yet, only one or two colonists can fit in each sector. There is a *politics of exclusion* at play here, as players vie for control over one particular area in each building, echoing imperial mentalities of inequality. In addition, various technology cards can move colonists from the privileged neighborhood to the less valued one. Everyone might have the chance to be in one of these special areas, but only someone who can play the right technologies can stay there.

Terraforming Mars: The Corporations Control Mars

In *Terraforming Mars*, currently (as of December 2019) the third most popular game on BoardGameGeek, the colonization of Mars has become firmly corporatized. In the game, the World Government decides it is time to terraform the planet. The Government creates a "terraforming committee" and institutes a global tax; according to the rulebook, this tax will fund "gigantic corporations that compete to expand their businesses and emerge as the most influential force behind the terraforming." In the game, each player controls a corporation that deploys different technologies to enhance various aspects of the Marian ecosystem. The game is played over a series of "generations," meaning the corporation supposedly lasts through 80–160 years or so. During the game, players gain resources (megacredits—a form of currency, steel, titanium, plants, energy, and heat), which they can spend to build technologies. The game ends when enough oxygen has been generated, oceans have been created, and the temperature has been increased to 8° Celsius. The theme of the game articulates a *neoliberal reliance on corporate interests to further technological progress*. That is, in the game, the fact that corporations are the ones in charge of terraforming the planet creates a discourse that normalizes industrial/capitalistic interests, and focuses on the way technological development and human progress can be tied to neoliberal economic policies.

The mechanics by which *Terraforming Mars* enacts this theme help to cohere this focus on capitalism and neoliberal policy. In *Terraforming Mars*, players focus on six main mechanics. We've already seen a number of these in previous games, including Hand Management (which rewards players for playing cards in certain sequences), Tile Placement (which rewards players for playing tiles in particular areas), and Variable Player Powers (which gives each player a different ability). As we've seen, each of these mechanics has contributed to general strategic advantages. Given a number of cards or tiles played in a certain order, one player may be able to control aspects of the board or the game. In *Terraforming Mars*, for example, players can spend eight plants to place one greenery tile. However, you can only place a greenery tile next to one of your tiles, so it is possible to block opponents from playing tiles.

Three mechanics that we have not yet discussed in *Terraforming Mars* are Card Drafting, Set Collection, and Take That. Card Drafting is a form of building a deck of cards wherein players take turns initially choosing cards from each others' hands. In *Terraforming Mars*, the "deck" a player builds contains all the different project cards they might be able to play. Different projects produce different effects. For instance, a project like "Wave Power" controls oceanic currents, increasing a player's energy production by one. However, it requires that three ocean tiles be played before it can be enacted, so perhaps the player played "Convoy from Europa" first, which brings water to the planet (in the form of an ocean tile). Each project builds on the ones before, and players can "chain" them together to enact various attributes. This mechanic helps reinforce the larger thematic construct that corporate control over technology leads to human development: some cards cannot be played until certain conditions (temperature level, oxygen level, ocean level, etc.) are met, meaning previous technologies have to have been played before them; and some later projects can cost more than earlier projects. Technological development depends on both previous technology and access to funding.

Set Collection refers to the mechanic that focuses on players' acquisition of a set of items. For example, one might be encouraged via end-of-game victory points (VPs) to collect all "star" cards. In *Terraforming Mars*, one of the sets could be collecting the most "science" tags on played cards. Collecting the most will reward the player with an additional five VPs and encourages players to continually play science projects. In and of themselves, science cards tend not to give direct benefit at the time they are played, but rather give additional VPs at the end of the game; for instance, "Mars University" gives players a chance to recycle their cards; "Breathing Filters" gives players additional VPs; and "Physics Complex" gives additional VPs for additional science cards. The key connection here between the theme and the mechanic lies in the idea of continued acquisition. Like a good corporation, players are encouraged to continue to develop and grow *for the sake of growth*. Scientific discoveries or educational facilities ("Mars University") exist not to better humankind, but rather for explicit profit.

Further enhancing this connection to neoliberal politics, the mechanic of "Take That" encourages direct player competition. Players can take actions that directly affect (usually impede) their opponent. For example, in *Terraforming Mars*, players can play projects that take resources from player cards, or they can play tiles in a way that blocks an opponent's progress. Take That reflects the very neoliberal idea that competition breeds value: that in striving *against* others, we become stronger and better (the flip side of this could be the philosophy that working together creates a stronger outcome).

An LDA of *Terraforming Mars*, therefore, sees how human progress, as symbolized in this game by the development of the Mars, is a job best suited for corporate competition, not individuals nor the government. The game could have focused on any number of ways to accomplish the goal of terraforming the planet: perhaps focusing on governmental agencies or international cooperation. But by focusing on the corporate, and engaging with direct and indirect superiority, the game creates a ludic discourse wherein neoliberal economics guide human development.

Conclusion

LDA reveals how the messages that a game's theme and mechanics create in conjunction with each other—messages that we can discover through a ludo-textual analysis and interactive potentiality—can mean something larger than just the game. Just as a discourse analysis reveals how language can shape the way we interpret the world around us, an LDA can illustrate how a game tries to convince us of a particular way the world functions. Because players themselves contribute to the development of this message through enacting the mechanics set in place by the game, they become cocreators of this discursive message, fully placing themselves within the larger discourse.

In this chapter, I've analyzed four games about Mars colonization that all give slightly different interpretations of the theme; and by comparing the differing mechanics in each game to the variations in each games' theme, we have been able to develop different readings of what the larger implications of the games are. They are about more than just colonization—they are about the experience of capitalism, of colonialism, of technological development, and of neoliberalism.

Looking at all four games simultaneously, however, can reveal even more about why this particular theme appears at this particular time in contemporary culture. In some ways, this LDA is similar to a *critical discourse analysis* (CDA), which critiques the role of discourse in "the (re)production and challenge of dominance," the "exercise of social power that results in social inequality."[29] CDA is a tool for understanding larger cultural paradigms, and the unequal power structures that undergird how we view contemporary cultural activities; for instance, the way one group of people may describe another group of people may reproduce racial or gender privilege, or the language used to refer to diasporic people ("illegals," "aliens") forces a dehumanizing framework on them. Board games have their own discourses that a CDA could examine: for instance, the way the language in the game refers to characters of different races might reveal underlying themes of dominance, or the roles given to women could reflect stereotypical gender roles.

So why Mars, and why now? We could examine any underlying rationale for these games all being released within a short period of time. One of the ways we might approach this from a discourse standpoint is by looking at where these games come from. Three of the games discussed in this chapter (*First Martians, Martians: A Story of Civilization*, and *Pocket Mars*) were designed by Polish game designers, and *Terraforming Mars* by a designer from Sweden.* That all of these games have come from Europe is no real surprise: Europe has a thriving board game culture, larger than the one in the United States. At the same time, the past few years of politics in Eastern Europe, as well as around the world, has seen the rise of populism and a return of conservative, right-wing ideologies. Poland's government in particular has become extremely right-wing when, in 2015, the Law and Justice Party came to power. This shift in governance has included changes to the country's laws, including punishment for anyone who makes the claim that Poland had culpability for Nazi crimes.[30] One could make the argument that the discourse of the games, especially those that come from countries that are tied to more conservative politics, reflects a discourse of economic and culture dominance. But at the same time, the games from Poland in particular are less tied to economic neoliberalism than the game from Sweden, perhaps reflecting a discourse *counter* to what is being enacted in Poland. Sweden is highly socialized and largely liberally progressive, although a particular strain of right-wing populist discourse has emerged in the latter half of the 2010s. Perhaps the neoliberal impulses of *Terraforming Mars* offers a critique of neoliberalism rather than a celebration; or perhaps it simply offers a different view of a contemporary political discourse.

The discourses of board games reflect different ideological implications which, when read in conjunction with the context they come from, can create different connections. Ultimately, an LDA emerges from the tension between the theme and the mechanics of the game. As Matt Forbeck writes of this tension, both have to match to be "true to the game and to serve the entertainment of the people who will play it."[31] But examining what happens when these two are read together reveals a larger story than just what the game describes; it reveals a discursive truth about the world from which the game developed. The game determines how a player's actions reflect a cultural reality.

---

* Jacob Fryxelius designed *Terraforming Mars* (working with members of his family), Michał Jagodziński designed *Pocket Mars*, Grzegorz Okliński designed *Martians: A Story of Civilization*, and Ignacy Trzewiczek designed *First Martians*.

4

The Designer as Créateur

The Board Game Industry and Constructed Authorship

Who wrote *Scrabble* (1948, Hasbro)? Who composed *Monopoly* (1933, Hasbro)? Who authored *Risk* (1959, Hasbro)?*

Board game players rarely, if ever, refer to the *inventor* of the game as the *author* of a game. "Designer" seems to encompass much more about game creation than authorship does, and while we might say that, for instance, Christopher Nolan *authored* a film, we'd rarely say that Nikki Valens *authored* a board game. But why might this be the case? And what can viewing game designers as authors bring to the study of board games?

Authorship seems more applicable to traditional media texts like film, television, and literature because of the strong cultural history audiences have with "reading" the text as the manifestation of the author's meaning. As cultural critic Michel de Certeau has written:

> The social and technical functioning of contemporary culture hierarchies these two activities [reading and writing]. To write is to produce the text; to read is to receive it from someone else without putting one's own mark on it, without remaking it.[1]

We are trained to see the author's voice as the ultimate authority (even the word "*author*ity" reveals the connection). In school we are asked to unpack "what the author meant" and "what the author intended." Reading (or watching) becomes a puzzle to solve, a venture to see into the mind of the author.

Games, and board games in particular, are conceived differently. First, they are not perceived as culturally valuable. Why bother to learn the author of a text that is not considered worthy of study? Second, for years, board games were seen as mass-market toys: products, not texts. We wouldn't say someone "authored" the yo-yo or the jigsaw puzzle, so why the board game? When games are perceived as low-value products rather than meaning-making institutions, the drive to investigate any deeper levels to authorship never materializes.

Importantly, there is an underlying rationale at work in these conceptions. As we have seen, the interactive nature of board games means that the *experience* of playing the game must always be understood to be part of the board game text just as much as the actual physical components of the text. In short, the game is like a toy because of precisely the same reason that it complicates media analysis: it is conceived from its start as fully dependent on the player. Colin Burnett calls this the "intentional flux" of games, arguing that attribution of authorship applies "with difficulty, or not at all, to these highly collaborative, popular arts."[2]

In many ways, then, board games symbolize a more complex, and more compelling, articulation of authorship that goes beyond De Certeau's "author-as-authority." In the last few chapters, I established that board games are not wholly the product of the text, but rather emerge from a cocreation with an active audience. This *interactive potentiality*—the idea that a board game is never a static text—has complicated our understanding of textuality and readership. Designers don't *author narratives*; they *design experiences*. It is the role of the *player* to author the game: "Board gamers themselves can be considered . . . 'authors,' given the narrative/tactical decisions they are encouraged to make."[3] This chapter uses an "industrial analysis" of the media industries to help understand both how an individual person can be seen as the construct behind a game author and how this concept strategically hides a number of other ways authorship can be understood in board gaming. Board games do not exist in a cultural vacuum, as they manifest the same complications with authorship that other media industry studies have revealed.

For the purposes of this chapter, I want to interrogate this denial of authorship by outlining three styles of authorship that board games *do* engender. Each one is marked by *simultaneous* authorship between the designer of the game (whose design may be meaningful but not actualized until the time of play) and the players of the game (whose play in and of itself authors the particular experience at the moment of play). Understanding the complexity of board game authorship is important because the board game hobby has well-known and successful game designers whose names are used—like authors—to market games. Hobby board games often proudly display the designer's name on the box top as a key marketing tactic. That is, games *use* the concept of the author to help players construct coherence, ascribing discursive meaning out of a body of work. Authorship is both eschewed and embraced. While traditional media forms may conceptually reveal the multiplicity of authorship, board gaming literally cannot be anything but.

Industrial Analysis

An industrial analysis examines how industry practices, economics, histories, and ideologies affect the production of a text. This type of research has an "interdisciplinary scope" and doesn't emerge from just one methodology.[4] For instance, John Thornton Caldwell's research into the film and television industries involved "textual analysis of trade and worker artifacts; interviews with film/television workers; ethnographic field observation of production spaces and professional gatherings; and economic/industrial analysis."[5] Traditionally, industry analysis has been used to "focus on film, radio, television, advertising, and digital media [and] this list could easily be expanded to include music, newspapers, book publishing, and even telecommunications"—note that games are not among those listed.[6] Board games, as with the other chapters of this book, have rarely been examined through this approach.

Authorship is a key function of an industrial analysis. As Michele Hilmes notes: examining the industry stems from "a concern for the creative forces of production *behind* the range of communicative texts and objects."[7] Further, "studies of *authorship* represent another significant way that film and television studies have probed the relationship between industrial organization and individual agency while also retaining a close attention to the textual dimensions of these media."[8] Focusing on authorship within production cultures allows the researcher to discover "the complexity of routines and rituals, the routines of seemingly complex processes, the economic and political forces that shape roles, technologies, and the distributions of resources according to cultural and demographic differences."[9]

Any discussion of authorship in industrial studies has to start with the concept of the "auteur." First championed by French film critics like André Bazin writing in the 1940s in the film journal *Cahiers du cinéma*, the concept of the auteur—or the idea that a film is the reflection of a director's singular artistic vision—was brought to contemporary English-language criticism by Andrew Sarris, film critic for the *Village Voice*, in the 1960s.[10] In classic auteur theory, all aspects of a film are centered on the director: the creative vision the director has shapes the meaning behind the film. The auteur theory has had significant influence on the way everyday people view films: audiences still tend to classify movies by the director and see themes across their works. However, it has been complicated over the years as additional industrial analyses reveal the impact and role of other individuals in the industry (i.e., the director doesn't necessarily control every aspect of the film): "Efforts to isolate the contributions of a particular figure must always fundamentally distort the realities of media authorship."[11] In television studies, as well, the traditional view of the producer/writer or showrunner as the "author" of a text has been shown to be problematic, as the multiple layers of production complicate any individual's contributions.[12] And within video game studies, authorship is also never clear-cut. Espen Aarseth opens an essay about the video game auteur by noting that such a category probably doesn't even exist.[13] Referring to the creation of video games as "distributed authorship," Stephanie Jennings argues that the video game industry is a complex structure where an "interplay of negotiated capacities of a number of actors (including but not limited to developers, publishers, and players) . . . create the content, structures, form, and affordances of video game works." She further notes that "these actors [don't] always work together collaboratively" or share power equally among them.[14]

Beyond simply the auteur, there have been many other views of authorship, each one differing in terms of the roles played by the writer, by the audience, by the creator, and/or by others that affect the interpretation of meaning within a text. One of the most significant theories of authorship emerged in 1973, ten years after the auteur theory came to the United States. Stuart Hall's *encoding/decoding* model, in which the author becomes merely one component of meaning-making out of many, illustrates a process by which media texts are *encoded* with the ideologies, beliefs, and backgrounds of the people making the media, and then *decoded* by those that may or may not share those same ideologies, beliefs, and backgrounds.[15] In this view, authorship doesn't create meaning; rather, meaning is cocreated by an author *and* an audience's understanding of a text. The encoding/decoding model has been influential in understanding the role that the audience can play in creating meaning—for example, in Hall's model, a producer might encode meanings that reflect an upper-class, white point of view, which is decoded quite differently by, for example, a working-class African American audience.

The encoding/decoding model is a compelling look at authorship; but it is not the only view of the interaction between authors and audiences. More specifically focused on interactive narratives (of which she includes games), Janet Murray's concept of *procedural authorship* offers another reading of the interaction between audience and author. With procedural authorship, the author creates a space, a framework, into which an audience can read/create their own meanings. For Murray, "procedural authorship means writing the rules by which the texts appear as well as writing the texts themselves . . . procedural authorship creates not just a set of scenes but a world of narrative possibilities."[16] In other words, the *author* of an interactive narrative designs the spaces in which the storytelling takes place, while the "interactor" (re: audience) is the "author of a particular performance within an electronic story system." Murray takes pains to differentiate this "derivative" authorship—as she refers to the work of the interactive audience—from the "originating" authorship, arguing it is "not authorship but agency."[17] Aarseth takes up this point when describing the so-called video game auteur, arguing that, rather than an author, designers are "master architects" who "create . . . stimulating tools and situations for others to explore, rather than being a strict director of actors and events."[18]

While Murray's model may work for electronic media (as, for instance, Ian Bogost attests),[19] I argue that it is also *limited* to electronic media, where the "essence of the computer . . . is procedurality."[20] As we saw in Chapter 2 and Bogost's analysis of procedural rhetoric in games, the fact that processes are already algorithmically in place in electronic media means that there is an structural order dictated by author/audience interaction. Both the encoding/decoding model and the procedural authorship model presuppose the author first, determining the resulting authorship situation. As Souvik Mukherjee attests, "The best way to describe authorship is not in terms of a primary all-encompassing authorship in which derivative instances are embedded; rather, authorship needs to be seen as an ongoing process of interaction between the game and the player."[21] Neither the encoding/decoding model nor the procedural authorship model readily explains the complex *and simultaneous* construction of meaning by authors and audiences with board games. Because the board game text is never complete until the precise moment of play, any authorship of the game by the designer is always latent. The board game isn't "complete" until the moment the players begin play and, in doing so, bring the game into being. The board game's analogue structure means that players can always think outside the algorithmic box that has been created: board game play is not just interpretive; it's creative. As Marco Arnaudo explains, "In gaming . . . one is more likely to see Luke rule the galaxy with Darth Vader, or Frodo keep the ring for himself. . . . This form of narration . . . has the considerable advantage of potentially generating narratives that other forms of storytelling are unwilling or unable to enact."[22]

In the rest of this chapter, I explore how authorship functions as both an element embraced and an element shunned in the board game industry. I provide a number of readings of board game authorship, including what I'm calling the board game *créateur*, the board game *crafter*, and the board game company's *branded aestheticism* as categories of authorship.[*] I analyze the work of Ryan Laukat of Red Raven Games as the créateur, or a board game designer with an identifiable style. I unpack the work of Vlaada Chvátil, a Czech board game designer, as the crafter who works in multiple gaming styles. And I focus on Fantasy Flight Games (FFG) as creating a branded aestheticism, or view where the board games company takes on the function of the board game author.

The Créateur of Games

I posit the term "créateur" to describe game designers who have a unique flair that can be observed across a range of games. If we apply the original *auteur* distinction—the auteur being a creative artist with a recognizable vision, as opposed to an author who is the originator of a work—to the term "game designer," we can interpret why "créateur" may be an appropriate term. The créateur is more than just a designer, as they might present a stronger-than-average thematic or aesthetic coherence, or recognizable gaming elements. In an interview I conducted in 2019, game designer Victoria Caña argues that some game designers "make a lot of games that are very similar and have a consistency to them. . . . You will be able to tell that they made the game." As the name of the designer is used by the board game industry as a shorthand for understanding quality game design, the concept becomes a useful heuristic for understanding discourses of game authorship. Yet, as I detail, the créateur can never be fully

---

[*] I'm using the *créateur* here both to link to the French *auteur* and to differentiate this conception from the word "creator," which tends to have a more "solitary genius" connotation. As I show, the *créateur* can never be the lone creator of a game.

conceived of as an "auteur," as any ludic discourse designed by the créateur will always reflect similar themes as other games, and even if only one person makes a game, it never comes into being without others, including players.

An examination of Ryan Laukat's games reveals the particular créateur discourse in board games. Laukat, the founder/owner of Red Raven Games, is aware that he has a particular style in his game mechanics and how much that can change his reputation among board game players. As he mentioned in our interview:

> Sometimes I try to branch out from what people in their minds think of as Red Raven Games. I have fairly eclectic tastes, so I want to try a bunch of different things. But it seems like anytime I sort of try to stretch a little too far, I end up alienating some of our audience. People have come to expect a certain thing out of Red Raven Games.[23]

This study of Laukat's games reveals three different ways his créateur status can be discursively constructed: through the game aesthetics, through the narrative worldbuilding, and through the interplay between theme and mechanics. I chose Laukat's gaming output to represent the créateur for a number of reasons. First, there is a manageable output of games to examine. Red Raven Games has published thirteen games, ten of them designed by Laukat.[*] Compared to the output of some designers, for example Reiner Knizia (who has published over 600 games), ten can be studied in a time-sensitive way. Second, Red Raven Games all have a recognizable aesthetic sense, mainly because Laukat does the art for all the games himself. Third, Red Raven Games has become a success in the board game industry: *Above and Below* (2015), their best-selling game, has sold around 50,000 copies, while the *Eight-Minute Empire* (2012) series has sold over 40,000 worldwide and has been translated into over fifteen languages. His highest-ranked game on BoardGameGeek (BGG) is *Near and Far* (2017), with a rank of 132 (as of December 2019). Fourth, on a personal level, I enjoy playing his games—while not a scientifically valid rationale, the fact that his games are fun while also retaining a sense of his particular style is a meaningful factor in the discursive construction of the créateur. The games that I researched for this chapter are all designed by Ryan Laukat, with art by Laukat as well: *Eight-Minute Empire*, *Artifacts, Inc.* (2014), *Above and Below*, *City of Iron* 2e (2016),

---

[*] At the time of writing. Currently, two games are in preproduction and will have been released by the time this book is published.

Islebound (2016), *Klondike Rush* (2017), *Near and Far, Empires of the Void II* (2018), *Megaland* (2018), and *The Ancient World* 2e (2019).

Upon first glance, all the games—with the exception, as I note in the following, of *Klondike Rush*—have a very clear aesthetic similarity. In an interview with me, Laukat noted that he has always "done the art for all my [game] designs, even since I was about 12, or 13" and the art is "one of the first things" he does, often before he "design[s] . . . the mechanics" (2019). Laukat's art is distinctive: not quite cartoonish, but also not realistic. His people have elongated faces; his animals are anthropomorphized (Figure 4.1). Buildings are squat; ships are tall. There are common elements throughout his games (which make sense given the narrative worldbuilding he engages in), like fish and jewels used as resources, human-sized animals, or colored banners as representative of different factions. Additionally, he illustrates his characters with different races, sexes, and species, representing diversity.

Many of his games revolve around exploration: of a country, a series of underground caverns, a mountain range, a galaxy, or an ocean. There are

Figure 4.1 Laukat's people and animals, from (top to bottom) *Empires of the Void II*, *The Ancient World* 2e, *Above and Below*, *City of Iron*.

therefore repetitions of aesthetic elements across games. Dotted lines connect circular locations, upon which tokens are placed; the names of locations are encased in banners. Huge mountains tower over windswept plains; magnificent oceans butt up against brilliant tundra. Often, landscapes are color coded to match in-game factions, or player characters. Laukat uses steampunk aesthetics at times to render androids and robots as characters, although most of his landscapes are pastoral. Even his buildings seem bucolic rather than urban.

While each game has unique elements, the aesthetic style of all the games is readily identifiable as *Laukatian*. This is true even of games he didn't design, but merely worked on: *Dingo's Dreams* (2016, Red Raven Games), for example, fits neatly into the Red Raven Games aesthetic. However, there are exceptions. The game *Klondike Rush* reflects a different style, with greater attention to realism and less cartoonish detail (although it, too, uses fish as a resource). Perhaps the reason for this is that, unlike his other games, *Klondike Rush* is seemingly located in a specific time and place—the 1890s gold rush to the Canadian Klondike. Although taking place on the fictional "Mount Titan," the game has a clear connection to a historical event. All his other games take place in more fantastical lands. In addition, it is the only Red Raven Game that relies heavily on an uction mechanic.

Laukat's games also share a story-driven element; they have themes that run the gamut from archaeological dig to deep-space exploration. Games like *Above and Below* and *Near and Far* take the storytelling literally. As characters wander through the landscapes offered in the game, they chance upon small decision points, where paragraphs of text offer choices of which direction the story will go. However, Laukat's narratives are not as fully realized as something like an RPG. Often, the paragraph will present a choice and once chosen, that topic will not return. *Near and Far*, one of the top-selling games of 2017 (Arizton 2018), presents some branching narratives, where one's choice of options will reveal a side quest, offering players a chance to explore the narrative more in depth. During one of my playthroughs, for example, a character encountered a magician turning people into rabbits and then cooking them. The side quest to stop the cannibalistic lapinavore took the length of an entire game.

Other Laukat-designed games also have narratives, even if not as developed as those in *Near and Far*. *Islebound* sees each player taking on a ship traveling from island to island, building buildings and developing resources; yet there are also small narrative events that can be solved on each island. In *Eight-Minute Empire*, players have an eponymous, if figurative, eight minutes to take over the world. *Artifacts, Inc.* is about rival archaeologists digging up fossils, statues, scrolls, and gems and vying to sell the most to four museums. *Klondike Rush* finds the players investing in different mining companies in the Klondike and searching for the abominable snowman. *Megaland* is a fully formed video game world where characters attempt to make it through different game levels carrying treasure. *Empires of the Void II* is a space opera about exploring and colonizing unknown planets. *The Ancient World* is about tribes of early people attempting to rid their world of giant monsters. *City of Iron* is a civilization-building game where different city-states vie to become the most powerful, earning a variety of common and not-so-common (bottled demon) resources. All these themes reflect narratives of exploration or adventure.

Many of Laukat's games (namely, *Above and Below, Near and Far, Islebound,* and *City of Iron*) take place in a shared universe called Arzium. This type of worldbuilding, as described by Mark J.P. Wolf, thrives because of "a wealth of details and events (or mere mentions of them) which do not advance the story but which provide background richness and verisimilitude to the imaginary world."[24] Laukat's Arzium isn't narratively complex, but it is filled with details that construct a meaningful alternate world. In this world, humans live with a smattering of alternate beings: hogfolk (human-sized pigs), fishfolk, lizardfolk, birdfolk, robots, and Glogos ("stone-skinned creatures with spine-covered backs and round, red eyes'"). The creation of Arzium ties together the games in a mutually augmenting environment with a developed history. For instance, Laukat's description of Arzium seems to link the titular "City of Iron" as a place where robots once roamed the streets to *Near and Far*, where many of these robots are "still running, despite their creators being long gone." Without directly telling the players, Laukat's world seems to detail the rise and fall of industrial cities (*City of Iron*), the rediscovery of civilization above and below ground (*Above and Below*), the reexploration of the world (*Islebound*), and a new age of mythic adventure (*Near and Far*). With a little squinting, it would be easy to place games like *The Ancient World* and *Eight-Minute Empire* in Arzium as well—both take place in different time periods that neatly slot into the universe Laukat has designed—and even *Empires of the Void II* might tell the story of Arzium into the future.

The final way that Laukat has invoked a discourse of créateur is through the interaction between the games' themes and the mechanics he integrates. As I

---

* https://redravengames.squarespace.com/arzium

described in the previous chapter, analyzing the interaction between the theme and the mechanic of a board game can reveal a ludic discourse. There are five main ludic discourses that seem to stretch across all his games, although all of these elements are not present in every one of his games, and not every game represents each element. Rather, these are general characteristics that seem to fit most of the time.

First, his games tend to present very short individual turns. Usually players have just one or two choices to make before the turn passes to the next player. For example, in *Islebound*, players move their ship to a new island and perform one action (usually, visit the island, attack the island, or negotiate with the island). While there may be instances where too many options on the board lead to *analysis paralysis*—the feeling of being overwhelmed with choices during one's turn—once the rhythm of the game is established, turns proceed relatively quickly. There is little downtime. The effect of this in the games, especially given their themes of exploration and adventure, is a ludic discourse of emphasizing readiness and reactiveness. Players always have to be ready to plan their next move quickly. The games are not particularly long—most Red Raven Games can be played in an hour or so—but reward total attention. There are some exceptions, however. When my game group played *City of Iron*, there were few turns (in total, everyone took just twenty-one turns: three in each of seven rounds), but due to the options available, there were long waits between turns.

Second, the reward in most Red Raven Games is not money, but renown or influence. Money does exist in these alternate worlds, and can be used to purchase things like scholarship or buildings (*City of Iron*), visit locations (*Islebound*), or recruit workers (*Near and Far, Above and Below, Empires of the Void II*). *Klondike Rush* and *Megaland* are the only games where the win condition is to earn the most money, and in both of those games, the "money" resource represents something else: investment in a corporation or video game acumen. In contrast, renown/influence can be earned in other ways—having more resources, building impressive buildings, attacking other characters or places, or defeating titans. Rarely does a Red Raven Game *necessitate* earning lots of money. In *Artifacts, Inc.*, for instance, while players do earn money for turning in valuable relics, the more important resource, the one used to win the game, is the reputation of the archaeologist they play. In *City of Iron*, money is used to purchase buildings, the more expensive of which allow greater access to rarer resources, which earn more influence. We can see a ludic discourse emerge when comparing this mechanic to the narrative worldbuilding, especially that of

Arzium: These are not games of pure greed, but rather games where capitalism can be harnessed in a variety of ways—both passive and aggressive—to triumph.

Third, Red Raven Games emphasizes indirect competition over direct competition. Indirect competition means that only one player can win the game, but players don't necessarily directly attack one another in the game. With the exception of *Empires of the Void II*, which I discuss later in the text, Laukat's games focus on each player building her own best strategy for winning, whether that's building more buildings than other players, defeating more bandits, or selling more artifacts. In *Megaland*, for instance, each player attempts to earn the most treasure cards (gear, eggs, carrots, stones, crystals, and fish), which they turn in to purchase buildings, which give them money by the end of the game. Players can't directly interact with other players. I can't take a treasure away from you nor could your character attack my character. Rather, the combination of buildings that one purchases leads them to victory. Combined again with the fantasy and adventure themes of Laukat's games, this indirect competition rewards strategy rather than aggression. A ludic discourse analysis might reveal a more pacifist reading of Red Raven Games, or perhaps, given the makeup of Arzium as an environment of human-, lizard-, hog-, and bird-folk (not to mention Glogos) working together, a ludic discourse of laissez-faire interactions ("you do your thing, I'll do my thing") guides the game play.

Fourth, while Laukat's games are always strategic, an interactive potentiality of luck exists in terms of dice rolling/card drawing. Dice can mean different things, depending on the score rolled. In *Above and Below* and *Near and Far*, for example, the number on the dice can lead in different narrative directions, as a dice roll determines which options may be available in storytelling. In *Islebound* and *Artifacts, Inc.*, the numbers on the dice allow different actions to occur: a four, for example, might mean a sea monster does two damage in *Islebound* or that an archaeologist can dive for the next treasure in *Artifacts, Inc.* Rarely will dice stop a player from doing a particular action, but they may determine how successful that action may be. This means that player decisions are more important than luck. The luck of the roll only rarely stops a player cold. A ludic discourse analysis of these games of adventure, then, reveals that there is always value in exploration. Although players may not always find themselves on the path they intended, they still progress through the game in important ways. Laukat seems to value exploration for exploration's sake: revealing the unknown reaps knowledge.

Fifth, and related to the others, many Red Raven Games involve a combination of Resource Management and Worker Placement as mechanics that guide the actions of the players. In *Islebound*, for example, players have to have a certain amount of fish to purchase a sea monster, and it takes sea monsters to attack an island. Players also need wood to hire new crew, who can be used to get fish. In *The Ancient World*, resources are ambrosia, coins, and knowledge. Players have three to five citizens (re: workers) who are placed on various action spaces to build, labor, draft, expand, learn, rebuild, recruit, grow, and explore. There are more actions than citizens, and it's important to consider all the actions during a round to expand your city, rebuild what's been destroyed, earn more resources, and develop your military—all while monitoring the monstrous Titan that threatens your empire. The need for control over both resources and workers throughout his games reveals a ludic discourse of balance and cyclically. In order to do one thing, a certain resource must be earned; to earn that resource, more of a second thing must be accomplished. And just as the resources the players take must be balanced, so too are the narratives in his games about balance, the circularity of life, and (re) emergence: for example, Arzium is about the rise and fall of civilizations. Other games have players moving literally in circles. In *Near and Far*, players continually have to go out to explore the countryside but then have to return to town to stock up on supplies. There is a constant back-and-forth movement. In *Klondike Rush*, players must always return to base camp in order to count up the mines they have built. *Artifacts, Inc.* shows players the resurgence of ancient relics but sees players continually returning to museums to sell their treasures.

Given these five ludic discourses, Laukat's games all seem to revolve around neoliberal or laissez-faire interactions of personal growth and self-worth coupled with the importance of venturing out into the unknown with a requisite return to home. Exploration—growth—is crucial for human development and civilization; but an individual's growth doesn't preclude the growth of others as well. Players are encouraged not to interfere with other players' progress, and what is attained rarely takes away from someone else. As he mentioned to me, "A good game is engaging. And it inspires at least some interaction between players, positive interaction that gets people talking to each other in a way that they wouldn't without the game." Throughout all his games, this sense of interaction flows from the combination of aesthetic style, narrative worldbuilding, and ludic discourses that Laukat creates.

Yet, at the same time, the existence of *Empires of the Void II* as a Laukat game runs counter to many of the above ludic discourses; and complicates the sense of authorship that Laukat has generated. In *Empires*, player-controlled space fleets can attack other space fleets, and players can either colonize or diplomatically influence the development of various planets. There is direct competition and a specific colonizing theme. It is far more strategic than Red Raven's other games, as players not only have a multitude of options to balance, but also must try to deduce what their opponents will need to do to succeed. And instead of Resource Management/Worker Placement, the game's major mechanics are Area Control (who has control over planets), Action Points (every player has a different number of points to spend on various actions), and Dice Rolling (in battles). In fact, of the ludic discourses identified earlier, only the strong narrative remains constant: not only are players invoking their particular alien race, but each planet at the fringe of the galaxy has its own mini-narrative (e.g., the people of Tan Fu are locked in a battle with the inhabitants of Meezle III, which means that all the mission and action cards for those planets focus on that war).

What this means is that, even if Laukat has an auteur-like vision for his larger oeuvre, there are some significant games that don't fit into that corpus of work. While Laukat has created a discourse of game authorship around his work, and there are some similarities between many of his games, the attribution of clear authorship serves mainly as a discourse for players to understand the content of the game before playing it. In addition, a complication to the créateur role is the fact that none of these mechanics are particularly unique to Laukat—hundreds of games are published each year that have short turns, limited resource management, indirect competition, and so on. Indeed, just as the cinematic auteurs didn't necessarily originate what made their films readily identifiable, so too does the game créateur take what is commonly used in board games and adjust it to fit into their own framework.

Finally, although each Red Raven Game may have a particular aesthetic similarity and play style, they necessarily and by definition must include players' inputs in constructing that sense of game. As we have seen, no board game comes into being without players, and none of the ludic discourses mentioned earlier has ludo-textual or ludic discursive meaning without a player actually producing the actions that manifest them. Although Laukat has created a definite style, theme, and discourse for his games, the ultimate authorship of each game lies in the simultaneous interaction that players have in cocreating the play session with Laukat's design.

The Crafter of Games

In contrast to the créateur, some game designers do not have a signature style within their board game oeuvre. These *crafters*, as I'm terming them, design games that cannot be typified into any one style or aesthetic sense. Crafters' games are seen to be quality because their name is attached to them, but they rarely repeat a theme, mechanic, art, or style. Each game is different. In this, the discourse around the crafter becomes a selling point because of the diversity of content they create.

There are many game crafters who might fit into this category—more than would be considered créateurs, even—but even in this, the crafter represents the same complex relationship with authorship as does the créateur. It is, at once, necessary for identification and unworkable in practice. Take, for example, the highly regarded game designer Vlaada Chvátil.[*] A Czech game designer, Chvátil's games are all very highly ranked on BGG: according to an informal ranking on the site, Chvátil is the sixth most popular board game designer.[†] The author of the ranking notes on this site Chvátil's ability to work in multiple genres and across different styles:

> To me, Chvátil games are basically Chvátilesque takes on existing games or genres. *Through the Ages* [2015, Czech Games Edition/CGE] is his take on *Sid Meier's Civilization* [2010, Fantasy Flight Games]. *Codenames* [2015, CGE] is his take on a party word game. *Dungeon Lords* [2008, CGE] is his take on a worker placement game. *Space Alert* [2008, CGE] is his take on a coop. Even *Prophecy* [2002, Altar Games] is a take on RPGs.

The point is that every game is different; players no more know what to expect from a game of *Bunny Bunny Moose Moose* (2009, CGE) than they do with a game of *Dungeon Petz* (2011, CGE).

Additionally, on many of his games, Chvátil works with different teams of artists. As we saw with Ryan Laukat, aesthetics can be a crucial element of the board game experience. It helps shape how players see and interpret the game and encourages participants to read the game in particular ways. While Chvátil has partnered with artist Milan Vavroň on a number of games (including *Mage Knight* [2011, WizKids], *Through the Ages*, *Space Alert*, *Prophecy*, and *Sneaks & Snitches* [2010, CGE], among others), Vavroň is far from the only artist featured

---

[*] My thanks to Brendan Riley for suggesting Chvátil for this chapter.
[†] https://boardgamegeek.com/geeklist/245399/all-time-designer-ranking-2018

on Chvátil's board games. Tomáš Kučerovský illustrated *Bunny Bunny Moose Moose, Galaxy Trucker* (2007, CGE), and *Codenames*. Flilip Mumak also worked on the art for *Codenames*, as well as *Through the Ages* with Radim Pech. Pech also worked on *Space Alert* (with Milan Vavroň) and *Galaxy Trucker* (with Tomáš Kučerovský). Andreas Resch did *Pictomania* (2011, CGE) while Chvátil himself worked on the art for *Graenaland* (2006, Altar Games). The point is that any *meaning* behind these games must come in concert with the art, the game design, and the actual play itself; it cannot be confined to just one person.

Yet, on every single one of Chvátil's board games (with the exception of his first, *Arena* [1997, Altar Games]), his name is displayed close to the title of the game (see Figure 4.2). It is obvious who created the game, and with whom the authorship of the game resides. This is especially true when the games are reprinted or released in a new edition.

These three games: *Codenames, Mage Knight*, and *Prophecy* join other Chvátil games like *Galaxy Trucker, Through the Ages*, and *Bunny Bunny Moose Moose* among many others as vastly different from one another. From

Figure 4.2 Three games, three themes, three styles, three aesthetics; same crafter. Image created by author.

party games, to heavy Eurogames, to real-time strategy games, to drawing games, to civilization games, to fighting games, Chvátil's work is impossible to typify.

But at the same time, they *are* typified by Chvátil's name on the box, by the authorial specter of his presence. Even as we know that games cannot be the result of one sole creator, Chvátil is established in this role. He is a designer, yes, but he is also poised as the voice of authority over the games he designed. If there are questions, he must know the answer. If there are concerns, he will address them. Similarly, his name—his authorship—is used by Czech Games Edition, the publisher of his games, to promote those games. The crafter may not be a singular voice, but they can be presented as one for industrial/economic reasons. Knowing who designed the game play may be like knowing who directed a film, or who produced a television series: it is a clear statement of the author-function, intended to consolidate all the texts under that name into a well-defined category. In effect, articulating such a deliberate sense of authorship over the game negates the power of the crafter, because it serves to highlight the similarities of the games rather than the differences.

Branded Aestheticism

In contrast to the créateur and the crafter, a style of board game authorship can also be seen in the way a particular game company imbues all its releases with a similar aesthetic and structural sensibility, what I'm terming a "branded aestheticism." Like a traditional corporate branding, where an easily identifiable aesthetic marks a particular company, different board game companies have developed diverse styles that are readily identifiable. Caldwell finds a similar type of branded authorship in the contemporary film/television industries in the "industrial auteur," a "negotiated and collective authorship," where multiple stakeholders in a text (producers, writers, studio heads, marketing, etc.) all contribute to the "production" of authorship.[25] Companies can create branded aestheticism through marketing a particular art style, through the work they do writing text in rule books and errata, which "work to retroactively enforce the producer's control over the game," or through the repetition of motifs, characters, or themes in their games.[26]

Branding has become a "go-to" corporate policy in the twenty-first century, as, according to Adam Arvidsson, brands are more than just symbols. They are "something of an omnipresent tool by means of which identity, social relations and shared experiences . . . could be constructed."[27] In other words, brands not only market a company, but also shape social activity.[28] Brands become a way for individuals to self-identify. Popular brands tend to develop fans rather than customers.[29] At the same time, Sarah Banet-Weiser notes, branding also represents "the loss of a kind of authenticity." We yearn "for anything that feels authentic, just as we lament more and more that it is a world of inauthenticity, that we are governed by superficiality."[30] We seek out brands to help us create a sense of identity, but that sense becomes flexible as brands shift and change. Brands and branding symbolize this loss of authenticity. Everything, it appears, is up for corporate marketing—including our sense of self.

Yet, I would argue that the brand aestheticism of board game companies embodies the opposite of this cynicism. Branding a game company through the brand aesthetic is different than merely turning the game into a commodity. Given the way the industry itself functions as a part of the board game hobby, branded aestheticism seems posited as a "marker of quality."[31] As we have seen with the previous conceptions of game authorship, a board game is more than just the pieces themselves—it is a packaged experience, at once created by those working behind the scenes and those playing on the table. The brand aestheticism isn't just about selling games; it's about turning the brand into a creative force.[32] The corporate brand identity can often mesh with an individual creative's role in the production process: Designers like Corey Konieczka have a créateur's flair, but also work for companies like FFG that come with corporate aesthetics and game play elements (although he left FFG in 2019 to set up a new studio with Asmodee, Unexpected Games).

Like the American film industry, the board game industry can be "characterized by three distinct classes of producer—the major studios, the conglomerate-owned indie divisions, and the genuine independents."[33] In this delineation, we might say that the "major studios" are the enormous corporations that produce board games in addition to creating other toys. According to Arizton, the largest vendors of board games in the global market are Hasbro, Mattel, Asmodee, and Ravensburger.[34] Hasbro, the largest publisher of board games in the world, bought game companies like Parker Bros., and now release games like *Monopoly, Risk, Scrabble,* and *Trivial Pursuit* (1981) under the Hasbro label. They also produce toys under a number of brands, including Nerf, My Little Pony, Play-Doh, Disney, Star Wars, and Marvel. In 2017, Hasbro had a revenue in excess of $5 billion.* Although Hasbro may produce more board games than other companies, board gamers in the hobby would not consider it a "board game company"—almost all the games it makes are all mass market, and do not have the kind of complexity or depth that hobby board gamers crave (with some exceptions: *Betrayal at House on the Hill* [2004] is a highly ranked game on BGG[†]). Mattel, the other major player in the toys industry, doesn't produce as many board game brands as Hasbro does, although it does own popular games *Uno* (1971) and *Apples to Apples* (1999).

As with Thomas Schatz's delineation of film studios, the conglomerate-owned indie divisions within the board game industry would be comparable to companies that have been bought up by a few larger board game-only companies.[35] Asmodee, a French publisher of board games, is currently the second-largest publisher of board games in the world. It has purchased a number of smaller board game companies that all maintain their own particular brand aestheticism, but are produced and distributed by Asmodee (Figure 4.3). According to their catalog, they currently sell almost 2,000 different board games, made under forty-two different brands.[‡] In 2013, Asmodee was purchased by Eurazeo for €143 million ($192 million),[§] and in 2018, Eurazeo sold the game company to a private equity fund, Pai Partners, for €1.2 billion ($1.4 billion).[¶] Pai Partners has over sixty different investments, including such diverse holdings as B&B Hotels (budget and economy hotel chain in Europe), Yoplait (yogurt company), Ethypharm (pharmaceutical company), Hunkemöller (women's lingerie retailer), and United Biscuits (snack company—handy for game players).[**] Yet, Asmodee retains control over its game division. As with many media entities, board games are becoming more and more corporate.

As Schatz notes, the final category of film production houses are the genuine independents, and the board game industry has many thousands of independent companies. Many have just one or two employees and market their games entirely on Kickstarter. Some are slightly larger and market and sell their

* https://investor.hasbro.com/news-releases/news-release-details/hasbro-reports-full-year-and-fourth-quarter-2017-financial
† *Betrayal at House on the Hill* is a fascinating case study in branded asceticism. It originated under the Avalon Hill brand in 2004, which is owned by Wizards of the Coast, itself purchased by Hasbro in 1999. But because Avalon Hill has long-standing brand pedigree with board and war game hobbyists, Hasbro includes the Avalon Hill brand logo on the box. Avalon Hill
‡ https://www.asmodeena.com/en/catalogs/
§ https://www.reuters.com/article/eurazeo-asmodee-idUSASA08DVE20131112
¶ https://icv2.com/articles/news/view/40926/eurazeo-finds-buyer-asmodee
** https://www.paipartners.com/investments/

Figure 4.3 Partial list of board game companies owned by Asmodee. Image by Asmodee.

games at conventions like Gen Con, through web retailers like Amazon, or even through their own websites. Others may turn freelance and sell their games to publishers. The difference between the major corporate board game and the independent, according to designer Rob Daviau, is like a "macro brew [beer] and micro brews." One creates a mainstream product that can be distributed farther and wider while the other is more niche but also generates greater audience attention. According to Brian Tinsman, game designer at Wizards of the Coast, "Most tabletop game companies don't have a staff of inventors creating new games. It's usually more cost effective for them to buy or license game designs from independent inventors."[36] In contrast to video games, where the cost of entry is high and the amount of knowledge needed to program a game is immense, board gaming has a much lower bar of entry. While making a good game may be difficult, it is not hard for a board game hobbyist to become a creator in their own right, and the Kickstarter revolution has allowed many to market their games.

Asmodee owns FFG, a company that exemplifies the branded aestheticism style of board game authorship. Established as Fantasy Flight Publishing in 1995 by noted game designer Christian Petersen, FFG is one of the biggest names in the hobby board game industry. It has published games as diverse as extremely heavy military games (e.g., *Twilight Imperium* [1997]) to miniatures games (e.g.,

Warhammer 40K [1993]) to licensed games (e.g., *Doom: The Boardgame* [2004]), and reprints of classic games (e.g., *Cosmic Encounter* [1977/2008]). When FFG was purchased by Asmodee in 2015, Petersen moved from being head of FFG to being president of Asmodee North America.

Although not all of FFG's games are identical—that is, there are different art styles, different designers, different mechanics—there is a general sense of discursive consistency throughout all their products. Arnaudo calls FFG "undoubtedly one of today's leaders in the hobby" as they have "managed to synergize production, game play, and theme in many of their designers, to the point of making such synergy one of their most recognizable traits."[37] Some of the branded aestheticism that FFG harnesses is the connection between strong thematic elements and emergent narratives: games like *Mansions of Madness 2e* (2016) or *Legacy of Dragonholt* (2017) are imbued with deep narrative structures, stories told through the game play. The stories are heavily structured by external elements: *Mansions* uses an app to help guide players through the world while *Legacy* has a paragraph-based story system, sort of like a choose-your-own-adventure tale. Both games were designed by Nikki Valens, known for her work in heavily thematic games.

Beyond individual titles, however, the interaction between theme and narrative finds root with FFG's use of an entire Lovecraft-inspired transmedia world.[38] Games like *Mansions of Madness* fit into what FFG calls the Arkham Files, a series of games that all take place within the same universe—*Arkham Horror* (2005), *Arkham Horror: The Card Game* (2016), *Eldritch Horror* (2013), *Elder Sign* (2011), and *Call of Cthulhu: The Card Game* (2008) all share characters and situations adapted from the work of H.P. Lovecraft, despite a number of different designers working on each game (Richard Launius and Kevin Wilson helmed *Elder Sign*, while Corey Konieczka and Nikki Valens worked on *Eldritch Horror*; Lanius, Wilson, and Valens have worked on various editions of *Arkham Horror*, Valens designed *Mansions*; Nate French and Matthew Newman designed *Arkham Horror: The Card Game*; and French and Eric M. Lang created *Call of Cthulhu: The Card Game*).

Despite the various creative inputs with the games, each iteration finds the same characters like Amanda Sharpe, student; Jenny Barnes, dilettante; Rex Murphy, reporter; and Wendy Adams, urchin. The characters often look similar across games and have attributes that affect how they are situated within each game. Jenny Barnes, for instance, appears in *Arkham Horror: The Card Game, Arkham Horror, Eldritch Horror, Elder Sign*, and *Mansions of*

Madness. In all of these games, she is portrayed as a woman born into wealth and privilege, influential over other characters and with easy access to money. In each game, these attributes are enacted slightly differently: in *Arkham Horror: The Card Game*, her special ability is to gain an additional resource in each phase; in *Mansions of Madness*, she can gain additional clues (the resource in that game); in *Arkham Horror*, she gains $1 during the upkeep phase; in *Eldritch Horror*, she has a very high level of influence; and in *Elder Sign*, she has the ability to use extra dice. Although manifested differently in each game, each of her abilities matches her particular characteristic of wealth and privilege.

Jenny Barnes, as with the other characters within the Arkham Files, becomes a "transmedia character," one whose "adventures are told across different media forms, each one giving more detail about the life of the characters."[39] These other media include images—Jenny Barnes is always wearing a fashionable dress and hat—and books as well, as FFG has released fiction under the Arkham Files banner. Jenny Barnes has her own book, *House of the Huntress* (2017).

FFG also demonstrates a brand aestheticism in their decision to use both licensed and original storyworlds as game fodder. In his dissertation, Nick Bestor describes FFG's use of licensed storyworlds as a form of transmedia worldbuilding, and in the FFG catalog are games related to *Game of Thrones*, *Marvel*, *Star Wars*, and *Lord of the Rings*.[40] This sort of "paratextual" game play highlights the ludic dimensions of contemporary cult texts as well as the placement of games within different franchises.[41] In a 2017 article, I discussed the way that the FFG game *Star Wars: Rebellion* (2016) refocuses and reexamines the narrative of the first film, operating as "a massive-scale fan fiction" for the franchise.[42] In addition, FFG have a number of transmediated fantasy games that within a world they themselves created, Terrinoth (*Runebound* [2004]; *Descent* [2004/2012], *Legacy of Dragonholt*)

The branded aestheticism of FFG isn't just in the style of art or the way games are constructed; rather, it lies in a particular ethos of the company. When players pick up an FFG box, they know what kind of game they are going to get: a heavily thematic, narratively driven experience, often with transmediated elements across multiple games and genres. It's not a decision any one designer created, but rather a company-wide brand that speaks not just to the authorship of any particular game, but to the authorship of the type of gaming itself.

Conclusion

In the first two decades of the twenty-first century, the board game industry has been hit by two contradictory developments. On the one hand, the consolidation of board game companies and mergers with larger corporations has led to a winnowing of the number of smaller, independent board game producers. On the other hand, new digital and social media technologies have opened up the board game play space to new innovations, both from companies looking to innovate in terms of game mechanics, themes, and styles and from individuals aiming to capture a slice of the millions of dollars crowdfunded for board games today. These two trajectories fit into the general theme of "convergence culture" that Henry Jenkins describes as both a "top-down corporate-driven process and a bottom-up consumer drive process."[43] We see it in the consolidation of media companies to just four or five major billion-dollar corporations; we see it in the rise of social media influencers and grassroots media production on YouTube and elsewhere. This intertwined culture of industrial consolidation/grassroots expansion has been happening for many years and across many different industries, and board games seem to be caught up in the same riptides as the rest of the media cultures.

The difference between the type of convergence culture Jenkins describes and the board game industry as discussed in this chapter, however, lies in the nature of the relationship between the industrial companies and the everyday game players. The board game industry developed, in large part, out of the board game hobby, and the two are still inextricably linked. Unlike mass media corporations, which are so immense as to be almost Cthulhu-like and unknowable, the board game industry is intimate. Composed largely of those who still participate in playing and designing games, who attend conventions both to present *and* to browse, the companies that I have been discussing in the book have not grown so big as to completely lose sight of the players themselves. The distance between the greatest game designer and the newest entrant into the hobby is not vast. Most designers have accounts on and are accessible through BGG. Game companies are staffed by people that love to play games; they are controlled by the designers.

What this means is that the grassroots development of independent games is intimately tied to, and in conversation with, the larger companies that develop their own brand aestheticism. The rise of niche publishing and small créateurs in board gaming highlights a change in the industry. The board game industry has never been as diffuse from its players as, say, the video game industry is.[44] But the distinctions between designers, players, and companies seem to be drawing closer and closer together rather than farther apart.

And this is why examining authorship in games is a relevant exercise. As we have seen, board games rarely call the person creating the game the "author," partly, I argue, because the concept of authorship is tied up with notions of authority and discourses of auteur criticism. What popular culture considers an "author," a person who controls the meaning behind a particular work of art, simply doesn't appear to work in the context of a board game, in which meaning is cocreated between those that created the game and those that play it.

But this is *precisely* how authorship can be understood in a variety of other media contexts too. Board games are no different in this respect from any other medium. Games are not some unique troubling entity in the history of authorship, but rather are *exemplars* of an already-troublesome concept. Meaning is never completely separated from the audience. The author may intend one meaning but the audience receive a completely different meaning. The audience has power to develop their own readings of any media product. "Authorship" is always a contested term, whether in book, film, television episode, or board game form.

Furthermore, that board game companies highlight the designer of the game on hobby board game boxes and in PR literature complicates this notion as well. Assigning a game to a particular person means ascribing to that person authority over the contents of that box. Vlaada Chvátil's *Galaxy Trucker* may be his design, and it is definitely his name on the box, but the game itself is the result of numerous people working on it (the artist, the manufacturer, etc.). And even in cases where the artist and the designer are the same person, as with Ryan Laukat, the resulting games are still not complete without the players stepping in and completing the game play. Laukat may be deeply embedded in writing stories into his games, but until they are enacted by the players, they remain undeveloped.

To be a board game designer—whether créateur, crafter, or brand aesthetic— is to fit into a niche category, between author and player; between industry and hobby. The board game industry, always closely tied to the players that make up its core audience, is both diversifying in terms of the types of games that are getting made, and consolidating in terms of the companies that are making them. But throughout it all, board games are never just gospel; they are mutable and moldable. Their meanings are always negotiated. And the industry is always part of the hobby that sustains it.

The Player as Fan

Ludic Fandom in Board Game Cultures

The notion that board gamers can be fans has been little interrogated in media studies. The majority of work that draws a connection between games and fans has concentrated on video gamers as a type of fan audience.[1] Indeed, as we saw in the introduction, video game players have obvious links to media studies—for example, as "paratexts," video games can become part of transmedia franchises and other mediated sites for audience consumption.[2] Video games are also quite obviously mediated through a screen, which links them to other common media technologies like television. Because video games are more obviously "media texts," the fan appellation arrives through the confluence of audience and medium. Video gamers become posited as that most active of audiences, as they interact in a more obvious way with their media texts.

As the next few chapters will demonstrate, however, board gamers can be— and are—fans. Given the rising popularity of board games and board gamer subcultures, it is surprising that few studies have argued for seeing board gamers as fans, even though the fan activity that board gamers engage in may be less obvious and less conventional than what fan studies has discussed in the past.[3] In this book, I have explored the opportunities that media studies scholarship brings to studying board games, and in this chapter I want to apply a fan studies lens to board gamers themselves. I interrogate the *a priori* argument that video gamers are a type of fan—that is, by assuming that video gamers (as implicitly opposed to board gamers) can be fans, media scholars actually prioritize video games and deprioritize board games as media texts. I don't think scholars believe no board game fans exist; but I do think that because board games are not generally considered in media scholarship, and the types of fan activities undertaken by board game fans are different than those discussed in traditional fan studies literature, those board game fans are elided and the field is undertheorized. Opening up fan studies to encompass board game players helps to underscore a diversity of fan experiences.

Limiting studies of fans and games to solely those of the "video" variety, however an unconscious a demarcation that may be, thus ultimately foregrounds only one type of reading. For example, in my previous book *Game Play*, I limited my analysis to what I termed "paratextual board games" that represent original versions of already-extant media text, and thus examined only how different media reflect different characteristics of the fan audience.[4] And, as Bethan Jones and Wickham Clayton write in their introduction to their special issue of *Intensities*, "board games based on audiovisual texts are often primarily aimed at cultures of interest and fandom that have developed around the *original* texts"—importantly, not of fans of board games in and of themselves.[5] One may be seen as a fan of, for example, *Game of Thrones* more than a fan of the board game based on *Game of Thrones*. This chapter is an attempt to explore some characteristics of board game fandom specifically, although it will necessarily be a limited analysis: no matter how many board game examples I use, there are thousands more (from the most heavily themed to the most drastically abstract) that further complicate this discussion. Further research into board game fandom (including the empirical research conducted for Chapters 6, 7, and 8) augments this theoretical and methodological exploration.

My argument will run in two directions. After a brief discussion of fan studies, my first argument shows the links between fan scholarship and board game play, and the multiple ways that board game players enact many of the same activities articulated by fan scholarship. I provide the term "ludic fandom" as a way of encompassing both the playful practices that fans engage in and the playful way that fandom can be harnessed for financial profit by the media industries. The second argument shows three ways that board game players can be interpreted as fans: first, through knowledge acquisition; second, through identification role-play; and third, through affective play. Ultimately, this chapter will explore the boundaries of fan studies, asking fan and media scholars to see fandom as a continuum of experiences rather than a media-influenced identity.

Fan Studies Analyses

Fan studies is a field focused on the investigation of the emotional (affective) work that fans participate in, as well as the value that popular culture itself places on these fans. "Fans," in this field, can be defined in many ways, and I prefer a broader term that encompasses much more of the population: fans are people that express or demonstrate an attachment to a media text (vs. sport, music, celebrity, etc.). Fan studies as a field largely emerged in the early 1990s with the publication of Henry Jenkins's *Textual Poachers* and Camille Bacon-Smith's *Enterprising Women*, although previous research into audiences and their emotional reaction to the media had been published before that.[6] These early-1990s fan studies works were largely ethnographic in nature, as both Jenkins and Bacon-Smith used interviews with fans to detail the emotional intensity and cultural practices of fan groups. In the twentieth anniversary publication of his *Textual Poachers*, Jenkins has noted that the book deliberately attempted to change the then "pathologized" view of "fannish enthusiasms and participations"; he did this partly by bringing his own fannish perspective to the ethnographic investigation (see Chapter 9 for my own autoethnography).[7]

In the years since *Textual Poachers* was published, fan studies has emerged as a multidisciplinary field, with methodologies drawn from ethnography, anthropology, textual studies, literary studies, economics, cultural studies, queer studies, critical race studies, big data analytics, and many more. Unlike some other methodological focuses, such as the ones used in other chapters in this book, "it is difficult to say that aca-fans are *producing methodologies*."[8] In other words, fan studies isn't itself a methodology, but rather encompasses multiple methodologies that all focus on the same subject: fans and fandom. Researchers can investigate fans through interviews (as Jenkins and Bacon-Smith did), through textual analyses of fan work (like fan fiction, fan videos, or cosplay), through historical methods, or through any other methodological focus that might lead to new insights about fandom, emotional reaction to the media, or the politics of popular culture generally.[9]

That being said, one consequence of examining board gamers as fans is the relative importance placed on the autoethnographic experience. Autoethnography, a focus on the self where "the tastes, values, attachments and investments of the fan and the academic-fan are placed under the microscope of cultural analysis," becomes an important facet of board game fandom, as understanding the processes at work through the individualized game play of a single board game session hinges on the individual experience of the fan.[10] Many board games create different experiences for players, even players playing during the same session. For example, in the game *Betrayal at House on the Hill* (2004, Hasbro), players cooperate to explore a haunted mansion, but at a certain point the game changes and one (or more) players become "haunted" and fight against the other players. Deliberately split, the game forces the haunted player/s to read a different set of rules which remain hidden from the others, and vice versa. The game experience is vastly different from one player to another. An autoethnography of this experience is the only way to get at this ephemeral experience.

Autoethnography, a relatively common methodology in fan studies, "asks the person undertaking it to question their self-account constantly" and reexamine their own place within a particular fandom or fan experience.[11] For Kristina Busse and Karen Hellekson, this means examining the fan-self as "an investment and as an awareness of . . . subject positions" which creates "affect" in the viewer/player.[12] Playing *Betrayal at House on the Hill* forces players into different subject positions. Using autoethnographic methods is not the only way to conduct fan studies analyses of board games, but it is a relevant methodology for integrating studies of fans within game and media studies.

In this chapter, then, I'm using a combination of textual analysis of games (see Chapter 1) and ideas drawn from a fan-centric autoethnography to investigate the ways that game players might be seen as a type of fan; or, in other words, how fan studies as a field might usefully offer a new perspective on the way scholars examine gamers.[13] In an article that unpacks the multiple layers of privilege within video game culture, Megan Condis questions "who is able to lay claim to titles like 'fan' or 'gamer.'"[14] In essence, she shows how video game culture—along with the cultural studies paradigms that emphasize video games and media—dictates the type of audience that is analyzed. I, too, wish to outline who gets to lay claim to names like "fan" or "gamer," but I'm curious to flip the analysis on its head: not to look at the meaning of the word "fan" per se, but rather at how the larger paradigm of media studies has reified the meaning of the term *fan* via *screen studies*, and not to analyze who gets to be called "gamer," but rather at how the types of games that are taken seriously in the academy fit into a particular technological narrative that actively prescribes video games as media.

Narrowing fan studies almost exclusively to screen studies links fandom and technology in a way that is both limiting and reductive; that is, fandom becomes linked to the *device* or *product* rather than the *experiences* or *affect* generated through the fan's interaction with the media text. Partly, this is because much fan studies work remains tethered to the digital, and partly because screen fandom is simply more visible to the scholar.[15] Fandom, however, isn't limited to screens and isn't only digital. This isn't to say that scholarly explorations of fandom don't take into account the larger fan experience—far from it. But prescribing a particular mode of reception necessarily limits the larger exploration of fannishness in the contemporary media environment. It's helpful to look at rhetorical scholar Kenneth Burke's discussion of terministic screens: "Even if any given terminology is a reflection of reality, by its very nature as a terminology it must be a selection of reality; and to this extent it must function also as a deflection of reality."[16] Any analysis must come from a particular selection of texts to analyze, and thus ignores the multitudes of other texts (or analyses) that might exist. Writing here about language, his point could be taken even more literally when applied to screens (and screen studies): studies of media that take the "screen" for granted close off additional concepts and experiences that might otherwise remain unexplored. It is easy to fall back on screen studies at the expense of other fan experiences, simply because moments with a screen are reproducible—it is hard, if not impossible, to replicate a particular "board game experience."

For example, it is easy to write a "fan/screen studies" analysis of the board game *XCOM: The Board Game* (2014, Fantasy Flight Games, and based on a video game of the same name) as it requires the use of a digital app—it is harder to approach this game through a "fan studies" lens given that each player will experience the game play differently, and there may not actually be a tangible product leftover after the fannish experience (e.g., the fan/player may not post about their experience online, write fan fiction, and make fan art about *XCOM: The Board Game*). The game focuses on an elite unit of officials who defend Earth from alien invaders. Each player in the game takes on the role of a leader of this group who must make use of ever-dwindling resources to develop new technology and defend the earth from attack. The app randomizes a number of elements, including the alien attack itself, and forces players to make "real time" decisions with a timer and countdown. The app is observable and analyzable, unlike the actual "in the moment" experience of playing the game. I've previously written about these multimedia board games, arguing that "the use of media products within paratextual board games reduces interactivity by tethering the game more closely to the media franchise."[17] By tying the mechanics of the game to an external mediated device as well as an extant media product, the unique characteristics of the board game are negated by the experience—and adherence to—the screen. A board game can veer in many different directions, prompted by individual player action (e.g., a group of players can decide not to use a particular card, or to not count certain dice rolls). The system is only as coherent as the players. When augmented with "interactive" media, however, the players must subsume their own experiences at the expense of the mediation. At the same time, however, the mechanics of *XCOM* and its reliance on external mediation actually enhance the board game's narrative immersion. There is a qualitative difference between, say, drawing cards from a stack (of which the remaining cards are visible, giving a tangible realization of the remainder of the game) and of receiving what might be an *unlimited* number of alien incursions via the digital app. This seemingly limitlessness narrative enhances the tension of the game and allows players to have a mediated experience akin to other media texts (although watching a deck slowly run out of cards can also be tension-filled). Although not all players will be "fans" of *XCOM*, the game itself offers multiple opportunities to engage in fanlike activities, not unlike other media texts. While playing a game doesn't (necessarily) make someone a fan of that game, it does emulate many characteristics that fan scholars have seen as part of a fan's behavior. Seeing how the screen affects but does not control the experience of the fan/player allows us to reflect on the differences between fan studies as focused on the screen and a more open fan studies that explores different facets of the fan phenomenon.

Ludic Fandom

There are other considerations that link fans and board gamers as well. One key aspect of fan studies that scholars have explored over the past thirty years has been a point that Jenkins originally made in *Textual Poachers*: fans "fill in the gaps" of the narrative, developing new ideas from the text and applying the lessons learned to their own lives. For fans, the media text isn't an unbreakable block; rather, fans

> are concerned with the particularity of textual detail and with the need for internal consistency across the program episodes. They create strong parallels between their own lives and the events of the series. Fan critics work to resolve gaps, to explore excess details and undeveloped potentials.[18]

We can see the same thing with board game players, and the way that individual players use the game to create their own stories, their own meanings, out of the text. As Marco Arnaudo argues of games that tell stories, "players [have] the crucial role of soliciting the narrative by manipulating the components, rearranging the blocks of the story, interpreting the content, and mentally filling in the gaps between the various thematic units."[19] That the characters in the game are enacted by the players at the table seems to make little difference. Take, for example, the cooperative game *Dead of Winter* (2014, Plaid Hat Games), a game in which a small band of survivors of a zombie apocalypse group together and must scavenge for goods. In the original game, there is no "cause" given for the zombie plague—players can make up their own minds about it. But the success of the game (as of December 2019, it is #88 on BoardGameGeek [BGG]) has led to sequels and expansions that flesh out the world. In one game, *Raxxon* (2017, Plaid Hat Games), players take on the roles of specialists who assist the corporation Raxxon in evacuating healthy citizens from the sick. The gaps between the game, its sequel, and its expansion all allow the players to create their own stories within the world created by Jonathan Gilmour and Isaac Vega, the créateurs of the game. There aren't clear answers given to the questions raised in *Dead of Winter*, but merely openings in which players can construct their own meanings.

In addition, in the game, each player is dealt a card that details whether their character is a "betrayer"—that is, whether they will secretly be working against the group to trying to sabotage some aspect of the plan. Throughout the game, players do not know who might be the traitor—or, indeed, if a traitor even exists. Only at the end of the game, or during the game if there is an accusation, is the traitor revealed. And once this happens, players will reevaluate all the actions that happened in the preceding game play session. Like fans who read through the media text looking for "clues" to the ending, the players of *Dead of Winter* (or any game with a traitor) can reread the game play in order to determine what they might have missed, or to fill in the gaps of that character's story.

The links between fandom and board games are strong, and they are enabled, not excluded, by the interactive potentiality of game play. In a piece for the *Journal of Fandom Studies*, I introduced the term "ludic fandom" as a way of describing both the playful way that fans work in the contemporary media environment, and as a term to describe how play culture has appropriated fanlike characteristics. The move to ludicize fandom serves to "turn fandom itself into a type of 'game' with the industries that produce media work."[20] The example I used in the article was Storium, an online game where groups of active participants wrote stories collaboratively using "cards" that affected the development of the story. That many of the stories on Storium were based in already-extant worlds meant that these writers were gamifying a type of fanfiction. At the same time,

I argued, because board games like *Star Wars: Rebellion* (2016, Fantasy Flight Games) were allowing fans to play the *Star Wars* story in various ways, it, too, was gamifying fandom. Yet, both examples hinge on the fact that fans as game players are enacting similar, if not the same, types of engaged interactions with the media.

Thus, on the one hand, ludic fandom presents a way of understanding fan work as based in game tropes. Board game playing mirrors the fans' style of affective engagement. When fans are engaging in the creation of original fiction, videos, cosplay, or other types of fan engagement, they are deliberately playing with the boundaries of the media text. Similarly, fans who "engage in . . . play enact an imaginative freedom to interact with media texts," using the boundaries of the media as mere suggestions.[21] Board game players, too, play. And while they may not (necessarily) be writing fan fiction or making videos of *Dead of Winter*, they too are pushing at the boundaries of the game text. Playing a board game well means finding the aspects of the rules that can stretch and bend; it means pushing the rules of the game to their limits. People who master board games know precisely how to play by the rules—and how to make the rules play for them. Breaking the rules means playing a different game, but knowing just how much play there is in the rules can mean the difference between winning and losing. For example, in the game *Empires of the Void II* (2018, Red Raven Games; see Chapter 4), players score twice in the game. The first scoring round can be initiated by each player individually, so knowing precisely when to play that score card is crucial. The rules of the game don't say when to play it, but having the sense to play with the unfolding of the game and the other players' progress can mean the difference between winning and losing. It's a different kind of playfulness from fan fiction, to be sure, because it's still playing within the bounds of the text (whereas fans can play outside the textual walls), but the interactive and play*ful* aspects between fans and board game players find concomitance.

On the other hand, ludic fandom also denotes play spaces that appropriate fan characteristics—what I've also called a "parody" of fannishness.[22] In this sense, mainstream media industries are using the tactics of fandom to generate more interaction with the media objects. Whether its interacting with Netflix's *Black Mirror* episode "Bandersnatch" (in which a choose-your-own adventure mandate guides viewers' digital engagement with the text) or crowdfunding a save-our-show campaign in order to receive the graphic novel that fleshes out *Wynonna Earp*, everyday viewers of media are being encouraged to embrace a particular fannish methodology in service of industry goals. Suzanne Scott's appellation of the "convergence culture industry" identifies one of the methods by which this occurs: through "industrial efforts to standardize the cultural category of 'fan.'"[23] Rather than encourage "transformative" fan work, work that exists outside the realm of the text, twisting and changing the canon, the media industries want "affirmational" work—work that supports the creator's vision and, as a corollary, encourages more authorized purchases. In Scott's work, the convergence culture industry's use of digital technology is linked to a gendered reading of fans, as the industry tries to cater to more masculine (re: affirmational, capitalistic) strategies of fandom. Board games fall into a similar pattern. Players literally must play by the rules—they must color in the lines—or they aren't actually playing the game at all. The rules dominate the tenor of the game and breaking the rules changes the game. Take *Dead of Winter* again—players have to roll a die after they move to see if they've been "bitten" by a zombie. To not roll the die, or to avoid rolling it because of an out-of-game narrative digression, risks changing the underlying structure of the game. This doesn't mean that players never break the rules, but rather that in order to be a "good player" one must abide by what the game suggests. In this way, board games are encouraging a ludic mentality *up to a certain extent*: you can play with the game only *so much* before it breaks. This form of ludic fandom mirrors the way mainstream media are courting fans today: the text is only malleable in ways sanctioned and set forth by the industry. A discourse of ludic fandom thus undergirds much fan and game player interaction in the contemporary media industry, both from the point of view of fans and from the point of view of the game industry.

T.I.M.E. Stories (Space Cowboys, 2015) exemplifies ludic fandom. In the game, players take on the roles of time-travel agents who go back in time and inhabit the minds of people from the past (so players can, in effect, swap characters throughout the game). Working together, the players must solve a mystery that unfolds as the game goes on. If they do not solve it within a specified time limit, their characters are ripped back to their original bodies and the entire game resets. Thus, it is a game of both mystery solving and memory, as players must learn facts on some iterations that they can apply in later ones. Each game experience is a single-play story. Once players have looped and solved the mystery, that set is effectively completed and there is no more narrative. As a business model, this means that players will need to purchase additional expansion sets with more narratives. At the same time, Space Cowboys have encouraged fans of the game to design and distribute their own fan-made expansions of the game, providing a "how-to" guide with card specifications and game play dynamics on their website. There are multiple fan expansions of the game (*Switching Gears, Submerged Atlantis,* and *Pariah Missouri* are the highest rated on BGG), with each recording a user-generated rating and reviews by players. This type of fan interaction is a form of creative fan work—but ultimately must fall within the structures of Space Cowboys *T.I.M.E. Stories* format in order to be played with the game system. One couldn't make elements that did not fit on the board, for example, or include mechanics that the game doesn't already provide for if one wanted to stay within the *T.I.M.E. Stories* universe. The fandom is playful, and encouraged to be so, but at the same time is constrained by the tenets of the original producer.

Fandom through Board Games

In terms of fandom and fan studies, games have many characteristics that tie directly into the larger academic study of fans. Ted Friedman notes that "game studies has picked up some concepts that could help us rethink the paradigms of media studies as a whole," and these apply to fan studies as well: play (ludology) and interactivity.[24] (In fact, the classic game studies "ludology vs. narratology" debate, as described by Gonzalo Frasca, Henry Jenkins, and Celia Pearce hinges on this "fundamental" difference.)[25] Going back to the beginning of fan studies, fans "play with textual materials"; are "interactive"; "perform" roles within their fandom; fans in many ways see the media environment as ludic.[26] Karra Shimabukuro argues that "one of the appeals of [role playing games] is that they extend beyond the canon, with . . . the Gamemaster (GM) and the players participating in an activity similar to that of fan fiction."[27] Ruth Deller explores how fans can make board games based on their favorite media texts.[28] One classic argument against the mediated aspect of board games is that board games don't have a narrative: Greg Costikyan declares that "there is no story in chess, bridge, *Monopoly* [1933, Hasbro], or *Afrika Corps* [1964, Avalon Hill]."[29] Yet, many board games augment our understanding of storytelling and narrative by breaking it down to its components: we see the *pieces* of narrative and as players construct the story together.[30] We become part of the narrative discourse.[31] Even if board gamers aren't labeled as fans, they are participating in activities that could be considered fannish. In much the same way, I've previously examined online "digital cosplay" on Polyvore using a fan studies methodology, even if "many of the users on Polyvore who create character outfits . . . may not consider themselves fans in the traditional way fans are defined."[32]

A huge community of board gamers exist that participate in fanlike activities. For instance, I've been citing the website BoardGameGeek (BGG) throughout this book. Consistently within the top 1,000 websites in the United States, BGG is a regular online meeting place for board gamers interested in discussing their favorite board games. It also serves as a community of players who help each other out with rules clarification and sharing (when an errant rulebook goes missing, fellow gamers often scan theirs and post online), with augmenting existing rules with variations, or even rewriting aspects of the game (in a type of fan-fiction-esque way) to facilitate different styles of play. BGG facilitates players to "become a fan" of their favorite games, highlighting the community of players as well as the affective reaction to playing board games that reflects fannish reactions. In many ways, BGG matches the definition of fan as posited by games researchers Katie Salen and Eric Zimmerman in their authoritative *Rules of Play*: "Participants co-construct communal realities, using designed systems as the raw material."[33] By neglecting board games, fan studies scholars have reinforced the view that board games are somehow "less than" other forms of media.

The first characteristic of board game players and fans that elicits a connection is that of *knowledge acquisition*. For example, many games include an enormous amount of detail and rules to memorize and understand. *Arkham Horror 2e*'s (2005, Fantasy Flight Games) thirty-two-page rule book details minutia and specifics throughout—and it is hardly the most complicated games on the market. In general, the board game landscape features very complex and difficult-to-learn games. In *Game Play*, I called this "unstructure"—the relationship between the rules of a paratextual game and the canon rules of the original text interact in meaningful ways. For board game players—much like for fans of a media text—knowing these rules requires a great deal of knowledge acquisition, either through investigating alternate extratextual sources (e.g., wikis or BGG) or through other research means (e.g., watching YouTube videos on game play or fan theories).

Fan studies examines how fans gain and use knowledge about the object of their fandom. Jenkins argues that "Fan communities were among the first to experiment with ways they could pool knowledge, build on each other's expertise, and trade insights within networked communities."[34] For example, fan knowledge can lead to greater cultural capital within fan communities; that is, the more knowledge one gains about a particular media text, the higher one may be on a fan hierarchy. This isn't true of all fan communities, of course, but it does become a way of establishing competency within a fandom.

Memorizing rules or knowing the "unstructure" of the board game allows fan/ players to position themselves within a community of other game players, both as "rules explainer" or "trainer" and as "question-answerer." Within board game circles, this role is often played quite literally though training videos, "how-to play" instructions that can garner tens of thousands of views. For instance, the aforementioned game *Dead of Winter*'s rule book is not long (about fourteen pages), but the game itself is quite intricate and involves a patterned flow of actions that must be followed exactly. Many online videos explain the rules; the popular "Watch It Played" video on *Dead of Winter* has over 225,000 views. As a player of complex games, I often watch these videos before—or as—I read the rulebook.

Knowledge about rules is one aspect of knowledge acquisition. Another is knowledge about the world of the game itself. The game *BioShock Infinite: The Siege of Columbia* (2013, Plaid Hat Games) is based on the video game *BioShock Infinite*. The board game pits two players (or four players playing on teams) against each other, one playing as a rebel force in the flying city of Columbia circa 1912 and the other playing as the political leader of the city defending their totalitarian policies. The board game flips the role-play around so that the narrative of *Siege of Columbia* takes place relatively simultaneously with the events of the video game, while never actually coinciding directly. *Siege of Columbia* therefore is situated rather peculiarly as part of the *BioShock* franchise, an already-transmediated experience that also includes transmediation within the narrative as a form of exposition.[35] *Siege of Columbia* presents knowledge acquisition through the fannish knowledge of the *BioShock* universe. Situated much like fan fiction as part of both a canon and "a fantasy based on the needs of individual writers," *Siege of Columbia* is board game fan fiction, a reimagining of a reimagining. Knowledge of the original video game helps to define and delimit the board game.

A second characteristic of board game players and fans that echoes between the two is the *identification role-play* that board games engender. For Kurt Lancaster, playing board games asks us to "enter imaginary environments" just as a fictional text invites "simulated environments that people can enter."[36] He investigates "how prospective participants become immersed in . . . fantasy play" as a form of identification with the game as a text. Identification with a cult world lies at the heart of much fan scholarship, and the interactive elements of board games—the pieces, the rules, the board itself—lend themselves to world building as well. *Siege of Columbia* uses multiple characters and unique abilities to help players enter the world and identify with the characters. Furthermore, as we saw, the game *XCOM* literally places characteristics onto each player, as the app has players take on the roles of Commander, Chief Scientist, Central Officer, and Squad Leader. Each player must role-play in order to win the game.

A board game like *T.I.M.E. Stories* also plays with the idea of character identification. In *T.I.M.E. Stories*, players doubly role-play, first as the time travelers themselves and secondly through the minds of the characters those time travelers inhabit. The players need to identify with the particular characters that they're playing as. At times, different characters will have different abilities—the ability to pick locks or pockets, for example—so to fully embrace the narrative, a player must get into the mindset of the character they are playing as.

A third characteristic of board game players and fans that unites them is the affective play between game and fan. For Matt Hills, fandom represents a relationship with a media text in which affect (the characteristic of an object to create emotions) becomes "playful, as capable of 'creating culture' as well as being caught up in it."[37] In other words, the media text generates a playing with emotion that connects fan with text. Board games reflect a similar sense of affective play—interactions with the game and with their fellow players allow fans to experience a playfulness with their own emotional response. In both *XCOM* and *The Siege of Columbia*, fans join with others to either beat back the alien invasion or defeat the rebels (or founders)—in both cases, play and affect become linked through continued interaction. The more one plays, the greater a connection to the text itself.

In *T.I.M.E. Stories*, this can be seen through the repeated playthrough of the same game session as a direct tie to the time-travel theme of the game. As we've seen, the game is built as a mystery—the original card deck and each expansion can really only be played by each group of players once as the affect and emotional connection to the game builds through trying to solve the mystery (and once the mystery is solved, it will forever be). The game is played through a mystery deck of cards. Players do not know what cards are coming, and characters travel to different locations to unearth items, maps, characters, and new locations (e.g., a hidden tunnel). To win, the game players must solve the mystery within a certain time limit, but if the time limit ends before the mystery is solved, the game is reset and players start again—but this time armed with the knowledge of their first (or second, or third . . .) play through. Simulating time-travel repetition, the game places the players within an affective relationship with the text itself. To win the game means not just playing the game, but *remembering* and *reliving* the experience of playing the game. Like fans' rereading and re-viewing of traditional media texts. *T.I.M.E. Stories* deliberately draws on the affect of players to guide them through the game multiple times.

Conclusion

In a piece for *Flow TV*, Friedman asks "what can media studies learn from game studies?"—in essence, seeing the two disciplines disparate rather than familial. Friedman notes that "scholars trained in cinematic and televisual textual analysis began to ask, what about this *new* form of entertainment on our screens? As the game industry has continued to grow, pulling eyeballs away from more traditional media, the question has become impossible to ignore . . . *game studies . . . seeks the approval of more traditional media scholarship.*"[38] The implication is that games and media are separate entities at odds with each other.

This larger academic lineage hinges on technology: since the invention of the printing press, media, and technology have been linked, and as more advanced (re: digital) technology emerges, new media studies attempts to keep current. The notion that board games, those old and dusty cardboard relics, might be media is often elided—or ridiculed—in academic literature. Partly, this may be because board games "are rarely narratively consequential."[39] Because board games are played intimately (i.e., with small groups playing games that might conclude differently each time), they cannot, by definition, all give the same experience. Even if we may all play *Catan* (1995, Mayfair) the same *way*, we still experience different game play *development*. Partly, as well, this division of board games from media may be because of the unique elements that board games bring into the field: specifically, the notions of tangibility and intimacy. But, as we've seen throughout the first half of this book, board games aren't "part" of media because the emphasis of a board game is on the player rather than on the content; that is, board game studies *must* focus on the players rather than on the game. Studying board game players as fans means we must continue to emphasize ethnographic methodologies melded with textual and ludic analyses. Each board game is a balance of game content (e.g., rules, pieces) and actual game play (e.g., with people). It is impossible to analyze a board game outside its immediate context. Video games are artifacts in the traditional media sense: if one buys a cartridge (or, more likely today, downloads a file), one is, by definition, purchasing an experience that can be replicated because it has been preprogrammed. The board game as a physical object can be replicated, but the experience of playing is intimate and social, and in many ways dependent on the group play rather than on the material of the game.

By focusing on players of games as a key element connecting board games to media, I have augmented fan studies through board game play. Game play has similarities to fandom, as sitting down to play a board game means necessarily interacting with it, learning from it, and cocreating the meaning with the designers of the game. Audiences become a way of exploring the medium of the board game. In the same way, we can think about media studies in terms of "play" as well. For Friedman, "Rethinking media as a form of play offers several promising avenues for us to reexamine some of the core concepts of contemporary media theory," namely interactivity, intertextuality, aesthetics, realism, learning, history, and narrative.[40] Indeed, gradations in types of board game players seem to have analog to types of media audiences as well, from the casual player/viewer to the enthusiastic hobbyist/fan. But perhaps this philosophy is even older than digital technology; the metaphor may work because games themselves have always been a form of media.

Board gamers may not traditionally be called "fans," but in all these cases there are particular characteristics for board games that draw on fan studies strategies for understanding gamers. Tying fan studies to screen studies, as has been done in the past, limits the types of interaction that can be seen through the type of autoethnographic and methodologically diverse analysis of board games. Although it's not my intent to castigate fan studies for this lapse—indeed, the multidisciplinary nature of fan studies means that any lapse could be seen as an opportunity for relevant and diverse scholarship—it is important to reflect on ways to expand the field. Ultimately, board games represent an ancient form of textuality that fan studies could usefully take up in future analyses. One of the ways board game scholars can do this is through a renewed focus on the interaction between the playful practices that fans engage in and the way that fandom itself can be used by media industries, what here I've termed "ludic fandom." By focusing on these points of tension within both game and media studies, new opportunities for investigating the impact of games on everyday players can be developed.

Part Two

Ethnographic Analysis

Surveying Board Game Players

Who Plays What . . .

Survey research is a methodology for making empirical observations about different groups of people by asking a random sample of a population to answer questions. According to a survey research method textbook by Floyd J. Fowler, Jr., surveys can be used to understand "the subjective feelings of the public" as well as "numerous facts about the behaviors and situations of people."[1] Unlike the largely textually-based research methodologies discussed so far in this book, survey research is statistical: that is, by quantifying participants' answers to questions, one can make general observations about what various groups of people think about a particular topic.[2] For the purposes of this book, I am interested in how hobby board gamers conceptualize the hobby and what types of games and activities they prefer to engage in.

This chapter and the next will report the results of a survey of board game players I conducted in April–May 2019. I was curious to get a sense of the landscape of board gaming and board gamers, to see what sorts of games, styles, mechanics, and attributes players liked the most. I asked both quantitative questions that could be answered numerically and qualitative "fill-in-the-blank" questions that must be analyzed to be understood. There are advantages and disadvantages to this sort of data collection—the survey was longer than most people wanted to fill out and people tend to get bored answering too many open-ended questions. But *only* looking at quantitative or *only* looking at qualitative data doesn't give the full story; it's better to have both. This chapter will largely report the quantitative results, with some broad statistical analysis, while the next chapter will look at the specific qualitative answers.

As Fowler writes, "Every survey involves a number of decisions that have the potential to enhance or detract from the accuracy (or precision) of survey estimates."[3] Some of these decisions include the sample size, the sample frame (those whom the survey actually reaches), the design of the survey, the rate of response, and the evaluation of the answers. I made some deliberate choices in my survey that affected the results: these answers do not reflect *all* gamers, but just those who saw the survey and took the time to fill it out.[4] In addition, as observed by George Beam, any survey research has a fundamental flaw: "answers to questions are not reliable [as] . . . people often give inaccurate answers" and "there's no way to distinguish those that are correct from those that are not."[5] This is not to say that all answers are always wrong, simply that people (being people) are inherently unreliable at reporting their own data. The observations and analysis that I perform may not be reflective of all board game players, and I hope that readers will take this chapter with a very large grain of salt, since it only represents the perspective of the 900 or so that filled out my survey.

This research both supports and expands the board game survey research run by Stewart Woods for his book *Eurogames*.[6] Woods targeted users of BoardGameGeek (BGG) to discover the demographic and habitual information about his participants, and had approximately 650 responses. In contrast, in order to collect my data, I used targeted social media posts and word of mouth to spread the survey. I also posted up flyers for the survey in my local board game stores and cafes. I wanted to survey people who already identified as hobby board gamers, so I didn't try to reach out to the full population. I also wasn't as interested in exploring role-playing games or collectible card games so I aimed my research at hobby board gamers specifically. I sent out some preliminary tweets and Facebook posts which gained some minor traction. In the initial push, I received about 200 responses. Toward the end of my data collection period, I sent out another round of tweets, this time tagging some online board game content creators and asking them to retweet it. In one week I received an additional 700 responses, for a total of about 900 completed surveys. (I discuss in the conclusion of this chapter some of the issues and problems with my data collection, and how we can learn from these mistakes to approach more diverse answers; and in Appendices 1 and 2, I include a breakdown of all the questions and quantitative responses I received.)

There are other methods that can be used to investigate board game players. In 2018, Dinesh Vatvani used data scraping techniques to harvest data from BGG. Data scraping is a type of Big Data analysis where computer algorithms are programmed to pull data and information from large databases. Rather than collecting data from filled-out surveys, then, Vatvani's research looked at what users had uploaded/posted to BGG itself. Vatvani's technique is useful for finding out what data is already out there, but it doesn't get at some of the underlying ideas that board game players themselves might have by itself—that is, he collected data that's already been posted but didn't ask new questions.[7]

Generally, what I found from the quantitative results of my survey is that board gamers are more focused on the social aspects of board games than on any one particular game style or mechanic. I also made some "planned comparisons" between different demographics, and discovered some differences in terms of age and sex/gender in terms of what types of games gamers enjoyed playing—generally, younger players and female players tended to enjoy less competitive, more social games, while older players and male players tended to enjoy more strategic and competitive games.[8] For the purposes of this survey, I also asked players about their race/ethnicity. The vast majority of people who filled out the survey were white—722 people out of 807, or almost 90 percent. Ten people identified as Black or African American, two as Native American; thirty-one as Asian; two as Pacific Islander, and forty-four as other (including fifteen Latinx people). Because of the huge disparity in white participants versus people of color, any sort of data analysis related to race will be heavily skewed and unreliable; however, I have discussed race and gaming in this chapter and in Chapter 8.

Understanding the Survey and the Results

I am not by training a survey research practitioner, and I am indebted to my colleague Dr. Kendra Knight who helped me frame the questions and gave valuable insights into the survey process. She made the survey infinitely better, and any mistakes within it are entirely mine.

Although everyone will approach creating a survey and understanding the results differently, it might be useful to follow my nascent exploration of survey research to learn from my success and to avoid my failures. I started by writing a series of questions that captured my intended topic. Finding the right questions can be difficult, but the right questions will lead to the types of answers you want to find. For my survey, I was particularly interested in understanding the thoughts of individual hobby board gamers, so I asked both open-ended and structured questions. For example, I wanted to find out what particular elements of board gaming were enjoyable, but I wanted to give respondents a chance to answer in as many different ways as I could. I asked a "Matrix"-style question where they rated on a Likert scale (a scale of 1–5) how much they agreed with a statement about *favorites*:

1. Do you agree or disagree with the following statements? (On a scale of 1–5, where 1 is not at all and 5 is very much)

    a. One of my favorite parts of a game is its table presence (figures, dice, board)
    b. One of my favorite parts of a game is its art
    c. One of my favorite parts of a game is learning the rules
    d. One of my favorite parts of a game is winning (or completing the game successfully)
    e. One of my favorite parts of a game is beating others
    f. One of my favorite parts of a game is learning the strategy
    g. One of my favorite parts of a game is luck
    h. One of my favorite parts of a game is socialization
    i. One of my favorite parts of a game is its fun flavor text
    j. Other

The "Other" category allowed them to fill in the blank with their own answers. Matrix-style questions offer a lot more information than a simple "What is your favorite aspect of gaming" because they allow for inter-question analysis and comparison, while also constraining the types of answers into just the ones that I'm interested in. (See Appendix 1 for a list of all the questions I asked.)

In general, about 900 people clicked on answers. Once I had closed the survey, I had to clean up the data. The data collection system, Qualtrics, compiled all the information together, but also recorded every time someone opened the survey and didn't fill it out. There were about 200 "blank" entries—entries where no answers had been given. I deleted those to give me a workable set of data (I kept in any survey responses that had at least one question answered). Qualtrics also provided summaries of all the data (with basic statistical analysis, like averages for numerical questions) and all the pretty graphs that you see in this chapter.

I then copied that data to a spreadsheet so I could work with it more easily. At this point, I could have started using programs like SPSS to provide advanced statistical analysis. For the purposes of this book, however, I merely wanted to give an overview of the information with some basic analysis that didn't require inferential analysis. The simple reporting of information is called *descriptive* statistics, in which a researcher uses statistics to describe the data rather than running tests on the data. This helps researchers see patterns in the data. (The other type of statistical analysis, *inferential* statistics, uses the data to make inferences about the population, and involves more quantitative analysis, such as finding out p-values, making hypothesis, and finding statistical significance.) Thus, the data in this survey reveals what *these people* answered, but we can't assume (or infer) how *all gamers* might respond.

The more complex part of the analysis was comparing aspects of the data. To do this, I would isolate two or more variables and compare them against one another. For instance, if I were interested in what different ages and sex/genders considered their favorite aspects of gaming, I would first sort the "age" data set so that all the answers from age group eighteen to twenty-four years were in a row, followed by the answers from age group twenty-five to thirty-four years, and so on. Then, next to each "age" answer would be their corresponding *favorite* answer, so I had a list of what each person answered for their age and their favorite, organized by age (note that because there were so few people aged sixty-four to seventy-five who answered my survey, I combined their answers with the fifty-five to sixty-four age range). I compiled the data the same way with the answers to the sex/gender question.

Following this I averaged out what each of these age groups considered *favorite*. (I also looked at the mode and standard deviation—mode represents the most common answer given, while standard deviation is how close to the average most answers are: the lower a standard deviation, the closer to the average—in order to assess how consistent the answers were for each age and sex/gender grouping.) This descriptive statistical comparison revealed only minor differences in how different demographics favored different aspects of games, but nothing hugely significant—that is, every age group tended to answer the questions similarly, and with similar modes and standard deviations (Table 6.1).

While there is some variation in all the answers, there is nothing at this level that says that there are significant differences between how different ages or different gender identities answered this question. The biggest difference lay in the "Learning the Rules" category, where age and sex/gender identity only reflected minor differences. In terms of age, the fifty-five to seventy-four demographic averaged 3.46 while the twenty-five to thirty-four demographic averaged 2.87. I suspect this has to do with the fact that twenty-five- to thirty-four-year-olds may not have as much time generally to learn and play games. And men tended to prefer learning the rules (average: 3.14) more than women did (2.54).

Table 6.1 Age Data, Favorites Question

	Table Presence	Art	Learning the Rules	Winning	Completing it Successfully	Beating Others	Learning the Strategy	Luck	Socializing	Fun Flavor Text
Average										
18–24	4.09	4.26	3.09	3.29	4.26	2.88	4.53	2.68	4.59	3.56
25–34	4.13	4.19	2.87	2.94	4.05	2.53	4.26	2.51	4.51	3.38
35–44	4.30	4.16	2.96	2.80	4.02	2.33	4.24	2.49	4.53	3.42
45–54	4.25	4.08	3.00	2.83	4.11	2.43	4.32	2.44	4.44	3.30
55–74	3.97	3.72	3.46	3.25	4.40	2.92	4.44	2.47	4.44	3.25
Male	4.23	4.08	3.14	2.83	4.05	2.44	4.37	2.48	4.47	3.33
Female	4.18	4.24	2.54	3.01	4.13	2.51	4.06	2.54	4.59	3.51
Nonbinary	4.24	4.34	2.97	3.03	4.00	2.45	4.34	2.41	4.48	3.39
Standard Deviation										
18–24	0.83	0.79	1.22	1.12	0.83	1.15	0.79	1.01	0.61	1.05
25–34	0.95	0.89	1.07	1.21	0.86	1.24	0.88	1.07	0.76	1.12
35–44	0.73	0.80	1.06	1.08	0.89	1.12	0.82	0.98	0.75	1.06
45–54	0.81	0.80	1.00	1.06	0.82	1.09	0.79	0.93	0.77	0.96
55–74	0.76	0.80	0.91	1.11	0.68	1.23	0.80	0.93	0.68	0.98
Male	0.82	0.83	1.04	1.10	0.86	1.15	0.75	0.97	0.76	1.07
Female	0.85	0.82	0.98	1.17	0.84	1.20	0.98	1.04	0.71	1.03
Nonbinary	0.82	0.88	1.16	1.22	0.91	1.16	0.88	1.22	0.72	0.98
Mode										
18–24	4	4	2	4	4	3	5	2	5	4
25–34	4	5	3	3	4	2	5	2	5	4
35–44	4	4	3	3	4	1	5	2	5	4
45–54	5	4	3	3	4	3	5	2	5	4
55–74	4	4	3	4	5	3	5	3	5	3
Male	4	4	3	3	4	3	5	2	5	4
Female	4	4	2	4	4	2	4	2	5	4
Nonbinary	4	5	4	2	4	2	5	2	5	3

For other questions, I also used Excel's "countif" and "countifs" functions to count the number of times different answers were mentioned by different ages. One of the most important things to learn about doing survey research is finding out how to use Excel effectively!

Survey Results

Demographic Questions

The data demonstrate that most of the people who took the survey were white (Caucasian) men, aged twenty-five to forty-four, from the United States and the United Kingdom. This is not to say that there wasn't great variance between the many people who contributed, or that there isn't diversity within the board game community as a whole, but the results of this particular survey were very heavily skewed toward that identity. There are many possible reasons for this. The most obvious is that the community *could be* mostly white and male. There are other explanations, however. For instance, the demographics of respondents that I had for this survey could also stem from my sampling technique—I didn't attempt to reach out to different board game groups online or target specific demographics with my survey. Using social media can have advantages; it can also mean that one's data is limited to the responses of those that are on, or have, a particular social media technology.[9] Additionally, different types of people are more likely to take surveys, according to William Smith:

> In general, more educated and more affluent people are more likely to participate in surveys than less educated and less affluent people . . . women are more likely to participate than men . . . younger people are more likely to participate than older people . . . and white people are more likely to participate than non-white people.[10]

It is hard to see the results of my survey as indicating that women were more likely to answer, and future survey research should deliberately reach out to underrepresented groups in order to have more representation. Not including these perspectives is a detriment to the data and misrepresents the hobby.

The majority of people answering the survey (745) were aged between twenty-five and fifty-four, with thirty-four people aged eighteen to twenty-four and thirty-six people aged fifty-five and older (Figure 6.1). Because of Institutional Review, I couldn't officially reach out to people under eighteen years of age, although obviously younger people are playing board games as well. Because of the time/cost associated with playing board games, it's not surprising to me that the most populous age range was thirty-five to forty-four; this is an age when one has (perhaps) settled into a career and family, and may have some extra time and/or money to spend on gaming. Additionally, this age bracket has grown up with and witnessed the rise of digital technology, which may make them more keen to spend time engaging in face-to-face social activities instead of looking at more screens (as I discuss more in Chapter 7).

I also asked people which gender they identified with, and 70 percent, or the vast majority of people (563 out of 814), answered "male," 222 people (27 percent) answered "female" with 18 people marking "non-binary," 4 answering "queer," and 7 answering "other" (Figure 6.2). Asking gender-related questions can be difficult because people interpret "gender" in different ways. As some people pointed out when answering "other," gender is a construct of culture (masculine/feminine) rather than biological sex (male/female). This is true, and surveys would do well to ask multiple questions to get a full range of identities (gender identity, sex, sexuality, presenting gender, etc.). However, the vast majority of surveys that people are used to taking still use this outdated language. In fact, Qualtrics, the software used to make this survey, defaults gender answers to *just* male/female, ignoring nonbinary entirely. In retrospect, I wish I had included

Q27 - What age are you?

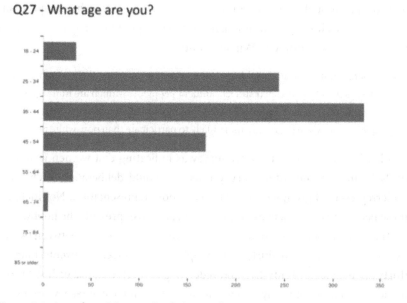

Figure 6.1 Age of participants. Qualtrics graph.

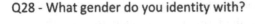

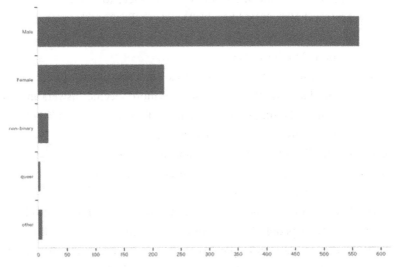

Figure 6.2 Gender identity of participants. Qualtrics graph.

an option for "transgender," as two of the "others" responded with that, and been more clear in distinguishing sex and gender.

However skewed this data is toward the male, it is significantly more diverse than Woods's survey of BGG, which found a 96 percent male response.[11] I suspect this has to do with the historical stereotype that more men play board games than women do (a point I take up in the next chapter), or it could have to do with the fact that, as Amany Saleh and Krishna Bista found, male participants are more likely to respond if they received a reminder (and the second tweet I sent could have served that purpose).[12]

In addition, I asked people what their race/ethnicity was. This is another tricky question for people to answer because there are many different ways of identifying. I opted to use what is, in the United States, a standard "race/ethnicity" survey question, to which I added an "other" category and asked people to fill in the answer if they wanted to. As mentioned earlier, 722 people out of 807 who opted to answer the question identified as white, 10 identified as Black or African American, 2 as Native American, 31 as Asian, 2 as Pacific Islander, and 44 as other. My own identity as a white researcher from the United States blinded me to the way people identity *differently* across the world and led me to default to these race/ethnicity categories, but in truth I should have had more foresight into the global experience of gaming today. For example, I didn't realize that in New Zealand the term "Pākehā" refers to nonnative people of European descent. I also should have reflected on changing demographics and included categories for mixed race/biracial identities. Table 6.2 summarizes all the races mentioned in the survey.

To have participants write in the answers to all race/ethnicity questions or all gender questions does offer the opportunity for more specific answers and user-generated responses. Letting everyone write in their own answer would have opened up space for greater diversity of content. For the purposes of this survey, however, I needed the information to be more quantitative, which is why I opted to use multiple choice. In the future, this would be helpful to dig down into the specific for individual participants.

Finally, I asked the open-ended question, "What is your country of residence?" The vast majority of people (531 out of 802) said they were from the United States of America (one person put "America," which I included in that list). The second most common country of residence was the United Kingdom, with 94 people stating it, although I should note that in that number I did *not* include England (15 people), Scotland (1 person), or Wales (1 person). Additionally, one person put the United Kingdom/United States. Table 6.3 outlines all the countries included in the sample.

Table 6.2 Race/Ethnicity, Other Answers

Race/Ethnicity	Number
White	722
Asian	31
Latinx/Hispanic	15
Black or African American	10
Mixed/Biracial	10
Human	4
Native Hawaiian or Pacific Islander	2
American Indian or Alaska Native	2
Jewish	2
Malay	2
Pākehā	2
Slavic	1
Mediterranean/Spanish	1
Filipino	1
Indian	1
Irish/British	1
[Did not answer question]	205

Table 6.3 Countries Represented in Survey

Country	Number
Africa*	1
America	1
Australia	17
Belgium	1
Brazil	3
Canada	59
Catalonia*	1
Croatia	1
Czech Republic	1
Denmark	1
England	15
Europe*	1
Finland	3
France	2
Germany	17
Greece	1
India	1
Ireland	4
Israel	1
Italy	1
Japan	1
Malaysia	5
Mexico	2
The Netherlands	4
New Zealand	11
North Macedonia	1
Norway	2
Poland	2
Romania	1
Scotland	1
South Africa	1
Spain	5
Sweden	2
Switzerland	3
The Netherlands	2
Turkey	1
The United States	530
The United Kingdom	94
Wales	1
United Kingdom /United States	1

(For the sake of completeness, I included the starred answers, although I am aware they are not countries.)

Board Gaming Questions

The roots of board gaming go deep, as most people have been playing board games as a hobby for over a decade. I also found that overwhelmingly, participants play once or more a week with the same group of people but enjoy playing with new people. Additionally, participants tended to have mixed feelings about using digital apps in games, but enjoyed strategic, cooperative, and Deck Building games the most. Participants enjoyed a great variety of mechanics, with Worker Placement being the most popular, although all this varies with age and gender.

Going into this survey, I assumed that a lot of people in the hobby had only recently gotten started. The past ten years have seen an explosion in the world of board games, with more games being produced and marketed than ever before. Yet, almost half of people who responded to the survey played board games longer than I had thought—435 people said they played games for ten or more years, while 454 people have played for fewer than ten years. Digging into the numbers a bit more, it became obvious that the older a participant was, the longer they had played games. The most common response for players aged thirty-five and older was that they have played for longer than fifteen years. The average length of time that someone aged eighteen to twenty-four had played was three to six years, and the data correlates the older players get. While there was some variance within the answers (most age groups had a standard deviation of 1.3, meaning answers generally were within a few years of the average), it seems safe to say that, at least for the people taking this survey, board games are *not* a new hobby. However, almost 10 percent of the respondents have played for fewer than three years, which speaks to that increasing popularity of board gaming. Additionally, while I didn't specifically ask this, the data would seem to suggest that most people start playing board games as a hobby in their late teens/early twenties (there were six people over the age of sixty-five who took the survey, so it's hard to generalize from that small a sample, although five of those six have been playing longer than fifteen years).

I was also interested to learn what game introduced hobby board gaming to people—what is often called a "gateway game." A total of 837 people answered the question, listing a total of 218 games (although many people listed more than one game, and some people listed "can't remember" or "don't know"). By

Table 6.4 Ten Most Popular Gateway Games

Game	Number of People
(Settlers of) Catan (1995, Mayfair)	132
Ticket to Ride (2004, Days of Wonder)	42
Monopoly (1933, Hasbro)	39
Carcassonne (2000, Z-Man Games)	35
Pandemic (2008, Z-Man Games)	35
Risk (1959, Hasbro)	31
Dominion (2008, Rio Grande Games)	19
Betrayal at House on the Hill (2004, Hasbro)	18
Dungeons and Dragons (1974, Wizards of the Coast)	18
Magic the Gathering (1993, Wizards of the Coast)	18

a huge margin, the game that most people listed was *(Settlers of) Catan* (1995, Mayfair), with 132 people naming it as their gateway game. At the same time, 139 games were listed just once, meaning that there were just about as many people who got started with more obscure/less popular games as started with *Catan*. Table 6.4 shows the games in the "top ten" while a full list can be found in Appendix 2.

In addition, nine people noted that Wil Wheaton's online series *TableTop* got them into gaming rather than any particular board game.

Social Activities

In the survey and in my interviews with participants (see Chapter 7), almost everyone mentioned that board games serve an important social function in the age of digital technology. That is, the argument seems to be, as we have become more and more physically separated from people (because of our phones/computers), hobby board game playing has increased because it gives everyone a good excuse to get together for an in-person social event that forces social interaction. I asked the survey respondents whether they tended to play with the same people or different people. My intention for this question was to find out whether people had a steady game group or whether they attended events in order to meet people. Perhaps unsurprisingly, the majority of people (603/856) played with the same group. Only 2 percent of respondents said they mostly played with new people.

But beyond just playing games with people, I wanted to dig down more, to find out *how* people played socially. I asked participants how they participated with

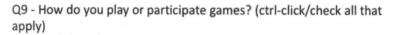

Q9 - How do you play or participate games? (ctrl-click/check all that apply)

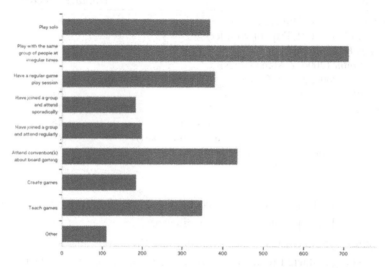

Figure 6.3 How do you participate in board games? Qualtrics graph.

board games and let them choose as many ways as they wanted, including adding their own: the answers thus reflected the variety in the hobby (Figure 6.3). This question wasn't asking what people preferred, but rather what people actually did. There are a variety of reasons that might affect how people answered, including where they live (if they are not close to many other people, that would affect whether they played regularly or sporadically) or financial situation (in terms of affording travel for and attendance at board game conventions).

Digging into this data a little bit, we can see that there is a great variety of ways that people participate in games—it's not *just* playing, but comes with a whole host of other attributes (Table 6.5). As a hobby, board gaming is creative (185 people said they have created games) and social (almost everyone wrote that they play games with people or attend conventions).

The "Other" category on this question was filled with a great variety of information, with over 110 people giving various answers, including playing board games online, play testing, moderating board game play, and (most commonly of all) playing with just a spouse. Overall 870 people answered this question with a total number of responses at 2,922. This means that the average number of ways an individual participates with games is 3.4 (although in the data, 183 responses listed only one way that the individual participated. By far,

Table 6.5 Types of Board Game Participation

Participation	Percentage	Total
Play with the same group of people at irregular times	81.72	711
Attend conventions about gaming	50.11	436
Have a regular play session	43.68	380
Play games solo	42.18	367
Teach games	40.11	349
Have joined a gaming group and attend regularly	22.87	199
Create board games	21.26	185
Have joined a gaming group and attend sporadically	21.15	184

the most common *single* response was "Play with the same group of people at irregular times.")

While many of the categories were consistent in terms of gender, some were more varied. For instance, a greater percentage of men than women (46 to 32 percent) played games solo, while a greater percentage of women played games with the same group at irregular times (85 to 80 percent). This may be a commentary on the gendered nature of leisure time: women still tend to do more housework/child-rearing than men do. People who identified as nonbinary/queer/other played solo even less frequently (23 percent said they do) but in groups even more so (91 percent). A greater percentage of men reported attending conventions (54 to 45 percent nonbinary/queer/other to 41 percent women). Interestingly, a greater percentage of nonbinary/queer/other people reported creating games (27 percent) compared with men (24 percent) and women (16 percent). Men tended to have a regular group of people they game with (47 percent report this) compared with women (32 percent) and nonbinary/queer/other people (41 percent). This gender breakdown seems to indicate that women and nonbinary/queer/other people tended to be more social with games, but men tended to play with the same group of people more often.

In terms of age, some additional correlations can be seen. For example, the older someone was, the more likely they were to play games solo, and the less likely they were to play games with the same group of people at irregular times. Eighteen- to twenty-four-year-olds were less likely than any other group to play with a regular group of people, which makes sense given that younger players are probably more likely to be mobile and exploring different communities. These younger players were also the least likely to go to conventions (only 32 percent), while the most likely to attend conventions were from the age group forty-five to fifty-four years, with 56 percent attending. This likely has to do with the cost of the convention coupled with the ability to readily travel. The oldest demographic in my survey (fifty-five to seventy-four) were also the most likely to create games, with 31 percent reporting that they do; interestingly, the next highest age group to create games were eighteen- to twenty-four-year-olds, at 26 percent.

Although the data on people of different races was scant (with only 89 participants out of 807 identifying as nonwhite) and thus cannot be seen as statistically significant, there were some unique differences among the participants identifying as Asian, Black/African American, or Latinx who answered the survey. Compared with the group as a whole, players who identified as Black/African American have a much higher percentage of playing games with the same people at irregular times (100 percent of Black participants noted this), while having a much lower percentage with playing with a group at regular times (zero Black participants identified this). This might be a reflection of the amount of leisure time available to different groups of people. Conversely, players who identified as Asian noted a slightly higher percentage of playing with a group at regular times (29 percent, compared with 23 percent of the total population). Also perhaps reflecting the level of leisure time available to different groups of people, fewer Black/African American players attended conventions than any other group (40 percent, compared with 42 percent Asian, 47 percent Latinx, and 50 percent population as a whole), or play games solo (20 percent Black players identified this, compared with 45 percent Asian, 47 percent Latinx, and 42.18 percent total). Finally, both Black/African American players and Latinx players noted higher percentages of creating their own board games (30 percent and 27 percent respectively, compared to 21.26 percent total and 26 percent Asian players). As I discuss more in Chapter 8, I would hypothesize here that groups that tend not to see games that appeal/cater directly to them are spurred on to create their own games.

Types of Games

The last group of questions I asked focused on the types of games people liked to play, as well as the elements of games that people most enjoyed. I wanted to interrogate the stereotypical notion that that board games are a palliative against the digitization of contemporary life, so I thought it would be worthwhile to find out whether people like to play games with digital apps. Quite a few games that have been released recently use apps or websites as central to the game play (see Chapter 5). The results were perhaps the most evenly distributed of any question

Q19 - Do you like board games that use digital apps? Why or why not?

Figure 6.4 Digital apps. Qualtrics graph.

I asked on the survey, with 364 people *liking* the use of apps, 201 people *disliking* the use of apps, and 240 people neither liking nor disliking (Figure 6.4).

A great many people offered rationales for why they did or did not like games with digital apps. On the one hand, apps can "add to the atmosphere and also tend to let there be no narrator role so everyone can play." They can also streamline aspects of game play that some players may find tedious, like keeping track of scores or randomizing enemy play. They also make the game experience "varied" and "easy to change." On the other hand, some players "don't like to look at my phone while I'm playing," while others think it feels "awkward and like lazy design." They can also "take away from the social interaction." Digital apps can be seen to be disruptive to the game play, and players commented on the lack of immersion they create. Some of the most passionate comments mentioned that people play board games specifically to "get away from the digital." Most of the middle of the road comments noted that it "really depends on the digital app and how it is integrated with the game." Many contributors mentioned specific games: *One Night Ultimate Werewolf* (2014, Bézier Games) was generally seen to use the app in a really positive way, as did *Mansions of Madness 2e* (2016, Fantasy Flight) and *Alchemists* (2016, Czech Games Edition). Almost nobody named games that used the app poorly. Appreciation of digital apps seems to be based on the app itself.

The last couple of questions dealt more generally with types of games and mechanics that people preferred, and they revealed a wide range of opinions. Respondents were given the option to check as many different answers as were applicable, so the data pool is enormous for all of these questions.

Question 21 asked respondents which style of game they preferred (Figure 6.5). Overall, 835 people answered the question, with a total of 3,685 responses. Only 84 people (about 10 percent) chose only one style of game, with Eurogame the most popular *single* choice by far. In general, Eurogames (644, 77 percent) and Cooperative games (589, 70.5 percent) were the two most popular styles of games, and war games (178, 21 percent) and collectible card games (CCGs) (184, 22 percent) were the least popular (Table 6.6). (I'm not surprised by this as I specifically reached out to hobby board gamers rather than war or CCG gamers.)

It's hard to make any sort of generalization about why different types of games might be preferred over other types of games. It could be that the popularity of particular games has affected the results, or the longevity of games in the market may make a difference. Some of the most popular board games over the past two decades have been Eurogames, and some players may find that they enjoy the hottest recent titles (although see Chapter 8 for a critique of Eurogames).

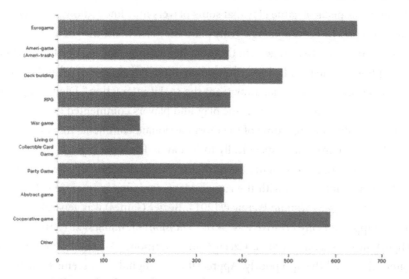

Figure 6.5 What style of game do you prefer? Qualtrics graph.

Table 6.6 Preference for Types of Games

Type of Game	Percentage	Total
Eurogame	77	644
Cooperative	70.5	589
Deck building	58	486
Party games	48	401
Role-playing	45	373
Ameri-game/Ameri-trash	44	369
Abstract game	43	360
Collectible card games	22	184
War games	21	178
Other	12	101

At the same time, as Dinesh Vatvani found, more players say they enjoy complex games like Eurogames because of that complexity. In other words, there may be a bias toward complexity.[13] Perhaps players rate more complex Eurogames higher because they are more challenging and take more effort to play—games that require little effort may seem less valuable. Of course, it is important to keep in mind that 90 percent of the participants chose multiple game styles, so very few people are wedded to just one style of game.

Some of the Other types of games mentioned included Legacy games, Dexterity games, Casual games, "Artsy" games, and Deduction games. One of the things this question and the next question revealed is the overlap in the way people talk about or describe games. Is a "Cooperative" game a mechanic or a style? (I included it in both questions.) How is an abstract game different from a Eurogame? What this revealed is that the way board gamers describe games can often be specific to the gamer; the overlap between "style" and "mechanic" is clearly present, as some said mechanics and styles were the same thing, and some saw them as quite different.

In fact, when I asked the respondents what mechanism/mechanic they preferred, answers were again all over the place (Figure 6.6). This time, I received 5,010 responses to the question, with 834 answering in total. Worker Placement (639 responses, 77 percent) and Cooperation (538, 65 percent) were the most popular mechanics, while Trick Taking (which I typo'd as trick tacking . . . oops!) was the least popular with 181 people (22 percent) clicking it.

Obviously, however, there is great variance in the mechanics that people enjoy playing, and almost every participant clicked more than one (Table 6.7).

Q23 - What mechanism of gameplay do you prefer? (ctrl-click/check all that apply)

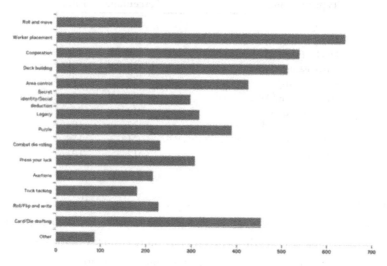

Figure 6.6 What mechanisms of game play do you prefer? Qualtrics graph.

Table 6.7 Preference for Game Mechanics

Mechanic	Percentage	Total
Worker Placement	77	638
Cooperation	64	538
Deck Building	61	512
Card/Die Drafting	54	454
Area Control	51	424
Puzzle	46	388
Legacy	38	317
Press Your Luck	37	307
Secret Identity/Social Deduction	36	297
Combat Die Rolling	28	232
Roll/Flip and Write	27	228
Auctions	26	216
Roll and Move	23	190
Trick Taking	22	181
Other	10	87

The Other mechanics that people enjoyed included Asymmetric Powers, Engine Building, Hand Management, and Storytelling, although there was a great variety revealed in the eighty-seven answers. (Indeed, a few people answered that it didn't matter because they just enjoyed the social connection with others.) I also wanted to dig more into the many varied responses to the question about game mechanics, and why players liked particular mechanics over others.

While many of the categories were relatively evenly preferred, male players hugely preferred Worker Placement (81 percent listed it) compared to female players (64 percent) (nonbinary/queer/other players were closer to the male percentage, at 79 percent); the same disparity is seen in Area Control games (men and nonbinary/queer/other players with 56 percent and 59 percent, respectively, and women with 36 percent). However, women greatly preferred Puzzle games (59 percent) compared to men (41 percent) and nonbinary/queer/other players (48 percent). Women and nonbinary/queer/other players also greatly preferred Roll and Move games (36 percent and 34 percent) when compared with male players (17 percent), but male and nonbinary/queer/other players preferred Auctions (31 percent and 28 percent) more so than did women players (13 percent). Just looking at these statistics, it seems as though men seem to favor games with more direct competition and strategy, while women seemed to favor games with more individual achievement (although, of course, players of all genders liked every type of game, so these are just generalizations).

Age didn't seem to make as much of a difference as gender did in terms of mechanics preferences; there were only a few types of mechanics that had significant differences. Most tellingly, the eighteen to twenty-four demographic heavily preferred Secret Identity games (with 53 percent reporting it as a favorite), while no other age group liked it nearly as much (twenty-five- to thirty-four-year-olds were the next highest, with 38 percent preference). This correlates with the social aspect of gaming; Secret Identity games are generally much more social and interactive than the other types. The older age group of fifty to seventy-four more heavily preferred Area Control games (61 percent) compared to everyone else (the next highest preference was forty-five to fifty-four at 54 percent). Worker Placement, again, had some variance, with younger players preferring it less (65 percent) compared to the thirty-five to forty-four demographic (82 percent).

Race, similarly, didn't seem to make too much of a difference in terms of the overall mechanics preferences, with some exception. There is a significant caveat that all racial data is extremely limited because of the extreme skew toward whiteness in the subjects. Players who identified as Asian (31 total, 3.8 percent) tended to prefer Cooperative games more than any other mechanic (83 percent, compared with 64 percent preference in the total population), and skewed higher on Puzzle games (57 percent, compared with 46 percent total population). Asian players tended to note that they preferred more mechanics than the general population, however; every preference was higher with the exception of Area Control (40 percent, compared with 51 percent total) and Auctions (20 percent to 26 percent total). Players who self-identified as Latinx (15 total, 1.9 percent) matched the general population's preference for Worker Placement, but tended *not* to like Cooperative games (47 percent to 64 percent) or Area Control (40 percent to 51 percent) as much as the total population. Latinx players, however, strongly preferred Press Your Luck games (47 percent to 37 percent) and Auction games (40 percent to 23 percent). Players who identified as Black/African American (10 total, 1.2 percent) were even more skewed, but that could be because the data is only drawing from 10 participants. For Black/ African American players, Deck Building was the most popular mechanic, with 80 percent of respondents noting it. Worker Placement was significantly less popular, with only 50 percent of respondents putting it down as a favorite. Area Control was also significantly skewed lower than the total population, with only 30 percent of Black/African American players putting it down. Other differences include Combat Die Rolling (for Black/African American players, only 10 percent noted it, compared to 28 percent of the general population) and Secret Identity/Social Deduction games, where 20 percent of Black/African American players put it down while 36 percent of the total population did. In Chapter 8, I discuss some steps that the board game hobby and industry can take to help make the industry more diverse and inclusive.

When combined with Vatvani's analysis of the most popular games on BGG, we can see some discrepancies between what is popular *now* (as indicated by my survey) and what has historically been popular (as indicated by Vatvani's scrape of data through all of BGG).[14] Vatvani reveals that the fifteen most frequently occurring mechanics in board games are the following:

- Dice Rolling
- Roll/Spin and Move
- Set Collection
- Hand Management
- Hex-and-Counter
- Card Drafting
- Tile Placement
- Variable Player Powers
- Memory

- Point to Point Movement
- Cooperative Play
- Simulation
- Modular Board
- Trading
- Auction

He also demonstrates that in the last twenty years, both Roll/Spin and Move games (games like *Candyland* or *Monopoly*) and Hex-and-Counter games (war game mechanics which allow movement in six directions) have decreased significantly, while Hand Management and Dice Rolling have increased significantly.

The most popular board game mechanics in my survey (which, admittedly, was limited to the choices that I included) are relatively low down in Vatvani's data—fewer than 1 percent of the games on BGG included Worker Placement as a mechanic while Deck Building is only slightly higher. Some of the least popular mechanics in my survey, Roll and Move and Auctions, are relatively high in Vatvani's scrape. Of course, we have to keep in mind that Vatvani is looking at *all* games in the BGG database, whereas my survey asked about contemporary preferences; what this means is that the past twenty years or so of board gaming as a hobby has seen an extraordinary growth in more complex mechanics that were not necessarily seen much in games from the past. In addition, I was asking a question about favorites while he was looking at overall data, including those who may *not* have liked something.

To return to the question that opened this chapter, I asked what players enjoyed the most about board gaming. I dig into the qualitative response to this question in the next chapter, but here I think the quantitative answers are revealing in the diversity of the board game community. I asked respondents to agree or disagree with various statements about their favorite parts of playing games: table presence, the artwork, learning the rules, winning the game, completing it successfully, beating others, learning the strategy, luck, socialization, or flavor text. I first assigned a value to "like," with "strongly like" assigned a 5 and "strongly dislike" assigned a 1. I averaged each of the categories to see which were the most liked and most disliked components of board games (Table 6.8). By far, the most liked aspects of playing board games was socialization, scoring a 4.5 out of 5, with a standard deviation of .74 and a mode of 5. The next highest categories were "learning the strategy" (4.28 out of 5,

Table 6.8 Favorite Parts of Games

One of My Favorite Parts of a Game Is . . .	Average	Mode	Standard Deviation
Socializing	4.504	5	0.744
Learning the strategy	4.283	5	0.831
Its table presence	4.208	4	0.825
Its art	4.128	4	0.835
Completing it successfully	4.073	4	0.862
Fun flavor text	3.379	4	1.057
Learning the rules	2.969	3	1.061
Winning	2.889	3	1.133
Luck	2.486	2	1.006
Beating others	2.464	3	1.168

mode of 5, standard deviation of .83) and "table presence" (4.2 out of 5, mode of 4, standard deviation of .82). The lowest categories—meaning the categories liked the least—were "luck" (2.5 out of 5, mode of 2, standard deviation of 1) and "beating others" (2.5 out of 5, mode of 3, standard deviation of 1.17). This data indicates general agreement with the data collected from BGG by Woods (2012).

The larger the average, the lower the standard deviation. This means that people generally agreed on what they liked, but there was more variance in what they didn't like. For example, "beating others" scored the lowest, but had more people differing on their ranking: more people ranked this 5 than ranked the *most liked* ("socialization") 1. The mode reflects a similar agreement; with the exception of "beating others" (which also had a larger standard deviation), the repeated values corresponded to the average. "Beating others" seems to be the most varied answer of them all, although still coming out with the smallest average.

Perhaps nothing illustrates why people like to play games than the entwined connections that this question illustrates. "Winning" is actually relatively unimportant to many game players; but completing the game is important. We like to work with others in order to complete a task, whether or not we're cooperating or competing. I think that says something really nice about the human condition. Playing with others is the most enjoyable aspect, but beating them is not. Game art and table presence is crucial, and flavor text is enjoyed, but relying on luck to get through the game is disliked. We like to be challenged, we appreciate the care and attention that goes into the things we like, and we like to be responsible for our own decisions.

Conclusion

Board gaming is obviously a massive hobby, and board gamers are an effusive group of people. In the next two chapters I pore over the qualitative responses to questions, including a follow-up to this survey that focuses on inclusivity in the hobby. If nothing else, this survey has indicated that there is a great deal of interest in finding out more about this hobby and the people that are part of it.

The results of this survey highlight a number of things. First, the demographics of board gamers (at least the ones who filled out this survey) are skewed heavily white and male. I am not surprised by this, having attended conventions and events and seeing the makeup of the others who attended. Greater care needs to be placed on both making board gaming a more welcoming space for people of color and women (as well as other absent voices, like queer and trans people) *and* on actually inviting marginalized people to the table. One of the purposes of this book is to present some avenues for how we might do this, like engaging with the industry on creating more diverse representations in games, or working with local groups to reach out to people not in culturally privileged positions. In addition, because of my survey technique, which relied mainly on social media, I may have only reached these voices because they are the ones who populate this area.[15] My "sample frame" may have excluded "some people in the target population who [did] not have any chance at all to be selected for the sample."[16]

Second, and along with the first, gaming for most of the people who took this survey, is about socialization—and not just socialization with people that you already know. Many people use board games to meet other people, to find friends, to seek out new relationships. We like to play games with people we know, of course, but we also enjoy finding new people through the hobby. Perhaps because board gaming is still a growing but relatively nonmainstream hobby, board gamers feel gregarious with others who enjoy it. Finding someone who is into this niche thing that one is also into bonds two people. And there's still a sizable population of board gamers who enjoy playing solo too.

Third, just because the demographics argue one type of identity doesn't mean that all board gamers are the same. There is an incredible diversity of interests and passions within the hobby. But overall, more people *agree* on favorites than *disagree*. Fewer people said that they didn't like particular aspects of board gaming. Board gamers tend to think more things are fun and enjoyable and fewer things are *not* fun or unenjoyable. Indeed, this represents another form of error that could be part of this survey: the validity of responses. Surveys ask respondents to answer "truthfully," but in truth is can be difficult for people to know themselves well enough to answer questions totally accurately.[17] Sometimes the questions may predict or even dictate the type of answers that may be given.[18] They may also answer questions in a way they think the surveyor might want them to answer. That is, empirical data is not always trustworthy data. At the same time, this survey also reveals a number of absences that should be filled in. As mentioned, the vast majority of people who filled out the survey reported being white and male. Much more data needs to be collected to ensure a diversity of viewpoints from all corners of the community. What are the unique challenges of the Black gamer? Or the queer gamer? Or the trans gamer? My survey didn't seem to reach many in those populations, and a more targeted approach in the future would be worthwhile.

Finally, as the board game industry continues to grow, and more and more games flood the market, there is going to be a very real problem of how to make new games different from what's come before. While Worker Placement might be the most popular mechanic for some people, other people may find greater enjoyment with different mechanics. Game creators are always trying to come up with new ways of exploring familiar mechanisms. Players seem to want innovative new mechanics, themes, and elements; one might think that integrating digital apps may be one way to go, but many people don't particularly like them.

Ultimately, this survey research presents just a snapshot of a particular slice of a community in a specific time and place. My hope is that readers will continue to investigate gaming communities in more depth, for board gaming's popularity means that these demographics and lessons will change significantly over time.

. . . and Why

Examining Motivations and Popularity of Board Games

In the previous chapter, I outlined some of the quantitative responses to the board game survey that I distributed in April 2019. However, I received more than just numerical data—I also collected thousands of comments on a variety of topics related to board games. In this chapter, I report the results of this information, focusing on the importance of socialization, intellectual stimulation, and analog (re: not digital) interaction across a range of board game players.

In terms of hobby board gaming specifically, the *social* and *intellectual* attributes of board gaming were the two most common motivations for why people played games. And yet, while the survey answers were overwhelmingly focused on these two motivations, the "long tail" of answers revealed a huge array of additional reasons why people like to play games.[1] This also connects with what the participants in my survey saw as the *ideal* experience playing games, which was largely seen as social rather than competitive. In addition, when I asked participants why board games were so popular, they articulated a tension at the heart of board gaming in the digital age—that board games represent an escape from the ubiquity of digital devices but also depend on digital devices for mainstream acceptance and growth.

In order to undertake the analysis in this chapter, I'm using a variety of qualitative research methods, relying most heavily on the analysis of survey data. Qualitative data analysis, "as much about social practices as about experience," looks specifically at nonnumerical data as articulated by individuals to understand their unique perspectives.[2] Qualitative data might come from an individual's answer to an open-ended question, a series of answers to an interview, or the observation of a group's behavior. Whereas in the previous chapter my quantitative analysis answered questions like "how many" or "how much," in this chapter my qualitative methods answer questions like "why" and "how" people participate in hobby board gaming. No qualitative study is generalizable to an entire population—in this case, even though I had 900 or so participants in my study, not only were they self-selected, but they were all largely approached through social media, and thus can't speak for all people, or all board gamers—but it is my hope that the answers to the queries in this chapter reveal both some commonalities across board gamers, and some unique attributes that paint a more complicated picture than we might normally have as to why and how people play games.

Qualitative Survey Methods

"Qualitative analysis" is a broad term to look at data that isn't quantified; and in this chapter the style of analysis I'm conducting could broadly be referred to as narrative ethnography, or the systematic retelling of information about different people and cultures.[3] In the previous chapter, I described some of the practices for designing and distributing a survey, whether that survey is quantitative or qualitative. In either case, when we investigate a foreign culture, a group of diverse people, or an unknown community, we practice ethnography, the "study [of] a culture's relational practices, common values and beliefs, and shared experiences for the purpose of helping insiders (cultural members) and outsiders (cultural strangers) better understand the culture."[4] As described by Jean Schensul and Margaret LeCompte:

> Ethnography attempts to understand social and cultural phenomena from the perspective of participants in the social setting under study. To do so, the approach builds conceptual models using a combination of experience, previous literature, and qualitative data collection techniques and then validates or "tests" these models.[5]

Ethnography is an iterative process, and includes asking questions, thinking about those answers, and then refining those questions for the future. The data I collected were the answers to the open-ended questions on the board game survey (see Appendix 1 for a full list).

One of the downsides of my survey was the amount of open-ended or fill-in-the-blank questions. People generally don't like spending more than five to ten minutes with a survey, and any time they have to add in their own answers (as opposed to clicking buttons or sliding a scale) can deter respondents from completing it. Including these open-ended questions meant that participants may have had survey fatigue. I saw this in my responses: the "click button" questions had a higher response rate than the "fill-in-the-blank" questions, and the response rate went down the further along the survey the respondents went. Generally, 900 or so people clicked on answers while 850 people filled in the blanks.

Qualitative survey analysis is different from quantitative survey analysis as it necessarily requires more interpretation. There are different ways to understand this type of data: Rafael Engel and Russell Schutt's textbook notes that while some scholars see this textual data as "the richness of real, social experience," others simply view it as different "perspectives . . . that can never be judged true or false. The text is only one possible interpretation among many."[6] Textual data is always going to be messier than quantitative data, because it is data inputted directly by the participants of the survey; it will reflect their voices, and may or may not actually reveal the answers that you seek as a researcher. Indeed, as Alan McKee notes, this type of qualitative data/textual analysis

> sometimes claims to find 'the reality' of the interpretations made by audiences . . . but this isn't exactly the case—at least, not in the way it's often understood. . . . Just because people *say* when you ask them that *this* is what they mean about a particular text, it doesn't mean that this is what it means to them in their everyday lives. This isn't to say that they're lying: it's just that the very process of telling somebody what you think about something isn't the same thing as thinking about it in your everyday life.[7]

Everyone's answers are tempered by their unique social and cultural experiences.

That being said, qualitative ethnographies are popular methods for research about cultural topics, especially because they "demand . . . that pretenses of objectivity be dropped so that emotions can be genuinely accounted for."[8] As researcher Harrie Jansen describes, "The qualitative type of survey does not aim at establishing frequencies, means or other parameters but at determining the *diversity of some topic of interest* within a given population."[9] While the quantitative research of the previous chapter attempted to describe the characteristics that most commonly *defined* this group of gamers, the qualitative data analysis of this chapter looks at *meaningful variations* within the group.

In order to write up the research in the following few sections, I have had to turn answers into a "narrative ethnography," which includes both the stories of the subjects and the "analyses of patterns and processes" within the answers.[10] What this means is that I've both chosen some aspects of the answers to focus on and made consequential decisions about what to leave out. With almost a thousand survey answers, there's no way I could keep everything in this chapter—written out, it would have been ten times as long as this entire book.

In the following text, I summarize the results, looking at what motivates people to play board games, players' ideal experiences with board games, and why people believe board games have become popular in the past decade and a half. The rationale for using these questions is to approach some key points about board gaming from different angles. Specifically, when asking about players' motivations, I'm specifically asking them about what they *do*; in asking them about their ideal gaming situation, I'm asking them about what is *possible*; and in asking them about the popularity of board games, I'm interested in their thoughts about *other people*. Of course, and as mentioned before, all these answers are reflective only of the community I surveyed. But my hope is that keen readers will see in these answers some connections to their own lived experiences, and perhaps understand a bit more deeply this community of players.

Results of Qualitative Analysis

In order to unpack the many thousands of answers I received, I inputted the survey into NVivo, a qualitative data analysis software platform that helps with coding the data. NVivo allowed me to categorize the information, which allowed for both a broad view and a more specific analysis. Some coding was relatively self-explanatory: if a person wrote that they liked to play games "to have social interactions," I could code that as "Social Interaction." Many people wrote multiple reasons (e.g., "to have social interactions and to learn strategy"), and in those cases I would code the sentence into both categories (with "Strategic Thinking and Puzzle Solving"). As with my previous chapter, this methodology just scratches the surface of the data analysis, and a longer, more detailed analysis would be possible with more space.*

---

* I have lightly edited answers for grammar/spelling, but have not changed the content.

Motivation for Playing Board Games

One of the open-ended questions I asked on my survey attempted to find out why people were motivated to play board games. The answers revealed both a wide variety of responses and a number of commonly repeated rationales. In total, I coded fifty-nine overarching reasons mentioned for why people are motivated to play board games, with 845 unique answers given. Coding answers can be a subjective experience, and not everyone would code all answers the same way. In this case, I initially went through all the answers to the question "What motivates you to play board games?" and initially placed every answer into a category that seemed to match its topic. After I completed coding the 30,000-word document of answers, I went back through all the categories to make sure that every answer ended up in the same category as others. For instance, some of the earlier answers might have been put in a category that morphed as I continued to code. Some of the subjectivity of coding can be seen by the following two answers, which on the surface look identical:

Social interaction, and using my brain in ways I don't in daily life.

Social interaction, and making strategic choices in a "play" setting.

Both answers obviously fit into "Social Interaction" and that part of the statement was coded the same way. The second part of each answer, however similar, ended up being placed in two different categories: I coded "using my brain in ways I don't in daily life" as "Diversion or Escape," while I coded "making strategic choices in a 'play' setting" as "Strategic Thinking or Solving Puzzles." As revealed in Figure 7.1, though, while some topics were mentioned by almost everyone, there were a great variety of motivations that only had a few mentions throughout. (Figure 7.1 is just the top fifteen categories, while Table 7.1 reveals all the categories coded.)

The most common response, provided 425 times by itself and 928 times in relation to others in the survey answers (and making up over 57 percent of the total coverage in the survey), was that people were motivated to play board games because of the social aspects—specifically linked to in-person, face-to-face interaction. I further divided the answer in more nuanced ways, as many people refined their answers into playing with *friends* (mentioned 276 times, the third most popular category generally), with *family* (mentioned 189 times, the sixth most popular category generally), with *colleagues* (mentioned 4 times), or playing to *meet people* (mentioned 34 times). Family can be further broken down, as people mentioned playing with their partner/spouse/significant other sixty-

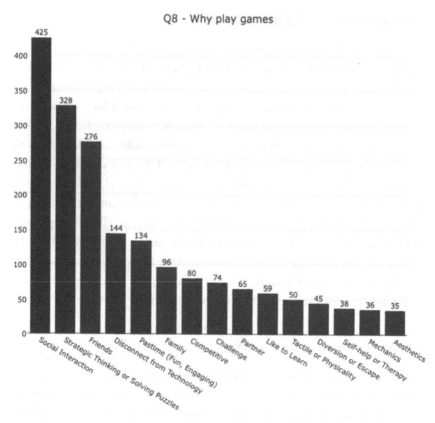

Figure 7.1 Top fifteen categories for "What motivates you to play games?" Nvivo graph."

five times and their kids twenty-eight times. While none of this is particularly surprising, what is relevant is the fact that more than half of the people surveyed responded that some aspect of socialization was important to their board game play. While many people simply responded with a quick "social interaction" rationale, some people wrote longer justifications; for instance:

> I enjoy playing board games because it helps me build meaningful connections with people. I have never had an experience of playing a board game with some people and that somehow making our relationship worse. In my case, it always makes people more relaxed and open.

Indeed, there were mentions of playing games with strangers, or playing games to meet people. For example, one participant mentioned that games are "extremely bonding, even with strangers," while another noted that games offer "the ability to meet a variety of people."

Table 7.1 All Answers for "What Motivates You to Play Games?"

Category	Mentions
Social interaction	425
Strategic thinking or solving puzzles	328
Social (friends)	276
Disconnect from technology	144
Pastime (fun, engaging)	134
Social (family)	96
Competitive	80
Challenge	74
Social (family (partner))	65
Like to learn new games	59
Tactile or physicality	50
Diversion or escape	45
Self-help or therapy	38
Mechanics	36
Aesthetics	35
Social (strangers or to meet people)	34
To win	32
New experiences	31
Storytelling or narrative elements	30
Thematic elements	29
Social (family (kids))	28
Creative	26
New worlds	24
Play well	23
Relaxation	22
Money	20
Variety	19
Food and drink (alcohol)	17
Childhood/nostalgia	16
Rules	15
New games	12
Gaming in general	11
Collecting	10
Help or teach	9
Food and drink	8
Accomplishment	7
Stay home (or don't go out)	6
Weather or seasonal	6
Entertainment	5
Accessibility	4
Social (colleagues)	4
Control	3

(Continued)

Table 7.1 (Continued)

Category	Mentions
Energizing or stimulating	3
Luck	3
Complexity of game	2
Flow	2
For work	2
Depth	1
Empathy	1
Fans	1
Gambling	1
Let out aggression	1
Negotiation	1
Online content creators	1
Possibilities	1
Repetition	1
Rewarding	1
Speed of playing	1

The second most common category for people's answers was the way board games focused on "Strategic Thinking or Puzzle Solving"—*strategy, puzzle-solving,* or *intellectual/mental simulation*—with participants mentioning this aspect of games 328 times in their answers. Participants noted the "mental challenges" of board games as well as the "intellectual stimulations"; games present "interesting problems to solve" while "exercising [the] brain." One participant expanded on this aspect thoroughly:

> I find most good board games to be deep puzzles that I can spend a lot of time thinking through, strategizing, and occasionally solving for specific moves or openings. I enjoy being able to explore strategies and solve puzzles. I dislike games of chance (e.g., poker, roulette) as overly random; and I dislike games of pure strategy (e.g., chess) as overly rigid, formalized, and more about time and devotion to study than about reading the situation and reacting.

This seems to be echoed throughout the other answers. "Luck" only showed up as a motivation for playing board games three times in the entire survey (or in 0.07 percent of the total coverage).

Although there were many aspects of the data to explore (and Table 7.1 illustrates the vast quantity of categories left to explore), there are two points that I want to iterate. First, there were 144 mentions of board gaming as a way to "Disconnect from Technology"—specifically, to "escape from screens" or to be "a good distraction from TV." Some people mentioned board games in opposition to video games, arguing that "I play to interact with others face to face without digital intermediation." Some people mentioned that, while video games can offer social activities, board games have a different "quality" to them "that we are sorely lacking in the digital world we live in now." Fully 10 percent of the survey answers were devoted to being anti-technology, with almost 20 percent of the respondents mentioning it at some point. Of course, this is a self-selected group of survey-takers, and I'm sure if you asked video gamers what they liked about video games, you'd have very different answers. But it does reveal how, for many of the participants in my survey, there is a belief that digital technology has both become a detriment to human socialization and engendered a passive audience. Board games, the feeling seems to be, "actually exercise the brain. They improve all types of cognitive functions."

Of particular note, one person directly compared the role of audience/player for digital entertainment versus board games: "If entertainment (e.g. video games/film) is *produced for us*, I believe fun (e.g. board games) is *produced by us*. Getting folks to a table face-to-face to share a laugh cannot be beaten" (emphasis mine). This quotation reveals an underlying belief across many of the answers—that the very interactive nature of board games is precisely what gives them cultural power. Popular culture, whether it is film, television, music, book, or web series, is largely made without direct interaction with the viewers (although of course as I pointed out in Chapter 5, audiences still have an important role to play, and active audiences/fans often participate with creators). Astute viewers will even pick up on times when popular culture caters to the audience; that is, when popular culture attempts to match the expectations of its viewers. The board game experience is cocreated between the designer and the player, and any particular iteration of a board game session is unrepeatable (see Chapter 4). Such interactive potentiality helps engender a stronger audience connection to the game.

Along with this anti-technology vibe, there was a strong emphasis in the survey results on the tactile nature of games, with the category mentioned fifty times. Many of the answers that focused on tactility also mentioned that earlier aversion to technology—"I value the intimacy of an in-person gathering around a shared table and enjoy the tactile facet of board game play, both elements that tend to be absent in playing digital games"—while others seemed to just focus on the physicality of the board game experience. For example, one person noted that they were motivated to play because board games are tactile. You HAVE to touch them. You get the satisfaction of moving pieces, cards, dice, etc. You have a physical representation of this fictional scenario for you and your fellow players to engage with. And that is unlike most other experiences.

A second point of analysis that the data revealed was how many people use board games for therapeutic reasons. It was mentioned thirty-eight times in the data. Participants revealed some of the mental, physical, and social afflictions that board games have helped alleviate, including social anxiety, multiple sclerosis, dementia, autism, PTSD, depression, cancer, and other chronic health issues. Along with focusing on developing intelligence and strategic thinking, board games in this sense teach serenity, compassion, relaxation, and traditional social cues, while also offering a focus for social experiences so that the focus is not on the conversation as much as it is on the game. There has been very little written about the health benefits of board gaming, and it warrants further study.

Ideal Experience with Board Games

In addition, I was curious about players' ideals with board games, so I asked, "If you could imagine a 'best' or ideal experience playing games, what would it look like?" The purpose of this question was not only to gauge how people perceived actually playing games, but also to reveal additional aspirational aspects of the hobby that may not be immediately apparent—that is, what is *possible* from board gaming. The question was intended to spark some creative imagining from the respondents. Because of the personal nature of the question, conducting an NVivo coding analysis would not have proven helpful, as almost every answer was as unique as the people that made them. Although some overarching themes could be observed, no one or two categories dominated the answers. In Table 7.2, I outline the twelve refrains that cropped up in the answers. In addition, I offer a representative quotation to illustrate how the theme was mentioned (although there were hundreds of unique answers among the participants).

Overall, the answers to this question were almost universally heartwarming, as players mentioned enjoying playing games with people they loved, in places they enjoyed, at peace with the world.

Of particular note, there is a great deal of overlap between the themes we see in the answers to this question and the themes we see in the answers to the question about why people play board games. What this means, at least on the surface, is that many players are getting the type of satisfaction they *anticipate*

Table 7.2 Common Themes Described as "An Ideal Experience Playing Games"

Category	Description	Example quotation
Avoidance of technology	Most of the people who mentioned technology as part of their ideal experience noted that they preferred a *lack* of technology, although one person said that using technology in games (like Augmented Reality) would be ideal.	"It's better . . . if cellular service was somehow shut off for the duration of the game."
Food and drink	"Food and drink" was mentioned as part of an ideal experience, either vaguely or more specifically identified (e.g., pizza, Cheetos). Alcohol was also mentioned, although quite a few mentions were about wanting to stay sober when playing.	"A 'game night' with a crock pot full of good food, a shaker full of great cocktails, several groups of people playing different games."
Furniture	Most of the furniture mentioned as part of an ideal experience were either "comfortable chairs" or "big tables."	"Big log guest house, edge of a forest overlooking the ocean. Wall to ceiling windows. Early spring. A few big tables. Lots of chairs. An open kitchen. Open fireplace. Bushwalk in the morning."
Knowledge of games	Some players commented on wanting to play games with people who had lots of knowledge of games (to avoid down time), but other players specifically mentioned teaching games to new players as part of their ideal experience.	"Getting to play new complex games without the struggle of reading/learning/ teaching the rules."
Length of time	There was little agreement about how long the ideal playing experience should be, but many people had their own ideas, from a number of short games to some marathon (more than a day) sessions. This category also represents responses that focused on the relative "heaviness" of the game (its complexity).	"Approximately 4–6 hours spent playing 3–5 games ranging between light and medium complexity (i.e. a couple 'tentpole' games of about 90 to 120 minutes each, interspersed with a few 'filler' games of up to 45 minutes each)."

(Continued)

Table 7.2 (Continued)

Category	Description	Example quotation
People	Quite a few respondents discussed the people that they would want to play with in ideal circumstances. Largely matching what cropped up in the motivation question, this included family, friends, children, and significant others/partners. Some people also noted the desire to meet people through board game play.	"Meeting people I don't know with my daughter and laughing through a game." "A quiet room at a convention with friends from across the country all in attendance. But, really, I'm very content to sit at my dining room table and play games with my partner after dinner. We also have a regular domino night with my 89-year-old grandmother that is really wonderful." "Playing at home, with my spouse only."
Place	Participants often mentioned places when recounting their ideal experience. Some of these places were specific and expansive, while others were more vague ("Home"). Some mentioned social spaces—pubs, game cafes, conventions.	"Rent a cabin in the mountains with a scenic mountain view." "Board game cafes, where several groups of people can help create a larger environment for game play."
Sensual experience	Some answers referenced how their senses would perceive the situation: the sounds that might surround them (birds singing, soft music), the smell, the temperature, or the weather.	"Long weekend at an all-expenses resort somewhere beautiful and warm overlooking an ocean with close friends. Private sea view room with plenty of A/C."
Type of experience	Participants would use specific phrases to elucidate their experience, hypothetically quoting what might happen in the experience.	"Surprise endings are the best. The kind that make you go 'you gotta be kidding me!'" "One that has a moment or moments that lead to conversations about it after the event. 'Remember when . . . You should have been there when . . .'"

Category	Description	Example quotation
Type of gamer	Answers that focused on the type of gamer mainly revolved around fairness and not being competitive. A few answers mentioned being inclusive and welcoming.	"Everyone gets along and no one is overly competitive. I also find that I enjoy playing games more when those involved don't use stereotypical 'gamer bro' language." "People who play honorably are important. This means a few things: we don't cheat. We play the game to win when playing a competitive game but don't get upset when we lose, at least beyond feigning umbrage. We want our 'best game play' to beat others' game play. There can be trash talk but kept friendly."
Unable to answer	A few participants couldn't think of an ideal situation, either because they said there wasn't one or because there were too many.	"I can't—there is no 'ideal' in such a diverse field ranging from *Happy Salmon* [2016, North Star Games] to *Twilight Imperium* [1997, Fantasy Flight Games].
Winning	Winning as a concept cropped up often in the results, with some participants talking about how much *they* wanted to win; however, most people that mentioned winning noted that they didn't care who won, or that it would be more fun if everyone had a chance to win.	"Much like my existing gaming group except I would win more often." "At some point in the game all players feel like they have a good chance at winning. Final scores are close so that everyone feels like one move could have made the difference for a different victor." "Everybody has fun, and my wife wins."

from playing by actually playing. That is, the reasons that people play are not that different from the idealized vision of board game play. Many people in their ideal experience mentioned the social aspects of play—wanting to play with more people, see their friends more often, or meet for regular game nights. Some people mentioned that they don't live close to their gaming friends, gaming cafes, or game stores, which makes it difficult to play on a regular schedule. This focus on the social seems to marry with the points that people make about what they enjoy about playing.

At the same time, there are some answers in the *ideal* that don't appear in the *motivational*. There seemed to be a lot more focus on *time* in the ideal experiences, where players seem to want to play for longer than their everyday lives allow—"Relatively long (8+ hours) uninterrupted session with the same group." Rarely did someone mention the length of time of play in their description of what they like about playing. Additionally, there were relatively few mentions of food or drink in the "why we play" answers. Some players mentioned that snacks or wine were part of why they played games, but quite a few described their ideal situation as one with lots of food and drinks. Coupled with the social aspects of gaming mentioned, this seems to be an indication that, often, the desired results of gaming isn't necessarily the game itself, but the experience surrounding the game. Finally, the ideal experience of board gaming rarely focused on the intellectual challenge of board games, marking a huge difference from the motivation for playing games. People seem to enjoy the challenge of games, but when it comes down to it, rarely see that as the main reason for playing. Perhaps we are mentally stimulated by so much in our lives today that board games are not unique in that; or perhaps, the combination of intellectual stimulation *and* social activity is what propels people toward gaming. Coupled with the decidedly anti-technology vibe that board games engender, they may seem a palliative against contemporary society's push toward digitization.

Why Are Games Popular Today?

Thirdly, I was interested in finding out what players of board games thought about the rise in popularity of board games today. Specifically, I thought this question might elicit answers that both touched on the particular facets of board game play that players thought that *other* players might enjoy (popularity encompassing the experience of others as well as the self) and focused on specific elements of games that were seen as culturally relevant. Only 695 people answered this question, fully 150 people fewer than answered the first question. As this was one of the very last questions on the survey, appearing after a number of other short answer questions, the fewer number of responses is probably due to survey fatigue. As with the first question, I conducted an NVivo coding analysis, placing each separate answer into one or more categories. Altogether, there were fewer total categories than with the motivation question, and fewer answers fit into more than one category—that is, while players demonstrated many reasons why they were motivated to play games, there were fewer reasons why they thought board games were popular today. Answers were also less skewed toward one or two themes throughout, and were spread more evenly throughout the categories, although socialization (here, most often noted as "face-to-face") remained the most popular category. Figure 7.2 shows a chart with the top fifteen categories, while Table 7.3 lists all the categories given.

Because of the inherently subjective nature of this question (how can anyone actually *know* what makes games popular?), these answers only represent what people hypothesize. But taken together, they reveal a spectrum of ideas that focus on what makes games appealing today.

Although face-to-face interaction was the most cited rationale for board game popularity, the second most common was that they offered a chance to disconnect from our digital devices, and indeed more answers indicated this rationale than mentioned it in either their motivation for playing or their ideal

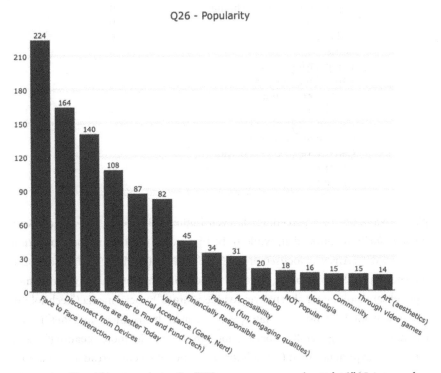

Figure 7.2 Top fifteen categories for "Why are games popular today?" Nvivo graph.

Table 7.3 All Categories for "Why Are Games Popular Today?"

Name	References
Social Interaction (Face-to-Face)	224
Disconnect from devices	164
Games are better today	140
Easier to find and fund (tech)	108
Social acceptance (geek, nerd)	87
Variety	82
Financially responsible	45
Pastime (fun, engaging)	34
Accessibility	31
Analog	20
They are NOT popular	18
Nostalgia	16
Community	15
Through video games	15
Art (aesthetics)	14
Intellectual	13
Cultural changes	12
Issues with the world today	9
Popular franchises and brands	9
Relaxation	9
Collecting	6
Stories	6
Enjoy staying home	5
Other things less popular	5
Positive well-being	5
Avoid politics	4
Diversity of creators	4
Companies can make money	2
Can choose who to play with	1
Creative	1
Novelty	1

playing situation (the percentage is even higher: 23.6 percent of the answers for *popularity* mentioned it, while only 16 percent of answers for *motivation* mentioned it). Answers focused on multiple types of technologies, including the internet ("people are looking for an escape from the Internet"), video games ("people are looking for alternatives to video games"), social media ("technology and social media tend to isolate people, games bring them together"), and technology more generally. Board games are seen as a "more meaningful and satisfying" experience than technology, which people seem to read as alienating. What seemed to be the consensus was not that technology itself was *bad*, but that it was *all encompassing*. Games allowed a "break" from technology to "reconnect with friends around a table."

At the same time, however, further analysis of these categories also reveals a tension regarding technology: specifically, as much as board games deflect from digital technology, they are also seen as popular today *because of* digital technology. In fact, the fourth most common theme in the answers was "Easy to Find and Fund," in which participants noted how much easier it is to participate in the gaming hobby because of technology. Participants in the survey noted, for example, the following:

> I do think the internet has contributed in some ways to board games' popularity. Crowdfunding sites like Kickstarter can get unique indie games published. Thanks to the internet, if you don't live near a dedicated game store, your selection is not limited to what you can find in Target, Barnes and Noble, etc. BoardGameGeek also provides a forum for game fans who might not otherwise have an outlet to discuss games.

Other participants specifically noted YouTube and podcasting as digital spaces for spreading news about games, as well as "play along" shows specifically focused on games like Wil Wheaton's *TableTop*. In fact, 108 answers (23.2 percent) focused on the fact that digital technology has made board games more accessible, more socially acceptable, and more available than ever before.

This concurs with what Aaron Trammell, in an article for *Analog Game Studies*, has noted:

> Analog games are emerging as a cultural phenomenon in our present moment because of their explicit relationality to the digital. They can only be understood and defined by and through an oppositional-yet-contingent relationship to digital media. . . . [The] milieu of digital media technologies . . . facilitate these games' production, advertisement, testing, and distribution. Understanding this relationship is key to understanding the scope of the analog game revolution and the urgency of its analysis.[11]

As with any niche interest, digital technology has enabled groups of people from disparate areas of the world to get in touch with each other. And shopping sites like Amazon—while admittedly eating into the business of local game stores generally—have also allowed access to games that many people may never have had contact with. Resell sites like eBay also help spread the word about games, as people can sell games with ease.

More than anything, however, two sites have helped to contribute to the popularity—or, at least, the widespread knowledge of—board games: Kickstarter and BoardGameGeek. In the survey, Kickstarter itself was mentioned sixteen times. Crowdfunding doesn't just serve as a way to make new games, but also as a way to advertise gaming: board game companies are still a relatively small cottage industry, and there are many companies that are really just one or two people working together on some small games. Crowdfunding is one of the best ways to get exposure for your game, and the model thrives because of digital word of mouth: podcast and video reviewers will review prototype games for Kickstarter, online rules videos provide context, and all financial interactions between the players and the company are handled digitally. BoardGameGeek, too, is a hub of game activity. At one time an encyclopedia of board game content, a forum for board game questions, a bulletin board for interaction, a social network for community, and a sales site for commerce, the website is one of the most consulted board game sites in the world.

All this is to say that board games, and analog game play in general, would not be as widespread without digital technology—and yet, players of board games use them to seek out spaces without digital distraction. The tension was rarely stated directly in the answers to my questions; perhaps participants saw a difference between board game-related content online and social media generally—that is, it's not technology that's the problem, it's the interruption. At the same time, there are times when digital technology can augment the gameplay experience: from a personal point of view, I often consult BoardGameGeek on my phone when playing a game to make sure we're getting a rule correct, or to check errata; but I would be loath to check my email or social media accounts as a distraction.

Three other categories require some additional context. One hundred and forty answers in the survey revolved around the fact that board games are of a higher quality today than they were in the past, with eight answers directly contrasting them to *Monopoly* (1933, Hasbro). This quality doesn't just refer to the components (although some people mentioned that the inclusion of more plastic figures and high-quality components was effective), but also to the sense of game play. Players commented on the new mechanics that board game designers were coming up with, or on the more complex themes in games:

> They have become radially better designed, and actual gameplay is way better than the 80s and 90s. Luck is down, thinking is up. Physical production, graphic design, presentation, themes, inclusive artwork, all these are better. Even just

having quarter boards so the boxes are square and deep instead of long and flat and bloody awkward is better.

In the past, responses indicated, games were less complex and less engaging; today, games are more impressive. Along those lines, eighty-two answers focused on the variety of games that were available today, saying that "They are becoming more sophisticated. There is a type of game for everybody."

Secondly, forty-five answers noted that board games were a more fiscally responsible entertainment choice than other entertainment, like taking the family to see a film. Board games can be expensive—the type of strategic hobby board game that the participants in this survey tend to play can run anywhere from $40 to upward of $140. But as pointed out by the responses, "while initial investment may be high at $50+ a game, you get many more hours of fun than taking a family of 4 to the movies for 2 hours." Other responses included "they are affordable," "it's an inexpensive hobby," and "millennials have no money and it's both cheaper than clubbing and much better." There were almost no answers in the survey that reflected angst about the cost of games, and everyone seemed to agree they were a good deal for the cost, indicating a certain level of privilege in the survey participation pool (see Chapter 8).

Finally, I should point out that eighteen answers reflected the idea that board games were *not* popular today, or at least, not any *more* popular than they have been in the past. "Are they?" one person questions, "I have not noticed a change." To the extent that more board games are being produced and sold today than ever before—a 2018 market report by Technavio Reports that it is growing at 35 percent rate, resulting in a projected $5.6 billion growth by 2022[*]—they are certainly become more ubiquitous, but these answers may seem to indicate that rather than spreading outward to appeal to more and more people, it is possible that board games are simply becoming more saturated within the already-extant market. One person noted:

> I do not think they are becoming that much more popular. The internet has brought together boardgamers and has created an echo chamber where we are surrounded or connected to others so we perceive this as an increase that is not really there in a significant amount.

However, research such as the Technavio Report does show growth among new audiences, mainly millennials. The opening of board game cafes, a recent

[*] https://www.technavio.com/report/global-board-games-market-analysis-share-2018

phenomenon in major metropolitan areas, also heralds a new popularity to games. So even if popularity of board games may be exaggerated at times, it is there, it is steady, and it reflects a changing generational shift, where "adults can play games for fun."

Conclusion

Understanding the culture of board gaming today means looking at more than just numbers. Quantitative data can effectively show how many people are participating, and can describe the relative weight of different types of participation, in board gaming today. But only qualitative survey data can get into the diversity of content and viewpoints, and can reveal some of the underlying tensions in board gaming culture.

The results of this survey reveal some patterns as well as some variations among the many participants. Overwhelmingly, across all the different questions I asked about why people play board games, the ideals of playing board games, and the popularity of board game play today, participants were focused on the social and community-oriented aspects of playing. Traditional representations and stereotypes of board games (and board gamers) often reflect a competitive element—when we see board game play in films and television, we often see a gleeful person slamming their piece on the table and exclaiming "I win!"—or, more likely, "You lose!" But the results of this survey reveal that most people play because they like being in contact with other, likeminded people. Said one participant: "I'm thrilled that other people are coming to love them the way I do. It may make their wallets a little lighter, but it's worth all the quality time spent talking and laughing with people." This was not an unusual comment; despite the fact almost 900 people took the survey, almost everyone mentioned the social benefits. In addition, survey participants noted mental and physical health benefits to playing games: board games engage the imagination, foster positive development in critical thinking and intellectual challenges for children, and serve as stress relievers in/escape from our "too-fast paced" and "increasingly isolated" world.

Second, despite the fact that the popularity of board games relies on the many manifestations of digital technology today, most players thought that they also served as a respite from a world increasingly made frantic by digital distractions. When discussing what they enjoyed most about playing, and how they imagined their most positive gameplay experiences, participants mentioned turning off phones, retreating to the comfort of home, and simply being present with friends, family, spouses, and children.

Third, the participants in the survey see board gaming culture as directly related to the growth of other nerdy/geeky/niche interests. As contemporary culture has diversified and engaged in multiple interests, what used to be considered cultish or nonmainstream has become more common. Partly, this is due to the rise of popular media that focus on board gaming, whether it's a web series like *TableTop*, a podcast like *Adventure Zone*, or the appearance of board games in shows like *Big Bang Theory, Parks and Recreation*, or *Orphan Black*. But partly it's also because fandom and geek interests are becoming more mainstream, more socially acceptable generally. Conventions like San Diego Comic-Con routinely have over 130,000 people attending the shows, superhero material earns billions of dollars in top-grossing films, and so-called "cult" texts like *Game of Thrones* or *Stranger Things* become some of the most popular shows on television and streaming. One of the participants in the survey argued that "one of the core causes" of this mainstream acceptance for geeky texts was

the *Harry Potter* series. There's a whole generation of kids—male and female, nerd and jock, black and white—who read those books, grew up with those books, and then were enamored with the movies. What was once a nerdy topic was thrust into the minds of many. I believe this made folks realize that alternate worlds/systems/etc. are enticing. Geek becomes acceptable.

Or, perhaps social media has made it more commonplace to *see* people's nerdy interests, so it's only become more visible today. Whatever the rationale, the cultural temperature is right for board games as a geeky interest.

As I mentioned in the previous chapter, this survey only barely scratched the surface of board game culture. It was only targeted to, and only reached, people already self-identified as board gamers. Thus, the qualitative answers given in the survey will reflect only this particular group. And given the demographics of the group (as shown in Chapter 6—largely white, largely male, largely from the United States and the United Kingdom), it doesn't get at the diversity that currently exists in the board game community. As a reflection of what this group of people believe, the survey helps us see the importance of socialization, intellectual stimulation, or disconnecting from technology; but as a survey of all gamers, it cannot approach speaking for everyone. Further surveys that reach a larger board gamer population—perhaps one for the 60,000+ attendees of board game convention *Gen Con*—would reveal more about the board game community specifically, while one that went out to a wide variety of people, not just board gamers, would show the relative interest in board gaming in the population as a whole. In Chapter 8, I continue this discussion of reaching more people as I focus more specifically on diversity and inclusion in board gaming cultures.

Cultural Studies of Games

Diversity and Inclusion in the Board Game Industry and Hobby

One of the main tenets of this book has been that, as a medium of communication, board games both reflect and create aspects of contemporary culture. Board games are not separate from the culture in which they are made (just as any media text can never be), and are designed by people that are influenced by their own cultural experiences. At the same time, board games can also be influential themselves, as they can convince players of particular points of view or inspire players in critical ways.[1] Games reflect the ideas of the era and demonstrate cultural relevance. For example, as game researcher Alex Andriesse notes:

> Games, like religion and song, have existed since before history began, and as with religion and song they are creations in which we cannot help but reveal our desires, prejudices, and fears. They may be overtly political . . . or they may unconsciously disclose cultural beliefs. . . . But in every case they generate an alternate space in which people can play through the anxieties of their daily lives according to clearly established rules and . . . without any fear of harm.[2]

The themes of games are one way of observing how different cultural anxieties or passions manifest. In a capitalist culture, for example, we often see games where the goal is to win the most money. We are encouraged to accumulate, echoing a culture where wealth equals success. But this is not necessarily the only way money can be used in games, and alternate ways of expressing victory can lead to different cultural readings. In the earlier chapters of this book, I explored this in depth—looking at themes of war, disease, mortality, and colonization—and provided different readings of games as cultural artifacts. In this chapter, I want to expand my focus outward from the games themselves to look at board gaming culture and, as such, how that culture impacts—and is impacted by—issues of diversity and inclusion. I'm defining board game culture as both the hobby and industrial aspects of gaming. I have engaged in ethnographic interviews with participants in board game culture at multiple levels to understand their views about diversity in the community and reflect on the problems that a lack of inclusion brings to the industry.

These ethnographic interviews were conducted with game creators and designers, online content creators, and game players. I contacted designers using the messaging function of BoardGameGeek (BGG), online content creators using Twitter, Facebook, and Discord, and game players through a follow-up email to my survey. The relatively small size of the board gaming community means that each of these groups can easily be in contact with the other; each of these groups frames the discourse around diversity and inclusion.

When I write about "diversity and inclusion," I am referring to opening up the types of games that are produced, the people producing games, and the people playing games to different identities, including (but not limited to) racial identities, gender identities, sexual orientations, physical/mental abilities, and national identities. Some might say—and indeed, some of my participants did say—that focusing on issues of inclusion is irrelevant, either because the hobby/industry is already diverse or because there are more pressing concerns. But research has shown that there is a significant overrepresentation of white, cisgender men—what Stewart Woods has called the "Aging Male Gamer" demographic[3]—in the industry, represented within games, and in the hobby; and as the majority of my interview subjects noted, this can have a deleterious effect on the community. For example, Tanya Pobuda's examination of gender and racial representation in the board game industry reveals that "the overwhelming majority of game designers and illustrators [are] white males, while white females or non-white designers and illustrators were under-represented."[4] Furthermore, in 2016, Erin Ryan famously wrote of representation that "you are more likely to see a sheep on the cover of a board game box than you are to see a group of women."[5] And Gil Hova's assessment of the hobby used a metaphor of invisible ropes—systemic patriarchal mentalities—to demonstrate that "boardgaming, while not [necessarily] overtly hostile to women, still has a bunch of invisible ropes that keep many women from enjoying the hobby."[6] Being committed to diversity and inclusion means that the board game community must be proactive in both changing the culture of the community to make a more welcoming space for marginalized people within the hobby and directly engaging with marginalized communities to join, rather than relying on any group of individuals to "find their way" into the hobby.

I have also used a critical engagement with two cultural artifacts to deepen this exploration of diversity in board gaming. A critical engagement methodology reads different objects within a culture—media texts, popular press news articles, fan discourse—to develop an understanding of how those objects reflect cultural trends. In this chapter, these cultural artifacts include the popular board game *Wingspan* (2019, Stonemaier Games) and the aborted game project *Scramble for Africa* (unpublished, GMT Games). In some respects, this engaged methodology borrows from other chapters in this book, like the textual analyses, rhetorical analyses, and discourse analyses from Chapters 1–3. As a form of cultural studies, which reads contemporary media texts as indicative of cultural shifts, this type of critical engagement sees game-playing as influenced and influential on cultural aspects of contemporary life.

Board Game Culture

What makes a board game culture? It is just the people that play games? The people that make games? As Adrianne Shaw asks of video game culture, "What does it mean to have a culture defined by the consumption of a particular medium? . . .[And] what are the implications of defining this culture in a particular way?"[7] Shaw's analysis uses cultural studies methodologies to examine three aspects of video game culture: who plays, what they play, and how they play. However, she does not include video game authors/designers as part of this culture, nor does she focus on those online opinion leaders who might influence video game players. This could be because video game culture has a highly stratified structure: players rarely make video games, and there are many millions of players that can constitute a highly engaged cultural group.

In contrast, board game culture has what we might call a flatter team structure. Because of the low barrier to entry, many board game players also design board games (see Chapter 6), and most board game creators are often highly engaged board game players (see Chapter 4). The community is smaller than that of video gaming, and is dominated by the use of BGG as an encyclopedia, discussion board, marketplace, review site, and aggregator of content. To only look at players of board games as part of a board game culture is to only look at one facet of this community. In my research, I found four, largely permeable, layers to board gaming culture. The first, and most numerous, layer is the *board game player*. The player is the person who sits down to play the game, often with other people. In the survey I conducted for Chapters 6 and 7, 70.4 percent of players played with the same group exclusively, 13 percent of players met regularly in groups, and 24.3 percent played with the same group of people at irregular times. This cultural layer is the most common and, probably, the most obvious: most people understand board games from this "bottom-up" position because it is the one most familiar to them.

The next layer of board game culture is the *online content creator*. These are influential players in board game communities who review games, explain the rules to games, play through games, or offers news about the game industry through digital content. The rise of these "intermediaries" stems from the confluence of two factors: the increasing popularity and complexity of games (which necessitate rules explanations, playthroughs, and reviews) and, as the previous chapter demonstrated, the simultaneous development of social media (which have allowed these productions to flourish). Most online content creators were largely unknown before becoming influential, but some brought their celebrity from other areas into this realm. For instance, Wil Wheaton was one of the most influential board game intermediaries with his online show *TableTop*, although he first became famous in the 1980s as a child actor. Many of the stars of these videos, like Rodney Smith of *Watch It Played* or Richard Ham of *Rahdo Runs Through*, have tens of thousands of subscribers and earn a living through these outlets. At the same time, these YouTube stars also function as gatekeepers, and their positive reviews and often make or break a Kickstarter campaign (they often receive advance copies of games to review for the Kickstarter). Yet, in my interviews with these intermediaries, one thing became abundantly clear—they consider themselves board game players first and foremost.

The third layer of board gaming culture is the *designers*: the créateurs and crafters who create the board games that the online content creators talk about. Some designers are full-time employees or freelancers, others are hobbyists who are able to channel their passion for board gaming into new creations. Both types have used crowdfunding sites like Kickstarter to fund their games, although the hobbyists are more likely to. Like the intermediaries, all the board game designers with whom I spoke would also consider themselves board game players, and some of them have influential online channels as well, making them intermediaries.

The final layer of board gaming culture is the *company*, which, as described in Chapter 4, can be large or can consist of just one or two employees. Within this structure, however, are companies that publish *only* board games and companies that publish many different toys, board games only being one. For example, Hasbro, the largest publisher of board games in the world, employs over 5,000 people,* but in addition to publishing mass-market games like *Monopoly* (1933), *Scrabble* (1948), and *Operation* (1965), they also release toys like G.I. Joe, Transformers, Nerf, and My Little Pony. The games Hasbro publishes are generally not considered particularly thematic, complex, or enticing, and the hobbyists I spoke with largely rejected these "mass-market games" (see Chapter 4). In contrast, the largest board game-only publisher, Asmodee, publishes more complex games like *Carcassonne* (2000, Z-Man) and *Diplomacy* (1959, Avalon Hill), many of which have been created by smaller board game companies like Plaid Hat Games and Mayfair.† Smaller, independent companies like Wren Games or Rattlebox Games (two companies I interviewed) may only release games sporadically. Many companies are peopled by board game players, although it is hard to know whether the executives in charge of companies like Hasbro would consider themselves part of the board game hobby. But even these companies influence board game culture.

Ethnographic Interviews

In this chapter, I use ethnographic interviews and critical engagement with cultural artifacts to outline some of the problems within board gaming related to a lack of diversity, and some solutions to those problems. In an ethnographic interview, the researcher engages in a guided discussion or "friendly conversation" into which she "introduces new elements to assist informants to respond as informants."[8] According to ethnographic researcher James Spradley, "rather than *studying people*, ethnography means *learning from people*"; the ethnographic interview facilitates learning as the researcher does not strictly adhere to planned questions,

---

* https://jobs.hasbro.com/
† As of March 2020, Plaid Hat Games left Asmodee, although many of the games Plaid Hat had previously designed stayed with the larger company.

but rather lets the interview subject help guide the discussion into unanticipated territories.[9] *Learning* instead of *studying* means engaging in dialogic practices by listening and responding rather than asking rote questions. Learning requires interactivity.

The interviews I conducted for this chapter included over forty game designers and online content creators (blogs, videos, and podcasts) about their experiences in the board game hobby. In addition, I followed up with about seventy survey-takers to ask them additional questions about diversity and inclusion in the board game industry and hobby. As a method, interviews are useful for understanding the experiences of these people; however, it is hard to generalize from these unique voices a full understanding of the industry because this group may not be representative of the larger community. Instead, these interviews "excel at achieving a detailed level of personal depth and describing a smaller, specific group."[10] Interviews like these help reveal the personal experiences that shape a community.

Practicing ethnographic interview methods actually helped shape the direction of this chapter too. While initially I had a list of questions, I found that having a conversation, where I could ask about whatever topic was emerging at any particular point, initiated a stronger bond with the interview subjects. I hadn't planned to write about diversity issues in board gaming initially, but so many people responded to my interview questions by discussing diversity that I started to ask more pointed questions about inclusion. In other words, not only did the participants answer the questions, but they also helped shape the direction of the research itself. This sort of interactive experience hearkens to some recent work by Benjamin Woo, a scholar of geek culture, who talked to members of card and board game clubs, stores, and conventions, "following" them and "trying to understand things from their perspective."[11]

One of the downsides of using interview methods is the sheer time it takes: each interview I conducted took thirty to forty-five minutes and often hours to schedule. Transcribing interviews can also be time consuming, often taking 1.5 or 2 times the length of the interview to transcribe.* Another downside is the individuality of interview answers. Interviews, at best, reveal what individuals believe about their personal experiences, but are influenced by prevailing cultural discourses. The interviews in this chapter are therefore

---

* In the instance of this chapter, however, I used an online program (otter.ai) that used artificial intelligence to transcribe the interviews (I merely had to upload the data and correct minor errors).

useful ways of noting the discursive forces that shape how board games are understood. In other words, interviews give a good sense of the participants' "*social worlds*, as evidence both of 'what happens' within them and of how individuals make sense of themselves, their experiences and their place within these social worlds."[12] Thus, for the purposes of this chapter, I look at the interviews as indicative of cultural discourses, rather than focus specifically on any one player's comments.

At the same time, as Matt Hills has shown, especially when interviewing people about culturally devalued activities (in his case, fandom; in my case, board games), asking questions about the nature of the activity "causes the fan to cut into the flow of their experience and produce some kind of discursive 'justification.'"[13] One of the ways I have found to help counter this justification is to invoke my own identity as a fan, gamer, and researcher during my interviews. People talk differently depending on whom they're talking to.[14] This can be helpful if one presents themselves as part of the same community they are researching. In a different set of interviews I conducted about *Doctor Who* fans in 2013, I found that it helped the research to note my own fandom of *Doctor Who*: people opened up more and spoke more willingly about their experiences in fandom.[15] At the same time, my identity as a straight, white, cisgendered middle-aged male (in other words, the most stereotypical "board gamer") might have prevented some people from freely sharing their viewpoints about diversity and inclusion in board gaming communities with me. We speak differently to people that identity differently than we do (see Chapter 9). Ultimately, as Alan McKee notes, "the amount of information gathered by the ethnographer can ensure that they are able to make very good educated guesses about the sense-making practices of the people they study. But this is still not the same thing as just reflecting reality."[16] All qualitative data, as with all quantitative data, must be taken with a large grain of salt.

When speaking with game designers and intermediaries, I sought out people of different races, ethnicities, and genders. More than half the people I spoke with (twenty-five out of forty-four) were nonwhite or non-cis-male (I spoke with fifteen women/nonbinary people and seventeen nonwhite designers). The interviews with players skewed male-presenting (judging solely by self-reported names and gender descriptors), with about the same ratio of female-presenting to male-presenting as in the original survey (sixty-eight people responded to my follow-up questions, and of them fifteen were female-presenting).

Diversity and Inclusion in Board Gaming[*]

The interviews I conducted made it clear that not only is the board game community aware of and responsive to issues of inclusion, but it is also concerned about the appearance of the "mono-cultural" stereotype of board gamers as older, cisgendered, male, straight players.[17] As the demographics of my survey revealed, the board gaming hobby is still largely white and male. Across the board, and with few exceptions (which I discuss later), there is a consensus that *something* needs to be done to make the community more systemically inclusive. At the same time, many of my respondents noted that simply pointing out that there was a problem wasn't enough, and some interview subjects also offered solutions. In order to ascertain what the interview subjects discussed about these topics, I organized the answers into five areas where the interviewees saw diversity issues in board gaming: player and game communities, in-game representation, types of games, the demographics of board game designers at the industrial level, and, finally, within larger culture itself.

Players and Game Communities

One of the most obvious ways that issues of inclusivity manifest in the board game hobby is through the actions and activities of the players themselves. As one player noted, there is a "lack of diversity at the table, specifically women and minorities." A lot of players noted that this lack of diversity stems from "gatekeeping" as "the community needs to do a better job about welcoming women, people of color, and people with disabilities to the table." Indeed, Hova's discussion of the "invisible ropes," that "most people in gaming don't notice, but that can turn off someone just entering the hobby," reflects the sentiments of many of the participants—the microaggressions, gendered assumptions, paternal attitudes, casual sexism at a gaming table, throwaway homophobic remarks, and mansplaining (as one of my participants recounted of her own experiences) all add up to an environment that can sometimes be implicitly or explicitly hostile or alienating to players that don't fit the "traditional" mold.[18]

---

[*] In this chapter, I am making the deliberate choice not to "call out" specific games, which unfairly gives the appearance that issues of diversity are limited to a single case study. In reality, these issues are systemic. Additionally, while I have kept the anonymity of the players I interviewed, I have included the names of online content creators and designers, all of whom gave permission for their names to be used and who have had the opportunity to read their responses in this chapter.

Christian Kang, a Korean-American board game player and online content creator, agrees, noting that a lot of hostility stems from "the old guard . . . the middle aged white male . . .. feeling like the mainstream is kind of invading and . . . transforming the space into something that does not reflect . . . the community that they were a part of." There is a sadness inherent in this sort of hostility, as it seems to stem from perceived threats to the status quo. If board gaming was formally a niche hobby, then the inclusion of new people—bringing with them different interests, different types of games, different play styles—might threaten "The Way Things Are." Danny Quach, an Asian-American, gay man who makes review videos, details that he first got into online content creation because "there wasn't a huge LGBTQ presence [in board games] online." But he goes on to describe the effect of social media on the *knowledge* that board gaming is diverse: "whether we realize it or not . . . on a bigger systemic level, before more women got into board gaming, before people of color got into board gaming: we've always been around, but we've maybe not have had that that space to make ourselves present or to make our voices present." So what changed? Namely, as board games have become more popular, and the "geeky" stigma has been eroding, the spaces that were formally populated by the "straight, white dudes" have seen an influx of new people into the hobby.

In many ways, board gaming can be used in socially progressive ways. For example, one player said that, "as a trans woman, there are few social activities that provide safe spaces for meeting people. . . . Board games help with that." The social interaction that board games provide can help social acceptance. Many players and content creators were quick to note that they had never had a problem in the community. That board gaming for these and other players can be a welcoming and safe space is laudatory, but as the data demonstrates, it is also not universal. For example, another player highlighted that an ideal board game experience would be one where she could "walk into my local shops and play with good people," but

> right now I can't do that because one, or more, or all of the following happens: everyone refusing to play with a new person; men refusing to play with women; men angrily explaining to me how to play games I've played for years because they don't understand or won't consider I have a strategy; women attacking me immediately to show dominance; a table welcoming new people only to gang up on them and kill them in round one.

The owner of a board game café noted that, in general, "stores are not doing enough to make everyone feel included" and they "need to make a conscious effort to curate the culture of their establishment." While some of these are issues with board gaming generally (overly competitive players may alienate any newcomers), these all-too-common complaints are heavily gendered and raced. Tiffany Caires, a nonbinary online game reviewer, had harassment campaigns started against them after they went on Twitter to speak out against gendered board games. They were attacked, doxxed, and harassed. It is easy to identify this as hostile and negative behavior, but the more insidious aspects of gatekeeping— the subtle use of language to alienate others (like calling all players "guys," or explaining game strategy to a woman who has played the game before), the tribal-like behavior of only playing games with people we know—can have negative effects. As game designer Sophie Williams describes, "There's still a long way for us to go in terms of acknowledging that we're not there yet. We as a community will call things out, but we don't necessarily notice our own failures."

While Caires's experiences reveal some animosity running throughout the board game community, it seems that the experience of most people in the hobby is more pleasant. There doesn't appear to be as much widespread and deliberate hate within the board game community as there is in the video game community; rather, and much like with other cultural institutions, there is a subtle and permeating sense of white, male privilege that shapes the discourse around games. Only when we stop thinking of game players and communities as *default* white and male can we make the space welcoming to everyone. As many of the interview subjects mentioned, one way to enable this is through creating a diversity of representations in games and throughout the gaming industry, as I touch on next.

In-game Representation

A significant number of people, whether players, online content creators, or industry professionals, identified diversifying the representations depicted within board games as being crucial to changing the industry. Diversification of representations can take many forms, including the images on the game box or within the game itself. Erin Ryan, in a piece for *The Cardboard Republic*, demonstrates extreme gender disparity within board games: she compiled data from the top 100 board games on BGG for each year from 2009 through 2016, noting the depiction of gender on game boxes. She found "only 5.1% of games released within a year of making it onto the BGG Top 100 featured women alone and no games featured a group of characters made up primarily of women" while "groups containing an equal number of men and women came in at 20.5%." Most games primarily featured men, or groups of men. (Ryan didn't set out to examine racial, sexual, ablest, or other types of representations on board games.)[19]

At its most basic principles, representation in board games—or in any media form—is important because how people act and behave "depends upon how they see themselves and their world, and this in turn depends upon the concepts through which they see."[20] Seeing oneself represented helps individuals picture themselves within that cultural sphere; it can lead to more positive social interactions and higher self-esteem among young people.[21] In board games, according to designer Sophie Williams, "people, when they can see people who are like them doing a thing that they want to do, that inspires them to do more. And we're only just beginning to get people from far more diverse backgrounds getting engaged in tabletop games. Representation can show us what is possible and what we are capable of." Representation can be as simple as the images we see in the games, or it can be as subtle as the words used in rule books: one player was adamant that games need to "stop assuming your players are male.... When some of them would reference players they always use the male pronoun." Using gender neutral pronouns helps generate universality—it is inclusive to all players.

Most of my interview subjects focused on the images they saw in games, and were vocal in their condemnation of the "hypersexualization of female characters and exaggeration of traditional gender roles" in board games. Many commented on how "off-putting" some games were because of the "chainmail bikinis" and the lack of playable characters that are not white or male. One player noted the racial stereotypes that can permeate some games:

> In [a] base game, there are twelve playable characters. Nine are white. The one Asian character is a martial artist. One of the two Black characters is a shaman from South Africa [the other is a Jazz musician]. . . . There is already a disproportionate amount of white characters. And the characters of color fit into what could be described as stereotypical roles.

As one respondent noted, this lack of diversity "is particularly true for fantasy games which begs the question, 'Whose fantasy is this?,'" illustrating how board games are idealized primarily from a white perspective. The types of characters available to play in a game affect who might see themselves as gamers, as Black game designer Tanisha Hall explains:

> There were not a lot of board games that had character that I could really identify with you without having to try so hard. I didn't have to imagine what would this character look like if they were Black? Or, what would it look like if this

scene was in New York City instead of you know, some grove or something like that? . . . We want to be represented correctly, fairly, honestly. We want to just have fun and not feel like we have to live up to a white standard of gaming in order to be fun, or in order to be valid.

Diversification and inclusion doesn't mean simply putting people of color or women into stereotypical roles, but in providing a full array of different characters and characteristics to choose from—treat people as people, not as stereotypes. One way to do this is to hire more people of color and women to work on games. This has the added bonus of preventing an appropriation of culture context, as online content creator Calvin Wong, a Malaysian board gamer and online influencer, discusses: "I will not buy games that have an Asian theme that didn't have Asian people working on it. I won't do it. . . . I've told companies straight up this is Orientalist. It's fairly racist. We shouldn't be doing it."

Again, this is not to say that there have not been steps in the right direction. As Kathleen Mercury, a game designer and educator, notes, the "meta discussions" that are happening about representation in the industry "are definitely appearing in games," and Mandi Hutchinson, a woman of color and contributor to the Dice Tower podcasts, argues that the community is becoming "a little more cognizant about how things are in the state of board games, I guess with in regards to representation and inclusivity . . . .[but] it's slow." For instance, game designer Nikki Valens is known for her gender and sexual inclusivity in her games. Her *Legacy of Dragonholt* (2017, Fantasy Flight Games) is one of the few games to have LGBTQIA+ characters. She described including this as important because "it's a part of many players' experiences." In addition to LGBTQIA+ characters, she also tries to include

> trans characters in my games, when it's possible to do so for the same reason that that is not only representing myself, but it's representing people like me, who don't really have representation in the large scale of the industry right now. And even in a lot of cases, the representation that we do find is done by people without the knowledge or the experience to do it well. And in those cases that can even harm those different groups of people, solidifying negative stereotypes or other harmful things.

Having a diverse range of characters to play can not only make more people feel included, but also bring, as one player noted, "a broader swath of humanity . . . into gaming. Many people play games to put themselves in a different role. What better way than to give the opportunity to play a person that is completely different than them." Some game companies make the diversification of characters in their games and on their box tops a priority and look beyond just race, gender, and sexuality to depict people of different social classes, ages, weights, and abilities. Game companies that reflect these diverse principles of representation seem to indicate that they are aware that the more inclusive they can make their game, the more people can be included as players (and, in a capitalist market, will possibly purchase the game).

Types of Games

Tanisha Hall's aforementioned quotation harkens to an additional area where issues of diversity can be seen in board gaming: through the types of games that get made. As my survey demonstrated, one of the most popular types of games on the market today is the Eurogame, a largely abstract game with indirect player interaction. Eurogames are so called because they emerged from Europe, largely Germany; many of the most popular hobby games of the past few decades, like *Catan* (1995, Mayfair), *Puerto Rico* (2002, Ravensburger), and *Carcassonne*, are Eurogames.[22] As I have been discussing throughout this book, if board games represent the culture from which they emerged, then it makes sense that there is a European cultural sensibility underlying the development of the Eurogame.

But how does this type of gaming sensibility manifest? Some of the players I interviewed were clear that "just using terms such as 'Euro-Style' game gives the impression of a white Anglo-Saxon view of the industry." Such a view leads to "probably the biggest issue . . . the treatment of other cultures and colonialism. The Eurogame picks a random indigenous or historical area and gamify them without doing proper research. . . . I would not feel great about introducing anyone from Africa or South America to Eurogames." Indeed, many Eurogames are about colonization (see Chapter 3). The way that players are positioned within these types of games can have often unintended ideological consequences, as the game can force players to complete actions that make them feel complicit in culturally insensitive ways. For instance, in an article for *Analog Game Studies*, Antonnet Johnson details her experiences playing *Small World* (2009, Days of Wonder), a game where players colonize an area of land, displacing the native inhabitants.[23] As a person of color, Johnson was put in an uneasy position through the game play, being forced to replicate an imperialist narrative in order to win. Other games glorify aspects of history that may be unpalatable to others: one player wrote, "I'm also not particularly comfortable with war simulations that ignore the moral ramifications. Playing as the Nazis for 'fun' is not a good look." (In a few pages, I'll talk about *Scramble for Africa* and its representation of African colonization.) Eurogames are not alone in including distasteful themes. For example, American games that are based in the Lovecraft universe have to tread carefully around the obvious racism within his work. As with Eurogames, many American games also feature "the enduring presence of colonialist themes of 'expansion,' 'conquest,' and 'taming the frontier,'" as one player noted.

Of course, there are many games on the market that do not share these themes, so diversifying the type of game that is available means discovering these other games—and purchasing them to support the designers, bringing them to game nights to diversify the collection, and encouraging people on social media to see this difference as a virtue. MaryMartha Ford, another African American designer, argues that "people make games that really reflect them. . . . There's something inherent in the DNA of the culture." Players can support designers by spreading the word about different types of games. Gerald King III, a Black game designer and vocal member of many board game communities, sees how differences in cultural backgrounds can influence the types of games that get made:

> It's not like the game I make is inherently marketed toward Black families or Black people or urban cultures. But there's elements of it that are just more relatable. . . . I just designed from my perspective.

Behrooz "Bez" Shahriari, a game designer living in Scotland, seconds King's perspective, saying,

> The world doesn't need just another game about farming that is done in basically the same way. . . . Like if you want to have a game that's all about Action Selection and Worker Placement, and then you basically make it about people in the restaurants or maybe it's about zookeepers, okay, boom, new theme. Or maybe it's about, you know, people trying to rejuvenate environments. . . . I just feel like you've got to seriously look at yourself and think, what is this game adding to the landscape of gaming?

Diversification of the type of game, through the theme or the mechanics, creates a healthier board game economy, as the greater variety of games available welcomes greater number of people into the community. Although the numbers of nonwhite players taking my survey were limited, they did show some significant differences in the types of mechanics preferred by different communities (see Chapter 6). Creating more games with these mechanics and advertising to these communities may help open up the hobby to different players. However, even if this wasn't the case, even if the motive of the industry wasn't profit-driven, there is still an altruistic, ethical need to reduce any impediments to gaming. For instance, many of the games I have discussed in this book can take two to three hours to play (and that's not including setup time or learning the rules) and can be expensive, often costing $60 or more. Having that sort of time or financial freedom is a privilege that many marginalized communities simply can't share, as King describes:

> You're asking people who already don't make any money, they don't have free time, they don't take vacations. . . . You're telling them, when every dime, when every moment you have during the day, if you spent every moment making them the maximum amount of money that you could make, you still wouldn't have enough to live—you want me to spend two hours sitting down doing a task that generate nothing? That is a huge barrier.

Another game designer, Victoria Caña, notes that she has a lot of colleagues from marginalized communities who "became designers because they're not always seeing the types of games that they want to see. They're not seeing games with them in, they're not seeing games that are accessible."

One clear obstacle that reflects this consideration of inclusivity is the issue of accessibility regarding physical and mental abilities. Simply put, as one player put it:

> Insofar as most games require someone to sit upright at a table and reach frequently, most board games are not accessible to people with any kind of disability that affects mobility. So a lot of people can't really play them, or they have to play in some way that turns lack of mobility into a problem for the game. Board game designers could design games with different roles or even roles that are made to come and go easily. They could also include accessibility notes in the instructions, and ask for audience experiences if games are inaccessible.

In addition, "games with extensive flavor text and convoluted setup can exclude people with different ways of thinking who would otherwise be able to engage with the game and have the ability to participate in the comparatively simple game play." In a blog post about their focus on inclusiveness, Stu Turner and Janice Turner of WrenGames consider hearing impairment, handedness (left or right), color blindness, and language and reading ability (dyslexia) when designing games.[24] Carla Kopp, a game designer, likes games "that are colorblind friendly to them makes it accessible." A number of my interview subjects mentioned the game *Nyctophobia* (2018, Pandasaurus Games) as designed in a way that blind people can play (in the game, everyone except one person is blindfolded and plays the game through touch). As websites like "Meeples Like Us," a resource for game accessibility, demonstrate, games like *Nyctophobia* herald a new approach to game design that manages to exclude fewer people.

Designers

Inclusion in the board game hobby has to be coupled with diversification in the voices of those that create games. If board games need to move beyond the stolid ideologies that have undergirded them for years, newer voices with different viewpoints have to be courted and encouraged to become part of the industry. Almost everyone I spoke to mentioned this fact in some way or another. One player said that "It's important for creators to come from a variety of backgrounds. People with different life experiences put different emphasis on their creations. Some infuse them with a sense of history and culture, some with a point of view that is not always expressed as prevailing, some with ideas and experiences I cannot name or quantify." Players remarked on the overwhelmingly white, male background of most game designers. In a 2018 survey of BGG, user TonyChen summarized the most popular board game designers, looking at how well a designer's games are ranked on the site. Of the top fifty names, only one person of color (Eric M. Lang) and one woman (Inka Brand) are listed.[*] When games are (almost) solely the purview of white male creators, like any media product they will tend to reflect the concerns and ideas of that particular identity, as designer Janice Turner notes.

Beyond simply seeing new types of games represented in the creative field, bringing more diversity into the design realm has other advantages. Young people who may be interested in game design can be influenced (or discouraged) by the presence (or lack thereof) of people that look like them in the field. And while more diverse representation in games is a stated goal of so many in the industry, there needs to be a sense of authenticity to games that reflect cultural experiences. For instance, Christopher Chung, an Asian-Canadian board game designer, focused on the "rich background [his] heritage has" and tied his game to that cultural background, but too few game developers look for that level of authenticity.

---

[*] Through my own research on the site, https://boardgamegeek.com/geeklist/245399/all-time-designer-ranking-2018

Developing more inclusion in game design is not as easy as simply saying "there need to be more people of color, or women, or LGBTQ people creating games." There has to be a systematic and deliberate courting of new voices, an encouragement of underrepresented groups, and a dismantling of structural inequities built into the industry. There are many hurdles to overcome for anyone wanting to design games, let alone someone from a non-privileged background. Designer Jonathan Gilmour sees "a huge disparity in the number of non-straight white dude designers, as opposed to straight dude designers. And we still have a huge step to overcome that. . . . Overall, diversity in our industry as a whole is nowhere representative of what the overall spread of diverse people in our culture is." But the issue isn't that there has been some sort of overt push to keep people of color or women out of the industry, simply a laissez-faire mentality that has let systemic social issues prevent large-scale diversification. For instance, Elizabeth Hargrave, a designer who has cultivated a strong following for her work on gender equality in the industry, attributed the gender disparity to economic issues. "So much game design is done as a hobby," she argues, and "everyone has their day job. And it's doing that on the side. And there are going to be certain demographic groups that have more time and resources to do that the other demographic groups." If the industry is truly committed to developing the work of new designers, then there need to be scholarships, design camps, tutoring, and mentoring for designers both new and old.

In addition, aspiring game designers often pitch their new games at conventions. The industry is still small and relaxed enough that many deals are made in such informal spaces. Designer Victoria Caña confirmed that "people only really became interested in me and the stuff that I was doing when I started to go to a bunch of conventions. And I think that that's what I would recommend to other people trying to enter the industry, is to try to go to as many as possible in your area." But, one of the players whom I interviewed noted that, "from a designer perspective, this is very challenging for anyone who can't afford to go, both in terms of time off from work and family responsibilities and money." It's the problem that Gerald King III mentioned earlier: higher levels of social and cultural privilege facilitate easier entry into industry-sanctioned spaces. Caña does note that there are scholarships that designers can apply for, but they not as common nor as widespread as they could be. More scholarships aimed at marginalized demographics would help increase attendance, and more activities designed specifically for those demographics would help everyone feel comfortable. But once a designer does go to a convention, there are other hurdles: feeling outside the community can be alienating. King, in fact, told me that he is used to being one of the only Black people at gaming conventions. One of the players I spoke with mentioned the following anecdote about her experience at a convention that alienated her from the community of creators:

> At tables to play test board games at GenCon half the creators (all male with no female creators in sight) would not listen to my critical feedback. I'm not shy and I hear I'm quite forceful with expression but it was as though they muted me. But when my (male) best friend repeated my thoughts verbatim? Suddenly these creators cared, taking notes and asking him for his email to follow up.

Obviously, this isn't going to be everyone's experience at conventions, but it speaks to the sense of gatekeeping noted earlier. Without deliberately inviting people into these spaces and making those spaces safe, including enforcing anti-harassment policies and creating policies that encourage diversity efforts, gamers erect silos around their work.

At the same time, while Kickstarter has been a massive disruption to the way the board game industry has traditionally functioned, as it has allowed smaller companies to create and market their own games without going through mainstream companies. African American board game designer Omari Akil ran a successful Kickstarter campaign for his game *Rap Godz* (2000, Board Game Brothas), after considering but deciding against pitching at a convention. If, as online content producer Jay Carmichael, a Pākehā from New Zealand, describes, "90% of board game content caters to 5% of the board game audience," then Kickstarter becomes a way to work outside of that system. However, it too needs a community of people to fund games. Game designers Rob Huber and Brendan Riley, who funded their first game on Kickstarter, noted that "you should [already] have people there when you jump." There are so many board games looking for funding on Kickstarter—as of August 2019, more than $1 billion dollars have been pledged to games, making it the number one category on the site—that without the community *already* supporting creators, the chances of success may be slim (only about 40 percent are fully funded).

Encouraging more diverse designers to enter the board game field doesn't mean the loss of traditional gaming—as many people have noted (over and over again in my survey and interviews), the board game industry is rapidly growing, with thousands of new games released every year. There is plenty of room for both contemporary and classic voices. Mandi Hutchinson reflects on how more content allows for greater empathy:

> I definitely think having these voices in the community is really important. And we have to take the time, people who are not part of a certain group or

maybe don't fully understand, need to just stop and think, okay, maybe I can understand and maybe empathize with this person or these groups and say, "Hey, I understand that they're not being represented, what can I do?"

If board games are becoming more popular today because they reflect a social interaction that's missing in today's society, then perhaps they also can demonstrate a meaningful return to empathetic understanding between people who, according to designer Kelly North Adams, might share some geek traits, but who don't necessarily understand each other's cultural background.

Culture

Ultimately, the board game industry and hobby are part of contemporary culture; they don't lie outside of it and are therefore influenced by changes in culture. Board games, as designer Daniel Solis has noted, are not made in a vacuum. These discussions about diversity and inclusion in the board game industry are also part of the contemporary cultural moment; fifty years ago, it wouldn't have been seen to be problematic if *only* white men were on the cover of a board game. It's not that inclusion has become an issue only recently; it's that, as an issue, it hasn't been seen as culturally valuable to discuss until recently. The same is happening across other entertainment industries, and my interviewees noted things like the #MeToo movement and the television industry's attempt to diversify as well.

At the same time, a push against diversification rings in board gaming cultures, just as it has in US politics, video game culture, and other aspects of life. Some of my interview subjects were concerned that efforts to diversify representations, for instance, would come at the expense of good game design (although those two things are not opposites). Some were vocal that there had already been diversification in the industry and there was nowhere left to go. Others thought that diversification would happen on its own, as the "market" called for more diversity. But as Lila Sadkin argues, "Ignoring a lack of diversity and assuming that it will work itself out 'on merit' is a willfully ignorant perspective that ignores the long history of white patriarchy that has reinforced inequalities and needs to be actively opposed in order for change to happen."[25] A number of people in my survey specifically mentioned that board games helped them *avoid* talking politics through play, noting that games gave a "safe space without getting political" or that they "mostly transcend political lines." As we've seen, however, games as cultural objects do not and cannot exist outside of politics:

and, indeed, when asked differently, my interview subjects *demonstrated* that board gamers are influenced by political and cultural events. For example, when asked "What are some issues you see with the board game industry today?" participants responded with a number of answers that were directly influenced by contemporary political discussions about the United States's increase in tariffs on goods from China affecting the cost of board games, largely mirroring a conversation happening in the news at the same time as I was conducting the interviews.[26]

One of the challenges of diversifying the industry is the danger that one person might become the spokesperson for an entire identity. In our interview, Sophie Williams said that whenever she is interviewed, she is almost always only asked about women in the industry:

> So people don't want to interview me as a game designer very often. I generally get, you're a woman in games design . . . so people assume that the only thing you're ever interested in talking about is being a woman in the industry, which then further polarizes people's attitudes, because then, "oh my god, all the women, that's all they have to talk about."[27]

Omari Akil described a similar experience:

> It's difficult being in those spaces and not seeing too many people that look like you. . . . And so I think the trickiest part is everybody is asking us how to make diversity happen. And we also don't know. So it's been difficult because you become a spokesperson in a way, and you don't necessarily have better answers than anyone else. That is a piece of the struggle, just being in the space.

Ultimately, the board game industry and hobby are themselves just systems. And if nothing else, board game players are very good at figuring out and mastering systems. One might say that it is what board game players are trained to do—to read the patterns of how something functions and try to find ways to either subvert or work within the system to enact change. Gamers take repeatable actions and call them mechanics. Learn the mechanics of a game well enough, and perform the system successfully, they call it winning. Successfully "gaming" the hobby could include changing the way people view diversity, not as an "add-on" expansion but as the base game itself. Imagine that the system was designed for a particular type of player—one that brought some cultural knowledge that others didn't, or that was geared toward making that type of player more successful. The game would be unbalanced. And that's what's happening in the hobby and industry today. The game is unbalanced. As Gerald King III says, "they didn't realize they were just building a system, but they built a system, and the system itself literally is forcing me out because I didn't belong there."

Wingspan and *Scramble for Africa**

How do these issues of diversity and inclusion play out in the games themselves? In this section, I want to critically engage with two representative game experiences that highlight how these issues actually function in game spaces. Elizabeth Hargrave is the creator of *Wingspan*, an engine-building game in which players are "bird enthusiasts—researchers, bird watchers, ornithologists, and collectors—seeking to discover and attract the best birds to your network of wildlife preserves."[†] Almost from its release, the game was met with accolades, and it won the 2019 Kennerspiel des Jahres award, aimed at "connoisseur or expert games." It has also had mainstream publicity, having been written up in the *New York Times*.[28]

Wingspan also highlights a number of the key precepts about diversity that my interview subjects have noted. First, and notably, Elizabeth Hargrave is a woman (one of only 8 in the top 200 of BGG), and has used her platform as a now-famous designer to deliberately engage with the board game hobby to promote diverse work, like her ongoing and oft-updated website highlighting women and nonbinary game designers.[‡] She uses Twitter to promote the work of other women and nonbinary designers, and to help up-and-coming designers to network. Indeed, *Wingspan* has an all-female creative group, as the art was also created by three women: Natalia Rojas, Ana Maria Martinez Jaramillo, and Beth Sobel. Second, the game has a theme that doesn't rely on imperialist or colonialist metaphors, and instead reflects an aspect of nature that is perceived as comforting. As an interviewee noted, it was the type of game his mom would play, because it didn't rely on players' knowledge of heavy board game thematics. Game publisher Jamey Stegmaier attributes an increase in women's participation with his games to *Wingspan*.[§] Hargrave wanted to design a game "tied to [a]

---

[*] The game's title comes from a phrase referring to a period of European colonization of the African continent.
[†] https://stonemaiergames.com/games/wingspan/
[‡] https://www.elizhargrave.com/women-nb-game-designers
[§] https://stonemaiergames.com/5-revelations-from-our-2019-demographic-survey/

subject [she] found interesting"—demonstrating that different identities on the creative side of board games can engender a greater variety of topics.[29]

Wingspan has also been popular, with 5,000 sold in its first week as a preorder and over 200,000 copies sold since. The game has been reprinted multiple times. The popularity of the game demonstrates that there is a market for diverse themes. It demonstrates a hunger in the board game community for alternate voices. And it demonstrates how the rising popularity of board games reflects a greater desire for games that do not fit the traditional pattern of gaming that runs the risk of alienating marginalized players.

In contrast, the aborted release of *Scramble for Africa* (unpublished, GMT Games) tells a different story. Designed by Joe Chacon, the game was intended to have players enact the colonization of the African continent in the late nineteenth and the early twentieth century. As part of this history, *Scramble for Africa* would have depicted—and forced players to participate in—human atrocities like slavery, torture, and other horrors of the era. The issue, as Jon Bolding writes in *Vice*, wasn't that the game depicted these uglier elements of human history, but rather that they were enacted

> without the due gravity that one should give to the situation. They do so without caring whether or not your "colonists" suffer and die after arriving on their "colonist ship," or are nearly exterminated by forced labor and disease as the Taíno were. They only care that you got enough points to win. The suffering that took place—and still takes place—is either ignored or has no repercussions.[30]

Antonnet Johnson's reflection on *Small World* once again reveals the imperialist attitudes that games like *Scramble for Africa* reproduce, as "games (re)produce dominant narratives and Western ideologies." For *Scramble for Africa*, an ideology of Western dominance ran throughout the game:

> Random events in the game included "penalties for atrocities," reducing the horrors of rhino-hide whips to a minor setback, an unavoidable consequence of being good at colonization. The game had you explore new "terrain tiles" and then build mines or plantations to exploit them, simply assuming a labor force would appear, as well as garrisons to guard against insurrections by the natives. Those natives could be incited to revolt by other players, but that was just a setback—there was no discussed mechanic to provide for something like Ethiopia's successful defense against invading European powers. You could even choose to play on a random map, fictionalizing a real place to better represent "the mystery of 19th Century Africa." Ultimately, the winner of the game was the one who had exploited the peoples and resources of Africa the best.[31]

About a month after *Scramble for Africa* was released, a backlash against the game led to GMT's owner Gene Billingsley to pull the game.

The creation of *Scramble for Africa* highlights all the issues my interview subjects noted about problems with diversity in the industry—a reliance on European-centric themes, a focus on violent, warlike strategy, and a blindness about the lived realities of people unlike the designers. This is not unusual, and, as designer Martin Wallace mentioned to me in our interview,

> You could do that in the 1970s or 80s if you wanted to do a game about Africa. And there have been various games about the Scramble for Africa, nobody would have batted an eyelid. But nowadays, you have to be really careful how you deal with certain subjects, you can't treat them in the same way as it used to be and you can't ignore people's feelings about these things.

This isn't to say that there can't be a game about the African colonization, nor is it to say that such a game can't be told from the colonialist point of view. But in order to make that game inclusive and avoid making people feel unwelcome in the hobby, that game has to recognize and acknowledge the gravity of the atrocities, and it cannot pretend like there weren't victims in history. Board games are always going to reflect back the ideologies of those that design them, and it is only through the active breaking of unconscious bias that the gaming hobby can become more inclusive.

At the same time, one could imagine a *Scramble for Africa* game told from a nativist point of view, created by people from African countries. The game *Spirit Island* (2017, Greater Than Games) already attempts this type of theme, as it presents players defending an island home from colonizing Invaders, including a Swedish Mining Colony and a Remote British Colony. According to Kevin Draper, in most African countries, "strategy board games are not a regular pastime."[32] But, he notes, there are the stirrings of some changes, as new conventions and board games cafes are opening in West Africa and Nigeria. Perhaps the next *Scramble for Africa* will tell of the Ethiopian revolt of the 1960s, or will at least not ignore the suffering of millions of enslaved people for a white, imperialist victory.

Conclusion

Almost universally, the people I interviewed for this chapter remarked on the overall friendliness and welcoming nature of the board game communities they are part of. Almost everyone talked about how open the industry was to getting feedback from its players. This isn't a surprise, as the board game industry is made up largely of those same players, and most people are able to communicate easily on BGG and social media. There's a feeling that, if you like board games, and I like board games, then we must have some sort of connection—we both like this niche hobby.

But as the population of board gamers grows, and as more games flood the market, the heady days where everyone knows your game will slowly start to make way toward a sense of gatekeeping and exclusion. In order to maintain a sense of inclusion, in order to fight against a creeping uniformity within board games, players, online content creators, and designers alike must actively work to include marginalized people, dismantle structural barriers, and create welcoming spaces. This is not easy, nor does it come naturally to everyone; it is incumbent upon all members of the community to look for areas of improvement. This is a lesson that gamers already know. As one interviewee noted, "The very diversity of board games to choose from is the best representation of what 'our culture' really is, which is a beautiful melting pot of diversity."

There are some clear paths toward more inclusion in the industry and the hobby that members of the board game community can enact moving forward. As players, try and buy more diverse games. This means a number of things. First, buy games created by designers who are women, LGBTQIA+, or people of color. If board games are part of our capitalist culture, then allow money to speak. Sure, spend money on games by your favorite designers, but also try games designed by a non-American or a non-European créateur. Try themes that are not typical "colonialism" or "expansionist" metaphors, and representations that demonstrate gender parity. While no one is saying you should never play games about colonization, break out of that mold to find themes that are nontraditional or different. Playing games with non-colonialist themes and/or nonsexist representations may also help bring more people of color/women to the hobby, people who, like Johnson, find that "as a player of color, I recognize in [a] moment of tension that *Small World* was not designed for me."[33]

Similarly, at a moment when the layers between the different board game cultures are still incredibly permeable, players can still talk back to the industry. Games like *Scramble for Africa* can be scrapped while games like *Wingspan* can be heralded. Learn more about game creators and about their points of view. The players' voice is powerful, even more so when the industry is made up largely of players as well. There is still a massive overrepresentation of white male game designers, and the only way to create more equity is to encourage women and people of color to go into game design. Hire people who believe in inclusivity; make it part of the interview process. Broadcast and follow through with a desire for diversity, seeking out new talent from previously underrepresented peoples.[*] This has to start at the educational level. In schools, teachers need to promote board game design as an educational tool, and encourage everyone in class to participate.[34] For instance, designer Kathleen Mercury both uses games in her gifted classes and provides an online resource for other teachers.[†] Early exposure to game design in education can result in people of color and women becoming involved in online board game content creation like review videos and podcasts. And the board game community has to support these efforts.

If board games are simply a system within this cultural sphere, what power do board game players have to change systemic racism, sexism, ableism, ageism, and so on? Obviously, board game players and designers are not going to solve all the worlds' problems by opening up a board game and laying out some pieces. But by examining the cultures that they *are* part of, and enabling small changes to come into effect within that culture, a ground-up approach to cultural change can occur. Learn from games themselves by turning inclusion into a gamified activity. What mechanics are necessary in order to win? Call out people who make negative comments. Include people of various backgrounds in gaming groups. Look beyond the obvious or mainstream games. Talk back to companies that don't do a good job promoting inclusion. Support scholarships to conventions.

As my interviewees have demonstrated, inclusion is a larger issue than just what happens in board game communities—fighting against entrenched white and male privilege is a systemic battle, not one that can simply be "solved" by buying a few games. But the more that the board game industry, board game creators, online content creators, and players alike all work together to enact real change in this small slice of contemporary culture, the more inclusive we can make one particular hobby, then systemic change at a larger level becomes that much easier.

---

[*] See game producer Jamey Stegmaier's 2019 blog post on diversity in game content: https://stonemaiergames.com/the-box-matters-how-publishers-can-prioritize-diversity/

[†] https://www.kathleenmercury.com/

The Epic Adventure of Grundy and Trixie

An Autoethnographic Journey through *Gloomhaven*

When the enormous box arrived on my doorstep, I knew exactly what it contained: a hot-off-the-presses copy of *Gloomhaven 2e* (2018, Cephalofair). I'd backed the Kickstarter for the second edition on April 9, 2017, for $99—not a small sum for a board game, but certainly not close to the eventual retail price of $140. After watching the video on the crowdfunding site and reading the details, I immediately joined 40,641 other backers who pledged almost $4 million ($3,999,795, to be exact) to helped fund the project. Eight months later, a twenty-two-pound box sat on my dining room table, waiting to be unboxed.

Two years later, I have completed nearly every scenario (of the almost 100) in the game—almost all of them playing solo—and I have finished about half of the solo-specific ones too. I've unlocked every character and upgraded nearly all of them. My board is covered in stickers of locations I have visited and achievements I have won. I have played every campaign, even if they were incompatible with each other (my city is paradoxically ruled by both the military and the merchant guild). *Gloomhaven* was my second home for a year and a half, a permanent fixture on my basement table, and the stories and adventures I had there continue to live on in my memories. I trade memes about the game with friends. As I write this, I eagerly await the expansion (preordered the day it was announced), which should arrive as this chapter continues to develop, and by the time this book has been published, I imagine I will have completed its scenarios as well. I have never played a game as often, as much, or as deeply as I have *Gloomhaven*. And yet, as I will show in this chapter, my explorations of *Gloomhaven* are intimately tied up with my own media experiences and cultural background. A deeper understanding of how I came to this place in my life—the influences and cultural biases that frame who I am as a game player and as a scholar—colors my interpretation of this solo journal; as any subjective experience changes an understanding of what playing board games today can be.

Throughout this book, I have been exploring different methodologies students and scholars can use to analyze analog board games. As part of the research for this book, then, I have used my own experiences playing games, both with my game group and by myself, to help understand what meanings games communicate, and how those meanings might be interpreted by a game playing community. In addition, I have undertaken conversations with game players, game designers, and online board game content creators to help deepen our understanding of how individual players might read board games and their place in our everyday life. These two overarching methods can loosely be summed up as textual, rhetorical, and cultural analyses, which offer a fresh perspective on the culture of playing board games; and ethnographies, which focus on studying people and the writing of those people's experiences as key to understanding interaction with a text like a game.

What I haven't done, and what I aim to do in this chapter, is turn the lens onto the person doing this research: myself. In this chapter, I use an autoethnographic methodology to examine my own history and play with the game *Gloomhaven*, a tactical dungeon crawler combat game with a heavy thematic narrative. Players take on the roles of different characters in the game, and these characters can level up to increase their skills. Characters go on different linked missions, often culminating in a fight with a "boss" enemy, an adversary who is extremely powerful. Each character has particular attributes that, in combination with other characters' attributes, present different approaches to battle. For instance, one character, the Quatryl Soothsinger, plays music and is excellent at supporting others (the songs can increase the damage wielded by other characters, the number of hexes characters can move, or the healing power of others, etc.), while another, the Vermling Beast Tyrant, comes with a beast companion who can also be controlled by the player. In addition, each character has a random "personal goal" to accomplish in the game, and when that goal is complete, a new game element (usually a new character) can be unlocked. There are eighteen characters to unlock in the game (including the six starting characters), and each one has its own play style, array of strengths and weaknesses, and particular goal. Thus, not only are "the characters . . . defined by attributes that can change during gameplay" but "abilities and equipment may be acquired or lost; personal traits may improve or worsen" over time.[1] *Gloomhaven* is precisely the type of game-that-tells-a-story that Marco Arnaudo describes in his analysis of narrative in games, as the character development in the game can engender closer player identification: it is precisely the type of game that *I* enjoy playing. As I played, I identified with some characters more than others, even while some of them felt more useful for the game as a whole. It is also meaningful that I have played *Gloomhaven* as a solo player for the vast majority of my time with the game.

Autoethnography is a research method that "invokes the *self* ('auto'), *culture* ('ethno'), and *writing* ('graphy')" to describe and interpret texts, personal experiences, ideas, and practices.[2] Importantly, autoethnography isn't just about describing my experiences playing *Gloomhaven* (solo or not); it also requires a "self-awareness of [my] partialities and positionalities as [a] cultural and media studies researcher."[3] That is, it requires an interrogation of who I am, and how my own experiences have shaped what I interpret.[4] In what follows, I critically reflect on my own experiences with *Gloomhaven*, both as a player and as a scholar investigating board games, to interrogate my positionality within the contemporary board game/cultural sphere. I also provide an analysis of the phenomenon of solo board gaming. Solo gaming has become a more visible form of board game interaction, and more games are being released that have "solo" modes or play styles.[5] Finally, I examine my autoethnography of *Gloomhaven* via some of the lenses that I've set out in this book to offer an "autoethnography of autoethnography," where my own preconceived notions of what might be appropriate studies of board games come under focus.[6] Ultimately, I hope to show the value of the critical self-analysis as a methodological tool for understanding board games.

Character Name: Paul Booth

An autoethnographic methodology engages two strands of analysis: the self and the self-in-context. When writing an autoethnography, researchers must "retrospectively and selectively write about epiphanies that stem from, or are made possible by, being part of a culture and/or by possessing a particular cultural identity."[7] The self is always contextualized by the cultural situation in which one is situated, and autoethnography requires the researcher to acknowledge and account for that cultural situation.

One area of cultural research where these strands have effectively been put in conversation is fan studies (see Chapter 5), where researchers have for over a decade been discussing the ways that the "aca-fan" (academic-fan) focuses on the self in order to understand the larger fandom of which one is part (see, as an example, Katherine Larsen and Lynn Zubernis focus on their *Supernatural* fan/academic identities).[8] For fan researcher Matt Hills's autoethnography, "the tastes, values, attachments, and investments of the fan and the academic-fan are placed under the microscope of cultural analysis," as the cultural background of the *researcher* affects not just the type of fandom one engages with, but also the type of *fan experience* one expects.[9] This is particularly relevant when the text under analysis hinges on personal experience, emotion, and affective engagement. For example, Hills begins his fannish autoethnography by charting all of his objects of fandom, past and present (e.g., *Doctor Who*, horror films, the band Toto). He then looks for common discourses within these objects to make connections about himself as a subject (e.g., "British," "cultishness," and "masculine"). By charting his emotional engagement with these texts, Hills observes his own growth in relation to the culture in which he lives. Autoethnography relies on the personal, the emotive, the affective; but always in conversation with the culture around the researcher.

With that being said, let me position myself culturally as a way of opening up an autoethnography of *Gloomhaven*. There are demographic characteristics about myself that resonate with my position as board game player and fan of (even before I played) *Gloomhaven*. I am a white (Caucasian), thirty-eight-year-old, divorced, heterosexual, cisgender man with masculine characteristics. I am in an upper middle-class demographic, especially given my job as a professor at an urban, private university, although given both the student loans that I took out to get an education and the location of the university in a major metropolitan area, my salary/social class is not enough to make me consider myself affluent. I am socially and fiscally liberal. By dint of my many years in school—I hold a BA in English Literature, an MA in Communication/Media Studies, and a PhD in Communication and Rhetoric—I am considered highly educated, although I still get imposter syndrome, as my major fields of research (communication, media studies, and fan studies) have traditionally been considered less rigorous or practical than other disciplines (e.g., hard sciences, business, and law).

I could go on, although at this point I think it's worth noting a couple of major connections between my demographics and my cultural situation. As Hills notes, this sort of "autoethnography asks the person undertaking it to question their self-account constantly, opening the 'subjective' and the intimately personal up to the cultural contexts in which it is formed and experiences."[10] To that end, given my demographics, I have obviously been situated within a particularly valued position within mainstream Western (re: American) society, which reaffirms and privileges whiteness, straightness, and maleness over other identities. This has given me the privilege to attend higher education without as much stress as many of my colleagues, to be able to teach/research culturally less-"valuable" subjects, and to advance in my career without having the additional disadvantages that other identity markers (e.g., female, queer, nonwhite) might make. Additionally, I come from a stable home and a socially privileged background: both my parents have graduate degrees, and both worked in higher education. Also, both my father and my material grandfather were professors, so there is a cultural knowledge about the workings of academia that have helped my career.

The fact that my hobbies have intersected with my academic life is a result of this privilege. I have been able to study/teach seemingly less practical areas because I bring a level of privilege, simply because of my own identity markers, to the conversation. Studying fandom and becoming a fan studies scholar resulted from my own (self-) interest in cult media (defined as media texts that are not considered mainstream). I am a fan of *Doctor Who*, *Star Trek*, *Babylon 5*, *Farscape*, and *12 Monkeys*, among many other cult science fiction shows; and I am a fan of other genres like fantasy and horror. My academic interest in board games sprung from the same well—I became interested in a leisure activity that was slightly off the mainstream (I have never been into sports) and that had cult appeal. Some of the first games I got into were based on those genres of which I am a fan. Yet, all of these interests, which then spawned my academic career, are inherently based in having both leisure time and extra money to participate (fandom, perhaps, less so than board gaming—one can be a fan of anything, but to formally attend conventions or purchase memorabilia, one needs a certain level of comfort in their daily life). To play board games as a hobby, one needs time (many games take multiple hours to learn to play, set up, and actually play) and money (hobby games often cost upward of $60). *Gloomhaven*, for example, now costs $140 retail; playing through the multiple campaigns in the game can take scores of leisure hours that some may not have the advantage of spending. Additionally, many games require having multiple people to play. I have a social circle of friends that have similar tastes as to my own, and a similar amount of leisure time and money to play a diversity of games.

As aca-fan Ross Garner describes, understanding the fan-self through autoethnography "can also assist in developing nuanced insights into . . . the affective fluctuations which form a normative part of long-term fan attachments."

In other words, one can chart the *changing* impact of fandom over time.[11] I've been a fan longer than I've been a gamer. I've been a fan when it wasn't cool to be a fan. I have only recently (in the past six years) became a regular player of board games. Many of the people I have spoken with for this book have been playing games longer, or have been more associated with board games than I have. In order to dive into my association with games, I need to explore my memory of gaming: "As autoethnographers, we use memory for much of our data; through memory we ground our analyses; our memories inform our epistemologies and methodologies."[12] However, I can't remember the first board game I played—it was probably *Candyland* (1949, Hasbro)—as I have been playing mass-market games since I was very young. (In contrast, I *can* remember the first episode of *Doctor Who* I watched: "Planet of Evil," rerun in 1984 or 1985.) As I grew up, I loved *Clue* (1949, Hasbro) and *Trivial Pursuit* (1981, Hasbro). In junior high school (age fourteen or so) one of my best friends started playing *Magic: The Gathering* (1993, Wizards of the Coast), but I didn't because I felt lost by the rules. I stopped being interested in games in high school both because I wanted to be seen as cooler and because I developed interests in extracurricular activities like speech team and theater (so my "cool" quotient didn't really increase anyway). I got back into fandom in graduate school, and back into board games when one of my best friends started to play hobby games with me in the early 2010s. At about this time, I also rediscovered a childhood love of jigsaw puzzles, and began to do jigsaws in my spare time. From puzzles (which may be where my love of solo gaming comes from as well), I drifted to hobby games.[13] My first hobby board game experience was *Pandemic* (2008, Z-Man Games), although I did play a lot of *Catan* (1995, Mayfair). I became interested in games that were based on media texts (what I called paratextual games) and published an academic book called *Game Play* about them in 2015, turning my hobby into part of my career. As I have developed my interest, I have been privileged to be able to afford to buy new games when they come out, to have time to meet my friends (or play solo) some long-form games, and to turn a hobby into part of my academic career, as I am with this book.

I locate this analysis in time because, as I have previously written, "an autoethnographic analysis is always constrained by a particular time and space, the temporal and spatial coordinates in which the researcher has undertaken the research."[14] Staring in 2016–2017, I became more invested in longer-form games like *T.I.M.E. Stories* because I enjoy the expansive narrative and player investment in both character and storytelling, and also in shorter-form games like the *Unlock* or *Exit: The Game* series of escape room games because of the puzzle-solving and intense engagement in the game. (Both of these games reflect in my earlier favorite games, *Clue* and *Trivial Pursuit*, and my love of puzzles.) I enjoy cooperation more than competition; story more than mechanics (although there has to be a great balance between them); strategy more than randomness; socialization more than solitaire gaming; and the physical more than the digital.

Your Board Gaming Style :

Low Conflict, Strategic, Immersed, and Gregarious

Conflict (24%)

Social Fun (82%)

Strategy (72%)

Fantasy (86%)

Your Board Game Motivation Profile consists of your percentile rank across a range of gaming motivations. Your scores are based on how strong your motivations are relative to other gamers. In this personalized report, we'll explain how to

Figure 9.1 My board game motivation profile. Quantric foundry.

In 2018, I took a survey from the Quantric Foundry that claimed to be able to tell me my "Board Games Motivation Profile."* It found that I heavily prefer social fun, fantasy, and strategy to conflict in my games, a profile termed "Low Conflict, Strategic, Immersed, and Gregarious" (adjectives that pretty accurately describe me as well) (Figure 9.1).

In 2017, I bought *Gloomhaven* as it reflected everything I learned I liked about board games.

Autoethnography

This discourse about myself is not, itself, an autoethnography; it is, instead, a critical autobiography. In the autoethnography that follows, however, I have applied this critical autobiography to the details of my own participation with *Gloomhaven*. Writing critical autobiography allows me as an autoethnographer to "construct . . . a certain sense of self" that necessarily impacts the way I read my own experiences.[15] As a methodology, autoethnography emerged in the 1990s as a way of writing outside traditional academic discourses; it is deliberately and authoritatively counter to mainstream academic thought. Post-structuralist, postmodern, and feminist writers used autoethnography to challenge standard academic orthodoxy: "Scholars became increasingly troubled by social science's ontological, epistemological, and axiological limitations."[16] These limitations include a rejection of the idea that every analysis can be objective or that ethnography is without bias. Autoethnography represents a discourse of acceptable subjectivity, acknowledged bias, and meaningful emotion. Indeed, autoethnography is deliberately feminized research (which may be why it has been criticized in the past, as I discuss later in this chapter[17]). According to Stacy Holman Jones, Tony Adams, and Carolyn Ellis:

> Traditional research often adheres to hegemonically masculine traits, particularly objectivity, control, and predictability. Other traits, such as subjectivity, uncertainty, and emotions, are often gendered as feminine and, consequently, considered inadequate, insufficient, and irrational.[18]

---

* https://apps.quanticfoundry.com/surveys/start/tabletop/

In academic discourse, as with mainstream society, the feminized tends to be marginalized. Yet these discourses are crucial for understanding people's everyday reactions to popular culture texts. We respond both rationally *and* emotionally, and to ignore affective engagement risks misrepresenting the human experience. In this, autoethnography is one of the few methodologies "that acknowledges and accommodates subjectivity, emotionality, and the researcher's influence on research, rather than hiding from these matters or assuming they don't exist."[19] Along these lines, autoethnography allows for a greater variety of voices to be heard by "engaging readers in first person accounts of experiences that are different, marginalized, or ignored."[20] Thus, autoethnography is not an appropriate method for attempting to engage in *objective* research; by design it is not intended to be considered outside the realm of human subjectivity.

The style of autoethnography that I practice follows my "personal experiences and perspectives."[21] In addition, it makes use of "thick description," a term popularized by researcher Clifford Geertz as a way of describing cultural experiences in richly detailed ways.[22] Norman Denzin expands on this definition, arguing that

> a thick description . . . does more than record what a person is doing. It goes beyond mere fact and surface appearances. It presents detail, context, emotion, and the webs of social relationships that join persons to one another. Thick description evokes emotionality and self-feelings. It inserts history into experience. It establishes the significance of an experience, or the sequence of events, for the person or persons in question. In thick description, the voices, feelings, actions, and meanings of interacting individuals are heard.[23]

In other words, thick description expands on the details of an experience to establish a connection to the larger cultural meaning of that experience. Autoethnography has been applied to game research in the past, most notably to video game scholarship,[24] although Graeme Lachance's master's thesis focused on his own autoethnography of game-mastering an RPG, and Moyra Turkington's "A Look Back from the Future" explored Live Action Role Play through an autoethnographic lens.[25] Jimmie Manning and Tony E. Adams have discussed the method as "valid, viable, and vital method for popular culture research," but even with the aforementioned exception of Lachance and Turkington, there have been very few autoethnographies of analog games and even fewer on board games specifically.[26]

Autoethnographies of *Gloomhaven*

Isaac Childres's game *Gloomhaven*, as I've noted, is expansive. As I've been playing the game for almost two years, I have built up a sizeable history in the storyworld of this game. In order to begin my autoethnography, I need to revisit my time with the game, both through tangible elements, like the gameboard, the scenario book, character sheets, the more than 1,500 cards and 18 characters,[*] as well as my own memories of playing the game. Part of the thick description I have of *Gloomhaven* thus depends on how I *remember* the experience of playing, which affects my sense of the game experience: as Grace Giorgia notes, "When writing through memory we find and create meanings and experiences of ourselves and others. . . . Writing from memory, we memorialize the past and present, creating new spaces for community and collective memory."[27] Memory is mutable, and thus my recollections are not always as exact as I may like. Yet, memory is also meaningful in its own absences—"One remembers best what is colored by emotion"—and *how* we remember can affect *what* we remember.[28] In order to organize my memories of *Gloomhaven*, some of which come straight from what I remember while others are recorded from writings I did while I played, I want to highlight my connection to the game via some of the methodologies discussed in this book. As a player, I found myself reflecting on many of the issues that I've mentioned so far; here, I want to explore some of these connections more deeply.

Gloomhaven is played over a number of linked scenarios, by characters who persist across each of them, changing and developing as they earn more experience. The map of a scenario is represented by a number of differently shaped tiles, each linked together to form a room; within the room exist any number of obstacles, enemies, traps, treasure chests, and loot. There is a goal in each scenario—for instance, in the first scenario, "Black Barrow," the goal is to kill all the enemies (in that scenario, the enemies are bandits and living skeletons, but throughout the game there are many other types of enemies: imps, demons, ooze, etc.). The game is scalable, which means the higher the level of the character you're playing, the more difficult the enemies become; the difficulty also grows depending on the number of characters playing in the game, so if there are only two characters, fewer enemies will be present on the board. Each

---

[*] The game starts with seventeen but can be expanded with one additional one, as I detail in the conclusion.

character has a deck of cards which gives them certain abilities. On a turn, a player plays two cards for each character, giving them two actions, which can be things like moving, attacking, healing, generating magical elements, or looting treasure chests. At the beginning of the game, characters start at level 1, meaning they can only use their level 1 actions, but as they level up, they have access to higher level cards and better actions (more strength, faster speed, etc.). However, players must choose which cards to add when a character levels up—there are more cards than can be added to the deck, so players have a choice of additional abilities. Further, players can use the money the character loots in the game to purchase permanent card upgrades to change the basic attributes of some cards. As the characters journey through different scenarios, they encounter different levels of narrative, from the individual scenario narrative (enter a room, kill a bad guy) to the campaign narrative (one of the first campaigns is to rid the town of the Gloom which has been infesting it) to the larger game narrative (how the town of Gloomhaven changes over time, as represented by stickers on a game board), to a meta-narrative (clues at various points within the game hint toward a larger out-of-game experience that I discuss in the conclusion).

Gloomhaven is designed to be played with one to four players; if playing with two to four, each player controls one character. If playing solo, then the one player controls multiple characters, but the difficulty level of the monsters increases. In solo mode, I started playing with two at once, but as I continued I ended up playing three characters simultaneously in order to open up more and more of the boxes and play the unique missions more quickly.

Playing a board game solo may appear odd. Studies on gaming find that most gamers are social, and board gamers even more so.[29] We perceive the activity of board gaming to be social even though many experiences reveal the unique pleasures of solo gaming. Yet, there are other media texts that are often experienced by oneself, and it isn't viewed oddly: we read books by ourselves, do crossword puzzles by ourselves, watch television by ourselves, even see films by ourselves (especially streaming). As George Elias, Richard Garfield, and K. Robert Gutschera identify, we even label games that are experienced solo differently—we call them puzzles.[30] Of course, anyone can do these activities with others, but it's not expected that one *must* do them alone.

There are many reasons why people might want to play solo. Perhaps players don't have a steady gaming group, but want to explore more games. It could be that a game like *Gloomhaven*, which is complex and time consuming (and space consuming), isn't feasible for the regular group play. Or perhaps there is a particular type of game that a group of friends doesn't like—in my case, my regular playing partner was playing *Gloomhaven* with his family and they wanted to work on the campaign together. I also wanted to get through the game/narrative more quickly than any of my friends/family did. In a 2017 quantitative study, Nick Yee found that solo gamers preferred playing games that were a lot like literature or film, games with

> a rich theme (whether horror, high fantasy, or island survival) with high production values in terms of the artwork and components. They allow a gamer to take on a believable role—typically a named character with a background story and unique set of skills—in a richly-detailed alternate world.[31]

In other words, *Gloomhaven*. In my survey, I found that 12.5 percent of players play games solo.

In my experiences, *Gloomhaven* plays well as a solo experience. Of course, playing solo contradicts my own Board Games Motivation profile, which noted that I preferred socialization and cooperative games to competitive, fighting games like *Gloomhaven*. And this is true—my favorite game experiences have involved moments of cooperative triumph of a brutal game system. I enjoy the elation of a group of players after successful communication has led to a well-thought-out plan. But playing *Gloomhaven* solo had its own pleasures, separate from the socialization I prefer. The scenarios become less about group communication/coordination and more about precisely what Elias, Garfield, and Gutschera identify: puzzle-solving.[32] As I play, I think, *what is the best way for me to utilize the unique attributes of my three characters in order to accomplish the next task?* not, *how can I work with others to accomplish this goal?* I view the game less as a play session and more as a chance to deepen my own knowledge of/enjoyment of the world I'm cocreating. Each scenario is a conundrum, and a chance to prove to myself that I have the necessary skills to complete it. Playing cooperatively can sometimes mean that one player dominates the conversation—often a player with more experience with the game world or system. Playing solo affirms my own abilities, as I win or lose depending on my own choices. There is no safety net, no other party to appease.

The style of play that I engage in with *Gloomhaven* reflects aspects of my ideology—perhaps some that I would prefer it not to. For example, it did not escape my attention that I began to play *Gloomhaven* solo at a time when I was going through a divorce. The game became practice for a solo future. Additionally, in my professional life, I prefer to write solo. I enjoy the comradery of colleagues but also revel in the individual feeling of achievement one can get from working on something alone. Analyzing my play of *Gloomhaven* reveals an underlying ideology of individualism that permeates my life and reflects the supremely Western characteristics of self-reliance and egoism—both aspects of my personality that stem from my cultural positionality.

An autoethnography of my experiences with *Gloomhaven* reveals the cultural limitations on board games and board gaming as a hobby: looked at through this lens, board games are specifically designed for *my* identity, within the sense of cultural privilege that I have. Given the lack of inclusion in board game culture that I revealed in Chapter 8, a game like *Gloomhaven* may not be as readily embraced by others, given the diversity of players in the hobby. As I've shown, there is a dependence on a number of cultural factors—price and game footprint, an implicit understanding of race and genre, a rhetorical focus on conclusive narratives—that complicate any cultural reading of the game. Being steeped in cultural privilege allows me easier access to these factors (That's not to say one without as much privilege can't access them, but rather it might be a harder journey to do so.) My autoethnography reveals, perhaps, that *Gloomhaven* is a game steeped in privilege; and the fact that it is still the number one game on BoardGameGeek speaks volumes about the makeup of the board game community. Board gaming is a privilege; it is an aspect of cultural privilege; it thrives because of privileged voices, classes, and interactions.

From a *ludo-textual* perspective, the range of characters in the game reveals an underlying assumption of abilities. As a fan of Tolkienesque stories of alterative lands peopled with various races, I come to *Gloomhaven* with familiarity to the basic structure of the characters. In the world of *Gloomhaven*, different species populate the landscape, and have different characteristics that help shape their play style (this is in addition to the multiple monsters that are simply anonymous, nonpersonified creatures). Like Tolkien's Middle Earth, which formed the structure of much of the *Dungeons & Dragons* landscape as well, each of these races has a particular expertise that determines a particular play style. For example, the Inox are "a primitive and barbaric race" that "lack in intelligence and sophistication . . . [but] make up for [it] with their superior strength and size, always eager to prove themselves in a challenge."[33] The Inox characters are the Brute and the Berserker, both large characters who move slowly but have great strength and superior hand-to-hand combat skills. As stated on the *Gloomhaven* website, the Brute is "very good at running around and murdering stuff. He's a Brute. That's what he does."* In contrast, the Quatryl are of a "diminutive size" and have an "affinity to engineering and machinery. Their long, delicate fingers allow them to build all manner of intricate contraptions to make life easier and augment their inferior physical strength."[34] The two Quatryl characters in the game are the "Tinkerer," who is adept at creating and using tools like flamethrowers, nets, and mines, and the "Soothesinger," who can play music to encourage/support others in the party. Altogether, there are nine playable "races" with key attributes in the base game of *Gloomhaven*—the Inox, the Quatryl, the Savvas (elemental), the Aesther (magical), the Valrath (rageful), the Orchid (meddling), the Harrowers (pestilential), the Vermling (scavenging), and Human (average, of course). Gamers familiar with traditional role-playing games may find some similarities between the different races and the characteristics they signify. As a player familiar with these sorts of experiences, when I started playing *Gloomhaven*, I was immediately attracted to two different races—the Tinkerers (possibly because I identified with their puzzle-solving/intelligent attributes) and the Savvas (control over the elements is just mystical enough to be interesting but not as fantastical as pure magical control). My first two characters were the Savvas Cragheart and the Quatryl Tinkerer.

Of course, as demonstrated by Dimitra Fimi, JRR Tolkien's work liberally makes use of "race" as a determinist factor in the particular characteristics of a type of person: for instance, the Orcs "undoubtedly have racial characteristics which are problematic: we never get a detailed description in the text, but recurring traits include slanted eyes and swarthy complexions. These elements sound straight out of Victorian anthropology, linking mental qualities and physique."[35] Taking this argument even further, one might simply note that determining *any* characteristics as part of a race—whether they are physical or not—is inherently problematic, as it equates biological attributes with cultural qualities.[36] I don't think Childres is deliberately setting out to make an ideological racial statement, but as a game that actively calls back to the genre antecedents of Tolkien, *Dungeons & Dragons*, and other role-playing games, *Gloomhaven* can't help but be caught up in the same dynamics that undergird the politics of race in other games.† Using *thick description* here highlights how the game connects to cultural issues.

---

* http://www.cephalofair.com/2015/04/gloomhaven-experience.html
† In *Gloomhaven*, for example, Childres does specifically call these categories "races" (see http://www.cephalofair.com/races-gloomhaven) instead of, say, "species."

As a liberal, pluralistic educator who values diversity and highlights systemic issues like racism in my classes as well as in my public and private life, the problematic racial elements of *Gloomhaven should* have bothered me. But the truth is, I didn't even acknowledge or think about this issue until my research started for this chapter on autoethnography. Partly, this is because of my own privilege to have my race and racial characteristics go unacknowledged; through no action on my part, I am not forced to confront race (I have the privilege to acknowledge race on my own time). But partly it's because my own interest in the narrative of *Gloomhaven*—and fantasy series in general like *Lord of the Rings*—overwhelms any particular focus on the characters. I enjoyed playing some characters more than others, but I am not as thoughtful or careful about my character development as some other players may be. For instance, I'm sure there's a way to figure out which cards would work best for particular maneuvers for the Brute or the Tinkerer, but I didn't study all the cards to choose which ones might work well for a particular race. I made some choices and simply played them as well as I could; I was more invested in the larger narrative than in trying to match the playable attributes of the characters. The emphasis on narrative happened as well because I was playing the game solo. Because I controlled multiple characters, I could mix-and-match the play strategy without having to communicate with someone else. Thus, I didn't have to rely on assumed characteristics (e.g., the Brute is strong) and could play with the specific cards in my hand.

From a rhetorical perspective, the *interactive potentiality* of the campaigns presented arguments about the different decisions I made as a player, both because they created "branching narratives" that developed in contradictory ways depending on my decisions, but also because any decision is (relatively) permanent in the game. This makes adventuring through the game of *Gloomhaven* a maze of possibilities that develops the world in specific ways. As an argument of interactive potentiality, it relies on the players' own actions to complete the rhetorical move and highlights the importance of strategy.

After beating any particular scenario, the players might be rewarded in a number of ways. The particular mechanic of a "reward" makes the player want to complete the scenario; a reward can work as a rhetorical argument for how a game is "supposed" to proceed. One reward is that new locations may become available, allowing the narrative of the game to be a "progressive revelation."[37] For a player like myself, invested in narrative development, this is the most exciting reward and the one I was most interested in following. For instance, after winning "Black Barrow," I was rewarded with opening up a new location—"Barrow Lair"—as well as an achievement for my party. This meant that on the giant board/map of *Gloomhaven*, I could place a sticker over Location 2, permanently affixing the location in my game, and that I could then visit that location (you cannot visit a location that hasn't been "unlocked" yet). In the "Barrow Lair," the goal was to defeat the Bandit commander and all the enemies that were revealed in the scenario. Upon completing this challenge, two new locations were opened—"Inox Encampment" and "Crypt of the Damned." Thus, the first narrative decision point opened up. Other rewards could include additional experience, additional loot, unlocking new items, increased experience points, and more.

The narrative of scenario 2, as detailed in *Gloomhaven*'s scenario book, gives a hint as to the type of story that might develop. Upon beating any scenario, a "conclusion" is read. This mirrors the type of "paragraph-based game" popular in the 1980s that included numbered paragraphs that described adventures in the storyworld. The stories in *Gloomhaven*'s scenarios provide information to deepen the storyworld and offer textual clues about the development of the narrative. In Barrow's Lair, the choice is stark:

> Shifting through the carnage left by the battle, you find a cache at the back of the room containing the scrolls you were hired to collect. . . . A bend in the Still River is clearly marked as a point of interest. Contemplating whether you want to find out more about this so-called "Gloom," you decide that the spot could be a point of interest for you, as well. [Location 4]. . . . But that can be forgotten for the moment. You pack up the papers and head back to Gloomhaven to collect your reward. Meeting Jekserah once again . . . you hand over the papers and are paid . . . [she says] "If you're interested, I may have another job for you. A tribe of Inox in the Dagger Forest has ransacked a couple of my caravans headed to the capital. . . . She places a crude map of the forest on the table and stands up, her jewelry clinking with the movement. "Come find me when it is done." [Location 3].[38]

Do we pursue the Gloom at Location 4? Or do we continue the life of the mercenary by hunting the Inox at Location 3? Each decision will lead us down a path that expands further and further.

There are other attributes of these decisions that my own experiences helped shape. For instance, because of my cultural background as an American, steeped (and academically trained to examine) popular culture, I find myself culturally predetermined to find narrative closure an important characteristic of media texts. I tend to expect my stories to have satisfying endings. In *Gloomhaven*, this comes to the fore because each character has a private "personal quest," which might be to kill a particular number of enemies (fifteen forest imps), to complete a particular number of scenarios in a forest, to have a particular number of items, or many others. If one is playing as their character, as the game encourages players to do, then the personal quest can guide the narrative, again creating an interactive potentiality.[39] My cultural background encouraged me to want to see my characters complete their personal quests. My first character, "Grundy" the Savvas Cragheart, had a personal quest to avenge its family,* who were killed by the forest-dwelling Orchids, by completing three scenarios in Dagger Forest. This meant that Grundy wanted to go to the forest. As it happens, my other character, Trixie the Quatryl Tinkerer, had a personal quest to complete fifteen scenarios (she wanted to see more of the world to satiate her curiosity). The choice was clear: we went to Location 3, to Dagger Forest, and did not explore the Gloom narrative. From the Inox Encampment, we then went to the Diamond Mine, then back to Gloomhaven Square, as we learned that the person sending us on these "errands," Jekserah, was actually a necromancer!

From a *ludic discourse* perspective, I was encouraged to advance through a particular route because of game mechanics and theme. Because of the permanent changes to the game state—stickers on the board, scenarios being played, bosses defeated—some scenarios become mutually exclusive (if one strictly played by the rules, which as I detail in the conclusion, I did not). I could not play the Diamond Mine *and* the Gloomhaven Warehouse, because the narrative conditions dictated the development of my particular game state. Additionally, if I had instead decided to ally myself with Jekserah and kill the Gloomhaven guards, I would have changed the "global achievement" of the game—an attribute of the game that can change the underlying political situation. In this case, I would have moved from the Militaristic Rule to an Economic Rule; this forced me to note whether I cared about the underlying political system of the world I was cocreating (given this choice, I would choose a system based on economic rule over militaristic, but this binary choice also erased other systems of rule that could have been present in the game, but weren't—democratic rule, socialist rule, totalitarian rule, and so on—that I might have preferred ideologically). Discursively, the game wanted me to create a system of governance over *Gloomhaven* through a forced choice.

---

* All Savvas are genderless

From an industrial standpoint, *Gloomhaven's* designer, Isaac Childres, could be considered a *créateur*. Childres has made two other games that both fit into the *Gloomhaven* world: *Founders of Gloomhaven* (2018, Cephalofair) and *Gloomhaven: Jaws of the Lion* (2020, Cephalofair). Both games take place *before* the original game, building up a narrative world. A fourth game set in the *Gloomhaven* world, *Frosthaven*, is set to be released in 2021. When compared to his other work (including his first game, *Forge War* [2015, Cephalofair]), all his games could be described as heavy gaming, with lots of decision making, open-ended outcomes, and intensely strategic thought.

Further, this autoethnography articulates how my financial privilege permits me to enjoy games with this much *stuff*. There is much to *Gloomhaven*, and Childres has noted in an interview how much he included in the game.[40] As Arnaudo notes, the "material nature of analog board games can contribute to make their content particularly vivid."[41] From an industrial standpoint, this enhances the appeal of the game. *Gloomhaven* is undeniably vivid, from the eighteen detailed plastic miniatures (which many players paint), to the artwork on the board, cards, and player sheets, to the thirty different map tiles, to the comprehensive scenario guides. All these elements, all twenty-two pounds worth of them, cost a lot of money, and while they enhance my pleasure of playing the game, I am also aware that that is a pleasure enabled by my position in life.

However, the digital has shaped my understanding of the material too. My first experience with *Gloomhaven* wasn't with the physical components; it was with the Kickstarter crowdfunding of the game. After I received *Gloomhaven*, I have been eyeing the purchase of additional material elements that individuals have made and sell on sites like eBay. Instead of using tokens to represent trees, for instance, I could purchase a three-dimensional (3D), painted plastic tree for $20. These material elements have been 3D printed by the seller, further enhancing the connection between the digital and the material. (If I had a 3D printer, I would probably print my own copies; I don't, so I consider buying them instead.)

From a *fan studies* standpoint, and by playing the game in solo mode, I participated in all three ways that connect fans to gaming: knowledge acquisition, affective play, and identification role-play. Most directly, I had to learn a huge amount about *Gloomhaven* to play, including detailed rules like which hero a monster might attack first, or whether a flying monster can land on a pillar. I also had extreme affective engagement with the game—as I describe in the following text, as I continued to play, I grew closer and closer to particular characters;

I also loathed some of the different monsters that would appear. Further, my knowledge of the game became immense and after a few plays I could stop referencing the rule book. In addition, my familiarity with fantasy and science fiction literature, film, and television made me aware of many elements that I could role-play in the game. One particular example stands out to me: the noble sacrifice. In much fantasy literature, the noble sacrifice is when a hero bravely dies (or suffers close to death) in order that his (and it's almost always "his") friends survive. Think, Gandalf in *The Lord of the Rings*, Obi-Wan Kenobi in *Star Wars*, Spock in *Star Trek II*, and so on.

Thick description of one of my early scenario plays of *Gloomhaven* reveals the connections to these three elements of fandom. We were reaching the end of the level and my two characters were struggling. It was Scenario 44, "Tribal Assault," and Grundy the Cragheart and Trixie the Trickster, would both complete their personal quests on this mission (it was Grundy's third mission in Dagger Forest and Trixie's fifteenth mission overall). In Tribal Assault, the culmination of a number of linked scenarios, the party has been joined by a new, temporary character, Redthorn, who is attempting to free his enslaved brethren from the Inox. The goal of this particular scenario is to kill all the enemies while also releasing all the slaves. We made it through the forest and found our way to the last room where, upon opening the door, an Elite Inox Shaman and an Inox warrior stood guard over the last two remaining Orchid captives. In what could only be described as a heroic effort, Grundy led the charge. He dealt damage after damage to this Inox Shaman, but the warrior fought back. If Grundy drew a powerful modifier card—the chances were slim, though—he would defeat them both.

Assuming Grundy would not draw the needed card, I knew what had to be done. He bravely moved himself between the enemies and the captive slaves, using his body as a shield to protect the innocents from the slaughter. His health at zero, he breathed his last breath, in my mind whispering to Trixie, "avenge me." And in her next turn, she did. With a frontal assault and one point of health left, she used her Net Shooter to attack and defeat both enemies at once. Both Grundy and Trixie fulfilled their personal goals, and two new characters were unlocked in the game: the Orchid Doomstalker and Aester Nightshrowd. The battle won, and the slaves freed, a personally and culturally satisfying narrative. In honor of the warriors, I recorded their last battle (see Figure 9.2).

As a fan of this story, I was able to make the game fit into the mold of my personal narrative. Although the ending could have gone any other way—I'm

Figure 9.2 Trixie and Grundy after their victory.

sure I could have won even if I hadn't "sacrificed" the Cragheart—it provided a more fulfilling narrative journey for me, especially as I had started to identify with these characters. As Jenny Sundén has described, one can relate emotionally to characters within a game.[42] I, too, had built up a connection between myself and these characters during the fourteen previous scenarios; I knew what their abilities were and I knew how they worked together. They are still my favorites. Games can "come to life" when "it possible to establish a deep connection with the theme and the characters in the game."[43] I felt like my characters were an extension of myself in this game world, and in playing them, in a way, *Gloomhaven* was also playing me. As an autoethnographer, I need to ask, "What can I learn about [my] self? Autoethnography can be turned back onto the research subject reflexively in order to examine the self who is doing the autoethnography."[44] Who I am is revealed through my autoethnography. I had become caught up in this world; I was starting to tell my friends stories about the adventures these characters were having as if they were adventures I was having. In taking a step back, in examining my experience through the autoethnographic lens, I can detail the different ways that *Gloomhaven* matched my personal and my cultural expectations, desires, and actions.

Conclusion: The Haven of *Gloomhaven*

Writing this autoethnography has told me things about myself. But, if I'm being completely honest, I haven't been completely honest. I cheated at *Gloomhaven*. At times I would grant myself a mulligan on a card draw, or I'd shift a character an extra space if it would make a more satisfying narrative. This type of interactive potentiality reflects on my own desire to get to the end of a narrative or to learn everything about a topic, I am impatient. Reflecting on my own play styles as I have written this chapter has made me resent some of the cultural elements that have encouraged me to seek out instant gratification. I try to resist this impulse, but I find myself getting frustrated with the longer temporality of meta-game puzzle-solving. I am on the tail end of the millennial generation, am used to being able to look up information on the internet since I was in high school, and have had a cell phone for my entire adult life. The world of information is available to me and I want it now, resulting in a conflict between the more traditional play style of board gaming and the instantaneousness of digital gratification.* If I had been playing with a group, I may not have cheated as quickly as I did; by myself, I valued the narrative more than the game. Does this make me a bad gamer? A poor sport? Certainly, an advantage of playing solo means that I didn't have to ask anyone's permission to cheat; but it also meant I wasn't accountable to anyone too. (And I justified by saying that it made a more enjoyable experience anyway.)

But writing this autoethnography has also revealed things about board games, and the board gaming hobby, as it is situated with my cultural milieu.

Throughout this book, in fact, we could look at the different games I've played and analyzed through this autoethnographic lens. I've generally focused on board games with narratives, board games with larger footprints, board games with many components and pieces, board games that take multiple hours to play. The games I've chosen fit into a general category of complex, hobby games. These choices reflect a particular emphasis within the board game hobby that not everyone may subscribe to. That most of these games are so highly ranked on BGG, that many of them are bestsellers in the game industry, that many of them are talked about online, means that the whole board game system is rigged toward a particular

---

* That being said, there is still one envelope I haven't opened yet. I need to find five ancient technologies before I can, and I've only found four so far. My rule breaking seems limited to the meta game, as I still play *Gloomhaven*, searching for that missing artifact.

player identity, a particular ideological viewpoint. Autoethnography can reveal that bias in the self, and it can also reveal it in the industry.

Earlier in the chapter I noted that autoethnography can enable unrepresented voices to be heard; and as someone whose voice is almost *always* represented, perhaps autoethnography isn't the most appropriate methodology for *my* study of board games. If anything, my autoethnography of *Gloomhaven* illustrates how someone who fits into the idealized mold of the board game player would read a game designed specifically for them. Those with different vantage points within and outside of contemporary board game culture may read the game differently. Thus, the true power of autoethnography emerges when multiple viewpoints on the same topic can be articulated. My journey through *Gloomhaven* is direct and unencumbered; perhaps yours will reveal a differently nuanced reading.

Like the other methodologies in this book, autoethnography is not without its own biases and assumptions. By eliding other experiences, I have presented just my own version of *Gloomhaven* as a stand-in for the universal. As a player with cultural privilege, this can be damaging for scholarship, as it risks reifying cultural hierarchies like masculinity and whiteness at the expense of a diversity of experiences. Additionally, my own perspective is of course colored by my self-awareness: by definition, I am only aware of the things I am aware of. What cultural biases am I not aware that I have? As I read back through this chapter, I realize I've left out an important part of my story—I don't have children. Would my experiences of the game be different if it had been family-bonding time rather than solo play? Researchers must be able to self-reflect, to examine who they are within a particular cultural system. Acknowledgment must be made about the lapses that a researcher may have.

Autoethnography also comes with assumptions about the method itself. By definition it is not objective, and thus doesn't meet many qualifications for purely scientific research. As I've pointed out, this also frees the method from being tethered to potential blind spots in the so-called objective research, but autoethnographers must be able to handle the criticism that comes with autoethnography:

> Critics want to hold autoethnography accountable to criteria normally applied to traditional ethnographies or to autobiographical standards of writing. Thus, autoethnography is criticized for either being too artful and not scientific, or too scientific and not sufficiently artful . . . as being insufficiently rigorous, theoretical, and analytical, and too aesthetic, emotional, and therapeutic.[45]

Yet, as Ellis, Adams, and Bochner go on to describe, these criticisms mistakenly position art and science at odds with each other. Autoethnography can be rigorous and analytical *while also being* emotional and self-reflexive.[46] As a "softer" methodology, autoethnography has been perceived as a more feminine style of research.[47] Perhaps the criticisms of autoethnography stem not from the method itself, but from the masculinized standards of "objectivity" in research that autoethnography attempts to correct. I learn much about myself, but I also learn much about the masculinized culture I am part of through my autoethnographic work. My personal valuing of an emotional experience is, perhaps, less important to others within this culture.

What I learned about myself—my privilege, my impatience, my love of narrative develop—stems from my place in my culture and affects my play of *Gloomhaven*. At the same time, *Gloomhaven* itself is culturally determined as well. It plays into the stereotypes of the genre from which it developed. *Gloomhaven* may be a game but it's also a city in a created, fantasy world. Both the game and I are from the same culture; we are both perfectly suited for each other. Autoethnography details this connection as an aspect of self-reflection.

Conclusion

The Board Gaming Environment

What does it mean to study a board game? And, relatedly, what does it mean to open up a box, punch out the components, read the rules, lay out the game, and engage in play? How do we—as scholars, as game players—begin studying something that is more than just a text, something that is an experience? In this book, I've shown that studying board games necessitates understanding multiple experiences of play, as well as developing a critical reading of the components, rules, and production of the game.

But what do we learn when experience itself is examined through media studies lenses? While scholars may argue about whether board games "fit" into media studies or not, I present a study of what we learn if we take that intuitive leap. And I undertake this merely to expand the scope of what media studies can be. Instead of reigning in the field by demarcating strict boundaries around what "counts" as media, we should look at the opportunities that arise for understanding each new invention, new developments in entertainment, and new types of mediation. New (and old) technologies modify and change media in unforeseen ways.

I believe we enrich our work by inviting new forms of media and mediation into the media studies canon. The diverse perspectives that new forms of media bring—however they are being defined—helps us engage in more meaningful scholarship. It results in work that not only explores new frontiers, but also becomes more accessible to those that actually experience that media. Media scholarship becomes legible to media audiences, becoming a space for engaged and meaningful connections with everyday communities. In other words, by opening up what "counts" as media, media scholars can have a stronger and more effective impact while also engaging with and learning from the people that use these new forms every day.

Throughout this book, I've explored different facets of studying board games, and I've presented some ways that the study of board games challenges traditional media studies scholarship to more effectively invoke the impact of the audience/player. We have reached a critical point in the media landscape, where audiences are encouraged to play with the media with which they engage.[1] We are expected to interact with our digital content, to deepen our commitment to what we watch. The media industries want to capture our clicks, to record our responses. The more we interact, the better we are able to demarcate our interests, demographics, and preferences. We become fodder for promotional material. Studying board games gives media scholars a unique insight into the way audiences interact with a text. For even though board games are analog, tactile, and create face-to-face social interaction, they also can represent the way that we respond to our digital media. Board games make physical the mental engagements our media consumption reveals—and make playful our media engagement more generally.

In the first half of the book, I've

- articulated how traditional media studies methodologies—textual, rhetorical, discursive, authorial, and receptive—cannot fully account for the experiential elements of the board game;
- discussed how a *ludo-textual* analysis of the interaction between the board game components and the themes of the game uncover new ideologies of game play;
- analyzed the *interactive potentiality* between strategy and luck in board games as argumentative strategies;
- focused on the *ludic discourses* that emerge from the tension between a game's mechanics and themes as revelatory about larger cultural values;
- developed three ways of examining the *complex authorship* implied in board game discourses; and
- examined the players of board games through a fan studies lens in order to unpack the concept of *ludic fandom*—a new understanding of what play can bring to fan studies.

And in the second half of the book, I've

- used ethnographic methods to explore fundamental questions about who constitutes board gamers and to bring to light diversity issues within the board game industry;
- interviewed and surveyed players, content creators, and game designers to outline who plays board games, why gamers like board games, and different ways the industry can develop as a more socially inclusive hobby; and

- focused on my own game play through an autoethnographic lens to interrogate the cultural aspects that have ideologically affected me, and how that, in turn, affects my game play.

Throughout the book, then, I've shown that board games reveal complex textual and social relationships that challenge traditional media studies methodologies to more fully encompass the interaction between players and the text. At the same time, this means I have remained focused on the board game as a *text*, and have not questioned the larger role of board games in the world. While the board game hobby has seen heavy growth over the past decade and a half, the impact of board gaming has been little discussed, either in this book or in scholarship in general. In this conclusion, then, I want to take a step back from the board game as a text to look more specifically at the effect of board gaming on the world around us.

To this end, I focus on the environmental impact of board gaming in order to illustrate some of the social consequences of the hobby. While it may not be as central a topic in board game studies as other, more thematic or mechanical issues, the environmental concerns of board games represent monumentally and philosophically significant concerns in terms of both the production of board games and opportunities to increase the visibility of the dangers of climate change. In this conclusion, then, I take a cue from Richard Maxwell and Toby Miller's concept of "ecological ethics"—the analysis of "the environmental impact of electronic waste (e-waste) . . . in media and communication studies"—and describe some of the ecological concerns with board games.[2] In their 2012 book *Greening the Media*, Maxwell and Miller unpack the environmental impact of media technologies like cell phones, televisions, and other electronic devices. Their book paints a damning portrait of the hazardous environmental effects of electronic media, and in this conclusion, I want to examine whether board games have the same deleterious effect, even without the electronic components. My goal here is not to provide hard data about the impact that board games have already had (I encourage environmental scientists to take up that mantle), but to develop insights into the way we gamers can mitigate our impact moving forward.

The Environmental Impact of Board Games

Climate change is happening. The overproduction of carbon dioxide is changing weather patterns. Pollution affects drinking water and breathable air. Less regulation of industrial dumping both in the United States and abroad affects the natural development of the landscape and biological growth. There has been a massive reduction in biodiversity due to deforestation (among other reasons). Impending, massive shifts in the environment have already started to affect huge swaths of human and animal populations. Rising temperatures and unstable weather patterns threaten both coastal regions and already-warming landscapes. Mass migration will put a strain on temperate economies and populations.[3]

When board gaming remained a niche hobby, the environmental impact was slim. And it is possible that its impact remains comparatively slim today. But any form of mass production has environmental impacts, and while the game industry may not have as much to contribute to climate change as, say, the automobile industry, it certainly contributes more than any one individual can anticipate.[4] And as board gaming has started to become more popular, it is important to start to think about the ramifications of the hobby in a more sustainable way to try to forestall any major impact. While perhaps board gaming isn't as popular as some other hobbies with even greater impact on the environment, the fact that it is growing more and more popular portends an increase in its role in climate change. Even starting this type of discussion can be difficult. This topic has not been heavily discussed in board game circles or in scholarship about games or media. There are occasional popular press articles and some online threads on BoardGameGeek, but on the whole, few gamers seem to want to think about the environmental impact of gaming. Partly, this is because people are notoriously bad at inferring huge consequences from small actions. If I buy one game, it is hard to see how it might make an impact—it's only one game, after all. In my survey with over 900 board game players, only a few people mentioned the environmental impact of games. One of the few who did write decried

> the use of plastic in games. Most games use cardboard when possible, but with the prevalence of desire for minis, I don't foresee increasing or continuing to use plastic in games as a good thing. With so many environmental issues out there, games using plastic at all, leads to problems. Finding alternative solutions is ideal.

Or, perhaps, as Maxwell and Miller elaborate, we have been conditioned to think of our consumptive behaviors as "a vital source of plenitude and pleasure, the very negation of scarcity."[5] Talking about the environmental impact of gaming is an "unwelcome buzz kill—not a cool way to converse about cool stuff."[6] No one wants to be reminded of climate change when they're sitting down to fight some orcs or take over the galaxy.

This isn't to say that no one is discussing these issues, however. Game designer Gerald King III, in my interview with him, discussed how

> the materials that we use to produce will have to change as well. The sustainability of producing hundreds of thousands of copies of something that will only be used four times? It's disgusting to even consider how many trees it takes to have this hobby, and the fact it's grown to the point where 6000 games a year are being released on the crowdfunding platforms alone.

Indeed, there are significant issues at many stages of board game development and production that have an outsized impact on the environment.

Even starting at the design process, board games have an environmental impact. Many designers today use online tools like boardgamedesignlab.com to begin planning their game on the computer before material production. As Aaron Trammell notes,

> During the prototyping stage, the game's components are often listed and balanced on a set of digital spreadsheets that allow designers a birds-eye view of the design. After this paper-prototyping stage (often mediated through digital design tools such as Adobe Photoshop and InDesign), the game's prototype is remastered through digital tools (almost certainly the Adobe suite again) and sent to a print shop which uses these digital proofs to print the game.[7]

Bringing games to Kickstarter may have revolutionized the industry economically (see Chapter 7), but has also brought more digital elements to gaming. All these electronic offerings rely on digital space like data farms, huge swaths of computer banks built across the world to hold all the world's data. These farms use huge amounts of electricity. According to a 2017 study by *The Guardian*, "The communications industry could use 20% of all the world's electricity by 2025," and while board game design programs certainly can't account for much more than a fraction of that amount, it still has an impact.[8] Data centers that house information—whether from smartphones, computers, or Netflix accounts—are huge endeavors. Just their construction costs around $20 billion a year. They consume as much power as a city of a million people. And they "emit roughly as much CO_2 as the airline industry."[9] Many are built in deserts, which means extra air conditioning is needed, necessitating even more electricity generation.

The physical production of both prototypes (often on paper and discarded when replaced) and finished game products can have an environmental impact. After games are designed, there's often the question of where to actually have the materials made. Constructing the game in China tends to be a cheaper option, although in that sense one is often subsidizing the low-paid wages of overworked employees.[10] In an industry where just a few copies of game might get purchased, however, producing for less helps keep overhead in companies low and profits high. However, China's record of environmental action is woefully inadequate.[11] The facilities that create the game components may not meet the more stringent environment standards that facilities elsewhere might.

The components of a board game also have an environmental impact. Most board games have some combination of cardboard tokens, plastic pieces, cards printed on cardstock, wood meeples, cardboard or plastic trays to hold all the pieces, and thick board for the playing space. In the previous chapter, I described my playthrough of *Gloomhaven*—all twenty-two pounds of it. That weight is generated by a huge amount of cardboard, plastic, and cardstock. The cardboard tokens usually come in large sheets that users can "punch" out—a pleasurable action, to be sure, but one that generates holey waste. Cards are wrapped in plastic cellophane wrap, which gets thrown away upon opening. Even the boxes themselves—often oversized to be visible on gaming store shelves—contain more "excessive packaging" paper products than necessary.[12] Expansions to board games are often no different. I've purchased an expansion for a game where the box was half the size of a regular board game box but contained only one small pack of cards. Card games come in plastic clamshell chases which get discarded upon opening. There is no guarantee that Chinese or American production facilitates are using recycled paper or other products, or that consumers themselves will recycle.

Plastic is often the cheapest way to produce components, but also one of the most wasteful. According to an article in *Tabletop Gaming Magazine*:

> To put it in context, plastics amount to 8% of the world's oil production. That's the same as the entire aviation industry. And plastic production is set to explode exponentially over the next 30 years. The extraction of oil from the ground and seabed has been linked to air pollution, acid rain and human cancer, as well as disrupting animal migratory patterns. . . . Plastic production is set to quadruple by 2050.[13]

All the plastic pieces in board games have become much less expensive to produce, which means more and more plastic production overall. But using wood for meeples instead of plastic may have its own share of environmental hazards. All that wood has to come from somewhere, and deforestation is both changing natural habitats for plant and animal life and reducing the amount of CO_2 that can be converted to oxygen by trees.

All is not so bleak, however, as some game companies are working to change the way games are produced. Blue Ocean, for example, created *Photosynthesis* (2017), a game about the growth of a forest, entirely from recycled materials—from the components to the box. In addition, as King mentions, they "recently signed a commitment to plant two trees in Ecuador's Amazonian rainforest for every one tree used in production. The result? Blue Orange will plant almost 2,400 trees this year."[14] Gamers can support companies like Blue Orange by purchasing their games, and by raising their profile on social media. The new game *Carbon City Zero* (2020, 10:10 Climate Action), designed by researchers Sam Illingworth and Paul Wake, has also been designed to be environmentally friendly. As their Kickstarter page notes:

> We have made every effort to ensure that Carbon City Zero does not have a negative impact on the environment. The game will be printed in the UK by Ivory Graphics, an FSC certified company, who ensure all of their products have the lowest impact on the environment as possible. In order to address the global issue of plastic pollution, this game will be fully reusable, replayable, and recyclable. This means that we will not be using any cello-wrap, and we will be asking gamers to find their own tokens for the carbon tracker (buttons, coins, and broken toys all work well). All copies of the game will be posted using eco-friendly packaging.

What Illingworth and Wake note about packaging reveals another environmental issue: shipping. Especially as many games are produced in China and yet sold around the world, those games have to be physically moved from one location to another. They are packaged in boxes, loaded into cargo containers, shipped on boats across the ocean, and then driven from the landing ports to distribution centers, where they are again shipped to stores or direct to people's homes. Beyond the environmental impact of travel (diesel waste, etc.), all the shipping packaging–plastic bubble wrap, more cardboard, and so on—increases the physical waste of game purchases. While it would be incredibly difficult to find games without shipping, the extreme low cost of Chinese production has only magnified the issue.

The Environmental Discourse of Board Games

If all this seems dire, it doesn't have to be. There are two areas where board gaming can actually start having a positive impact on the environment. One, as I mentioned earlier, are game companies that actively promote their eco-friendly games. The more that companies start to consider the environmental impact of their products, and the more gamers pay attention to—and purchase from— companies that are having a positive impact, the more robust the industry response as a whole can be.

The second positive impact that board games can produce is more pedagogical in nature. Quite simply, board games can help *teach* people about the dangers of climate change.[15] Games have always had a pedagogical bent. In *Analog Game Studies*, Antonnet Johnson cites historian Bruce Whitehill's discussion of *The Mansion of Happiness* (1843): "American board games were once designed as tools intended to teach players (usually children) how to live in the world, and have only recently become reframed as mere leisure activities characterized by play and fun."[16] While I'm certainly not advocating for a return to the moralizing strictures of those older games, I do believe that game play can be a space for meaningful, informal learning. As I have discussed in the first half of this book, board games have the potential to focus player's concerns on particular discourses, ideologies, or beliefs. And at the same time, the second half of this book demonstrated that board games offer a "safe space to have meaningful dialogue" between players.[17] Quite literally, board games can affect what people think about the world around them. Sam Illingworth and Paul Wake discuss the impact games can have on discussions about climate change, arguing that they are an ideal medium for discussion.[18] In addition to their *Carbon City Zero*, Illingworth and Wake have also been instrumental in triumphing games that depict or develop ludic discourses of environmental concern. Their print-and- play expansion for *Catan* (*Catan: Global Warming*) offers players a "unique scenario that focuses attention on the complex interplay of individual and collection actions in the process of global warming."[19] Of note, in the expansion, global warming isn't attributed to just one or two "bad guys," but rather becomes emblematic of systemic issues—issues that require systemic change. By invoking player investment in the outcome of the game, the ludic discourse of *Catan: Global Warming* articulates a meaningful experience where individual players are interpellated into environmental agency.

Games that promote biology, biodiversity, and environmentalism can help teach players about the fragile nature of their environment, and they don't have to be didactic. Blue Ocean's *Photosynthesis* isn't a treatise about environmentalism, but simply shows the beauty and importance of trees. Games like *Evolution* (2014, North Star Games) show how species can change over time, and

Evolution: Climate (2016, North Star Games), the impact of a changing climate on species' development. The game CO_2 (2012, Giochix.it) places players in the role of CEO of an energy company which has to try to meet the rising demand for sustainable energy.

In fact, the media have often been the voice of change. Sean Cubitt notes that television and film often create "popular mediations of frequently voiced concerns" like environmental activism.[20] Films about climate change can have "a significant impact on the climate change risk perceptions, conceptual models, behavioral intensions, policy priorities, and even voting intentions of moviegoers."[21] In his study, Anthony Leiserowitz surveyed viewers of the film *Day After Tomorrow* and found that the film

> led moviegoers to have higher levels of concern and worry about global warming, to estimate various impacts on the United States as more likely, and to shift their conceptual understanding of the climate system. . . . Further, the movie encouraged watchers to engage in personal, political, and social action to address climate change and to elevate global warming as a national priority.[22]

Television shows like *Blue Planet II* have been shown to change consumer attitudes toward plastic.[23] And celebrities of film, television, and other media can also "amplify" the public's understanding of environmental issues, although this can also become a detriment if the celebrity's persona changes.[24]

Of course, it's also important to remember that board games are the paradigm reusable resource. Once purchased, many games remain in play in households for years; one doesn't buy a new copy every time they want to play. (Does everyone have a closet at their parent's house where a dusty copy of *Yahtzee* (Milton Bradley, 1956) sits?). At the same time, the advent of "one-play only" games like *Exit: The Game* (Kosmos, 2016) or *Unlock* (Asmodee, 2017)—Exit Room games that are meant to be played only once—or even Legacy games that can only be played a set number of times complicate this reusability. For example, *Exit: The Game* often involves cutting up components, ripping up instruction booklets, or otherwise destroying aspects of the game, making replayability impossible. A player's only choice upon finishing the sixty- to ninety-minute game is to throw it away. And although the box itself might be recyclable, the plastic-coated cards and other errata in the box usually aren't recyclable at all. They just become landfill.

Ultimately, board gaming is still a small enough community that if there were a concerted effort to change the design, production, distribution, or sales processes to make it more environmentally sound, it wouldn't take long before the whole industry changed. Companies like Blue Ocean are already getting there. The first step is not being afraid to talk about the problems and issues. Find out if your favorite companies are outsourcing their production to China; ask whether their components come from recycled products or not. Once the board gaming community sets its mind to solving a problem, there's no stopping them. Because solving problems is exactly what we've been practicing this whole time.

Conclusion

I've focused in this short conclusion on the ecological impact of board gaming because it illustrates one of the key tenets of the book—that board games offer media studies scholars a new way of examining some fundamental insights into contemporary life. An ecological ethics analysis of board games is important not just because of what it tells us about the board gaming hobby, but also because it is so rarely done in *any* media studies scholarship. Simply put, it has rarely been a concern for media scholars. Framing board games through this study reveals its absence in other media scholarship; it emphasizes aspects of the media that have long been ignored.

If board games are a form of media, as I've been arguing, then by understanding the way individuals directly interact with and affect the changing state of the board game offers new perspectives on the assumptions of interactivity given to all new media. Audiences have always been interactive with their media; studying board games just makes it explicit. Playing a game allows us to become cocreators of the individual moments along the way. We imbibe the game, take it into our selves, and, in doing so, we change it as much as it changes us.

I started this project because I was curious about why board games had seemingly become much more popular; because I was seeing more and more hobby board games on the shelves of my local Target; because I was going to bars and cafes and seeing people play games. My students were playing games and I was curious about what they were learning. What I discovered in the process of research and writing it is that the world of board gaming is so much richer and more varied than what people normally think about. It's a way to bring families together, to meet new people, or to spend time with old friends. It's a social activity on the rise during a time when social media, cell phones, and other technology commands more of our daily attention than ever before. It's tactile in a digital world; it requires patience in a time of hyper-immediacy. Board games teach us how to think, how to interact, and how to deal with loss. They show us how to laugh at our own failings and show compassion to those who are struggling.

I'm not saying board games are a panacea to all that ails us. But in that magical moment when a roll of the dice goes the way you want, when you draw that card you needed to score, when your best-laid plans come to fruition, it certainly does feel that way. There's a reason there have been board games for as long as there has been human civilization. They are a part of us, and they reflect us. So let's play.

Appendix 1

Survey Questions

Section 1: History with board games

1. Do you identify as a board gamer?
2. How long have you been playing hobby board games?
   a. Less than a year
   b. 1–3 years
   c. 3–6 years
   d. 6–10 years
   e. 10–15 years
   f. 15+ years

3. What game got you into board gaming?
4. What are your favorite games?
   a. Why?

5. How often do you play board games?
   a. Every day
   b. A few times a week
   c. Once a week
   d. A few times a month
   e. Once a month
   f. Less than once a month

6. How often do you purchase a board game?
   a. Every day
   b. A few times a week
   c. Once a week
   d. A few times a month
   e. Once a month
   f. Less than once a month
   g. Never (I don't buy board games)

7. I'm curious to know why people like to play board games. Please tell me a bit about what motivates you to play board games?

Section 2: Relationship with games

8. How do you play or participate games? (check all that apply)
   a. Play solo
   b. Play with the same group of people at irregular times
   c. Have a regular game play session
   d. Have joined a group and attend sporadically
   e. Have joined a group and attend regularly
   f. Attend convention(s) about board gaming
   g. Create games
   h. Teach games (explain what you mean)
   i. Other (fill in the blank)

9. Do you mostly play with the same people or different people?
10. If you could imagine a "best" or ideal experience playing games, what would it look like?

Section 3: Social aspects of games

11. In general, how much do you like or dislike teaching board games to others?
    a. 1= most dislike, 5 = most like

12. When you're playing a game you've played before, how do you feel about playing with people who haven't played before?
    a. 1= most dislike, 5 = most like
    b. Is there anything you'd like to add to elaborate on the previous question?

13. Tell me a little bit about the board game club(s) that you are part of (logic question)
14. If you are part of a group, did you start the group or join one? (logic question)

Section 4: Opinions about gaming

15. How well do you learn games depending on the method? (Not very well to very well)
    a. Reading the rules
    b. Watching gameplay videos
    c. Being taught by someone who knows how to play
    d. Figuring it out with others
    e. Are there other ways you learn games not listed above?

16. Do you like board games that use digital apps? Why or why not?

17. Do you agree or disagree with the following statements?
    a. One of my favorite parts of a game is its table presence (figures, dice, board)
    b. One of my favorite parts of a game is its art
    c. One of my favorite parts of a game is learning the rules
    d. One of my favorite parts of a game is winning (or completing the game successfully)
    e. One of my favorite parts of a game is beating others
    f. One of my favorite parts of a game is learning the strategy
    g. One of my favorite parts of a game is luck
    h. One of my favorite parts of a game is socialization
    i. One of my favorite parts of a game is its fun flavor text
    j. Other

18. What style of game do you prefer? (check as many as apply)
    a. Eurogame
    b. Ameri-game
    c. Deck builder
    d. RPG
    e. Wargame
    f. Living or collectible card game
    g. Party game
    h. Abstract
    i. Cooperative
    j. Other

19. What mechanism of gameplay do you prefer? (check all that apply)
    a. Roll and Move
    b. Worker Placement
    c. Cooperative
    d. Deck Building
    e. Area Control
    f. Secret Identity/Social deduction
    g. Legacy
    h. Puzzle
    i. Combat Dice Rolling
    j. Press Your Luck
    k. Auctions
    l. Trick Taking
    m. Roll/Flip and Write
    n. Card/Die Drafting
    o. Other

20. Of one of those that you selected, what do you find compelling about that mechanism?
21. Why do you think board games are becoming more popular?

Section 5: Demographics

22. Demographic questions
    a. Age
    b. Gender
    c. Racial/ethnicity (categories)
    d. Country of residence

Follow-up Interview Questions

1. What are some issues you see with the board game industry today? How could we fix them?
2. Can you talk a little bit about how the board game industry does or does not have issues with diversity and inclusion?

3. Can you talk a little bit about how the board game hobby does or does not have issues with diversity and inclusion?
4. In what ways do you think board games reflect aspects of our culture?
5. Is there anything else you want to add?

Appendix 2

Data from Survey

Do you identify as a board gamer?

Answer	%	Count
Definitely yes	84.49	752
Probably yes	12.13	108
Might or might not	1.80	16
Probably not	1.01	9
Definitely not	0.56	5
Total	100	890

What age are you?

Answer	%	Count
18–24	4.17	34
25–34	29.94	244
35–44	40.74	332
45–54	20.74	169
55–64	3.80	31
65–74	0.61	5
75–84	0.00	0
85 or older	0.00	0
Total	100	815

What gender do you identify with?

Answer	%	Count
Male	69.16	563
Female	27.27	222
Nonbinary	2.21	18
Queer	0.49	4
Other	0.86	7
Total	100	814

What is your race/ethnicity?

Answer	%	Count
White	89.03	722
Black or African American	1.23	10
American Indian or Alaska Native	0.25	2
Asian	3.82	31
Native Hawaiian or Pacific Islander	0.25	2
Other	5.43	44
Total	100	811

What country are you from?

Country	Count
Africa	1
America	1
Australia	17
Belgium	1
Brazil	3
Canada	59
Catalonia	1
Croatia	1
Czech Republic	1
Denmark	1
England	15
Europe	1
Finland	3
France	2
Germany	17
Greece	1
India	1
Ireland	4
Israel	1
Italy	1
Japan	1
Malaysia	5
Mexico	2
The Netherlands	4
New Zealand	11
North Macedonia	1
Norway	2
Poland	2
Romania	1
Scotland	1
South Africa	1

(*Continued*)

Country	Count
Spain	5
Sweden	2
Switzerland	3
The Netherlands	2
Turkey	1
The United Kingdom	94
The United States	530
United Kingdom /United States	1
Wales	1

How long have you been playing hobby board games?

Answer	%	Count
Less than a year	0.34	3
1–3 years	8.77	78
3–6 years	23.06	205
6–10 years	18.90	168
10–15 years	13.16	117
15+	35.77	318
Total	100	889

How often do you play board games?

Answer	%	Count
Daily	4.20	37
A few times a week	38.14	336
Once a week	22.36	197
A few times a month	25.09	221
Once a month	6.47	57
Less often than once a month	3.75	33
Total	100	881

How do you play or participate with games?

Answer	%	Count
Play solo	12.56	367
Play with the same group of people at irregular times	24.33	711
Have a regular game play session	13.00	380
Have joined a group and attend sporadically	6.30	184
Have joined a group and attend regularly	6.81	199
Attend convention(s) about board gaming	14.92	436
Create games	6.33	185
Teach games	11.94	349
Other	3.80	111
Total	100	2922

Do you mostly play with the same people or different people?

Answer	%	Count
Same	70.44	603
Different	2.34	20
I play with both groups about equally	27.22	233
Total	100	856

In general, how much do you like or dislike teaching board games to others?

Answer	%	Count
Like a great deal	33.41	285
Like somewhat	41.03	350
Neither like nor dislike	16.76	143
Dislike somewhat	7.50	64
Dislike a great deal	1.29	11
Total	100	853

When you're playing a game you've played before, how do you feel about playing with people who haven't played before?

Answer	%	Count
Like a great deal	26.35	225
Like somewhat	36.18	309
Neither like nor dislike	33.61	287
Dislike somewhat	3.75	32
Dislike a great deal	0.12	1
Total	100	854

Do you like board games that use digital apps?

Answer	%	Count
Like a great deal	16.27	131
Like somewhat	28.94	233
Neither like nor dislike	29.81	240
Dislike somewhat	16.77	135
Dislike a great deal	8.20	66
Total	100	805

What style of game do you prefer?

Answer	%	Count
Eurogame	17.48	644
Ameri-game (Ameri-trash)	10.01	369
Deck building	13.19	486
RPG	10.12	373
War game	4.83	178
Living or collectible card game	4.99	184
Party game	10.88	401
Abstract game	9.77	360
Cooperative game	15.98	589
Other	2.74	101
Total	100	3685

What mechanism of game play do you prefer?

Answer	%	Count
Roll and move	3.79	190
Worker placement	12.75	639
Cooperation	10.74	538
Deck building	10.22	512
Area control	8.46	424
Secret identity/social deduction	5.93	297
Legacy	6.33	317
Puzzle	7.74	388
Combat die rolling	4.63	232
Press your luck	6.13	307
Auctions	4.31	216
Trick tacking[taking]	3.61	181
Roll/flip and write	4.55	228
Card/die drafting	9.06	454
Other	1.74	87
Total	100	5010

How well do you learn games depending on the method?

Question	Extremely well (%)	#	Very well (%)	#	Moderately well (%)	#	Slightly well (%)	#	Not well at all (%)	#	Total
Reading the rules by yourself	24.52	205	32.66	273	32.06	268	7.66	64	3.11	26	836
Reading the rules with others	8.29	69	29.81	248	38.22	318	15.02	125	8.65	72	832
Watching game play videos	28.09	232	36.32	300	23.00	190	7.87	65	4.72	39	826
Being taught by someone who knows how to play	44.26	370	38.40	321	14.47	121	2.63	22	0.24	2	836
Figuring it out with others	13.34	111	31.61	263	34.25	285	15.02	125	5.77	48	832
Are there other ways you learn games not listed above?	25.49	26	30.39	31	26.47	27	4.90	5	12.75	13	102

Do you agree or disagree with the following statements?

Question	Strongly agree (%)	#	Somewhat agree (%)	#	Neither agree nor disagree (%)	#	Somewhat disagree (%)	#	Strongly disagree (%)	#	Total
One of my favorite parts of a game is its table presence (figures, dice, board)	40.21	337	45.47	381	10.38	87	2.74	23	1.19	10	838
One of my favorite parts of a game is its art	35.73	298	47.00	392	12.35	103	4.20	35	0.72	6	834
One of my favorite parts of a game is learning the rules	7.41	62	24.37	204	34.05	285	26.05	218	8.12	68	837
One of my favorite parts of a game is winning	6.34	53	26.79	224	29.67	248	23.80	199	13.40	112	836
One of my favorite parts of the game is completing it successfully	32.70	274	48.45	406	14.08	118	2.98	25	1.79	15	838
One of my favorite parts of a game is beating others	4.18	35	16.71	140	26.97	226	25.66	215	26.49	222	838
One of my favorite parts of a game is learning the strategy	46.66	391	39.98	335	9.31	78	3.10	26	0.95	8	838
One of my favorite parts of a game is luck	2.15	18	13.84	116	32.22	270	34.01	285	17.78	149	838
One of my favorite parts of a game is socializing	62.01	519	29.39	246	6.21	52	1.79	15	0.60	5	837
One of my favorite parts of a game is fun flavor text	13.43	112	36.57	305	29.50	246	15.47	129	5.04	42	834
Other	62.10	77	10.48	13	18.55	23	4.03	5	4.84	6	124

What game got you into gaming?

Game	Count
(Settlers of) Catan	132
Ticket to Ride	42
Monopoly	39
Carcassonne	35
Pandemic	35
Risk	31
Dominion	19
Betrayal at House on the Hill	18
Dungeons and Dragons	18
Magic the Gathering	18
Munchkin	17
Axis & Allies	11
Chess	11
Agricola	9
Arkham Horror	9
7 Wonders	8
Clue/Cluedo	8
Stratego	8
TableTop (Geek & Sundry show)	8
Cosmic Encounter	7
Hero Quest	7
Careers	6
King of Tokyo	6
Puerto Rico	6
Talisman	6
Acquire	5
Battlestar Galactica	5
Forbidden Island	5
Small World	5
Candyland	4
Diplomacy	4
Eldritch Horror	4
Last Night on Earth	4
Parcheesi	4
Robo Rally	4
Warhammer	4
Citadels	3
Civilization 1e	3
Harry Potter Hogwarts battle	3
HeroScape	3
Legendary	3
Life	3
Lords of Waterdeep	3
Mastermind	3

(Continued)

Game	Count
Pandemic Legacy	3
Scotland Yard	3
Scrabble	3
Shadows Over Camelot	3
Stone Age	3
Trivia Pursuit	3
Ascension	2
Battle of the Bulge	2
Battle Tech	2
Blokus	2
Cards against Humanity	2
Codenames	2
Coup	2
Dark Tower	2
Exploding Kittens	2
Fluxx	2
Game of Thrones 2e	2
Hotels	2
Kill Doctor Lucky	2
Lord of the Rings CCG	2
Lost Cities	2
Luftwaffe	2
Mouse Trap	2
Outdoor Survival	2
Power Grid	2
Qwirkle	2
Rail Baron	2
Risk 2210	2
Risk Legacy	2
Shogun (A.k.a. Samurai Swords)	2
Shoots & Ladders	2
The Lord of the Rings	2
The Omega Virus	2
Tigris & Euphrates	2
Zombies!!!	2
52-game chest	1
Above and Below	1
Advanced Civilization	1
Alhambra	1
Apples to apples	1
Balderdash	1
Bang!	1
Battleship	1
Bermuda Triangle	1
Bohnanza	1
Buccaneer	1

Game	Count
By Jove	1
Cacao	1
Car Wars	1
Carrom	1
Castle Ravenloft D&D	1
Caverna	1
Caylus	1
Cesar and Cleopatra	1
Champions of Midgard	1
Clank	1
Concept	1
Condottiere	1
Cranium	1
Cyclades	1
Dawn Patrol	1
Dead of Winter	1
Drakon	1
Dungeon!	1
Eclipse	1
Elder Sign	1
Empire Builder	1
Epic Spell Wars	1
Escape from Colditz	1
Escape From The Valley of The Dinosaurs	1
EVO	1
Evolution	1
Finca	1
Flash Point: Fire Rescue	1
Formula 1	1
Ghost Castle	1
Gloom	1
Good Cop Bad Cop	1
Guess Who	1
Guillotine	1
Hare and Tortoise	1
Heimlich & Co	1
Hunters and Gatherers	1
Illuminati	1
Imperial Assault	1
In the Year of the Dragon	1
Jyhad Card Game (later changed to Vampire: The Eternal Struggle)	1
Kingdoms	1
Kingmaker, Avalon Hill Bookshelf Edition	1

(Continued)

Game	Count
Knights of Charlemagne	1
Le Nain Jaune	1
Legend of Zagor	1
Legends of Andor	1
Lord of the Rings LCG	1
Mage Knight	1
Magic Realms	1
Marvel Munchkin	1
Memoir 44	1
Metro	1
Midnight Party	1
Military History	1
Mississippi Queen	1
Mr. Jack Pocket	1
Mühle (like Nine Men's Morris)	1
Myretuen	1
Mysteries of Old Peking	1
Operation	1
Othello	1
Palladium Fantasy RPG	1
Panzer, Yaquinto Publishing, 1979	1
Patchwork	1
Pictionary	1
Pillars of the Earth	1
Pokemon Monopoly	1
Primordial Soup	1
Quelf	1
Railway Rivals	1
Rat Race	1
Ricochet Robots	1
Risk: Star Wars Original Triology	1
Rivet Wars	1
Rogue Trooper	1
Russian Railroads	1
Scene It	1
Secret Hitler	1
(Settlers of) Catan Junior	1
Seven Wonders	1
Shut Up and Sit Down	1
Silverton	1
Skull	1
Solar Trader	1
Sorry	1
Space Alert	1
Spirit Island	1
Squad Leader	1

Game	Count
Star Wars Armada	1
Star Wars X-Wing	1
Starfarers of Catan	1
Starquest	1
Stranger on a Plane	1
Strategy & Tactics	1
Stratomatic Hockey/Baseball	1
Supremacy	1
Survive: Escape from Atlantis	1
Sushi Go	1
Tactics II	1
Takenoko	1
Terra Mystica	1
Texas Hold 'em	1
The Duke	1
The Hobbit Boardgame	1
The Resistance	1
Thirteen Dead End Drive	1
Thunderstone	1
Thurns and Taxis	1
Ticket to Ride Europe	1
Titan	1
Tobago	1
Tokaido	1
Tripoly	1
Trouble	1
TSR Dungeon! 1983	1
Twilight Imperium	1
Twilight Struggle	1
Ursuppe	1
Warhammer quest advanced	1
Wild Life	1
Wizard's Quest	1
Wooden Ships and Iron Men	1
World in Flames	1
World of Warcraft Board Games (FFG)	1
World of Warcraft Trading Card Game	1
Zombicide	1
Zombicide: Black Plague	1

Notes

Introduction

1 Clara Fernández-Vara, *Introduction to Game Analysis* (New York: Routledge, 2019), 5.
2 Frans Mäyrä, *An Introduction to Game Studies* (London, UK: Sage, 2008), xii.
3 Sonja Sapach, "Let's Play with Research Methodologies," *First Person Scholar* (2018), http://www.firstpersonscholar.com/lets-play-with-research-methodo logies/3.
4 Fernández-Vara, *Introduction*, 26, emphasis mine.
5 Petri Lankoski and Staffan Björk, eds., *Game Research Methods* (Pittsburgh, PA: ETC Press, 2015).
6 Katie Salen and Eric Zimmerman, *Rules of Play* (Cambridge, MA: MIT Press, 2004), 310.
7 E.g., Marco Arnaudo, *Storytelling in the Modern Board Game* (Jefferson, NC: McFarland, 2018); Paul Booth, *Game Play* (New York: Bloomsbury, 2015); Paul Booth, "Board, Game, and Media: Interactive Board Games as Multimedia Convergence," *Convergence* 22, no. 6 (2016): 647–60; Adam Brown and Deb Waterhouse-Watson, "Reconfiguring Narrative in Contemporary Board Games: Story-Making Across the Competitive-Cooperative Spectrum," *Intensities* 7, no. 1 (2014): 5–19, https://intensitiescultmedia.files.wordpress.com/2014/08/2-b rown-and-waterhouse-watson-reconfiguring-narrative-pp-5-19.pdf; Irving Finkel, *Ancient Board Games in Perspective* (London: British Museum Press, 2007); Bethan Jones and Wickham Clayton, "Introduction to the Special Issue: The Transmedia Relationship Between Film/TV Texts and Board Games," *Intensities* 7, no. 1 (2014): 1–4, https://intensitiescultmedia.files.wordpress.com/2014/08/1-jones-and-clayto n-editors-introduction-pp-1-41.pdf; Mary Pilon, *The Monopolists* (New York: Bloomsbury, 2015); Stewart Woods, *Eurogames* (Jefferson, NC: McFarland, 2012).
8 E.g., Klaus Eisenack, "A Climate Change Board Game for Interdisciplinary Communication and Education," *Simulation and Gaming* 44, no. 2–3 (2013): 328–48; Ted Friedman, "The Play Paradigm: What Media Studies Can Learn from Game Studies," *Flow TV* (2008), http://www.flowjournal.org/2008/12/the-play-paradi gm-what-media-studies-can-learn-from-game-studies-ted-friedman-georgia-stat e-university/; Jones and Clayton, "Introduction"; Jeanne V. Russell, "Using Games to Teach Chemistry: An Annotated Bibliography," *Journal of Chemical Education*

76, no. 4 (1999): 481–8; Tara Whalen, "Playing Well with Others: Applying Board Game Design to Tabletop Display Interfaces," in *ACM Symposium on User Interface Software and Technology, vol. 5* (New York: ACM Press, 2003).

9 Woods, *Eurogames,* 46.

10 Woods, *Eurogames,* 79.

11 Stefen Fatsis, *Word Freak* (New York, Penguin, 2002); Philip Orbanes, *Monopoly* (Philadelphia: DeCapo Press, 2007); Pilon, *The Monopolists.*

12 Booth, *Game Play.*

13 Dinish Vatvani, "An Analysis of Board Games: Part I—Introduction and General Trends," March 5, 2018, https://dvatvani.github.io/BGG-Analysis-Part-1.html#BGG -Analysis-Part-1.

14 Maria Cassano, "The 10 Best Strategy Board Games for Adults," *Bustle,* January 2019, https://www.bustle.com/p/the-10-best-strategy-board-games-for-adults-1 5561360.

15 Shephali Bhatt, "How India Caught on the New-Age Board Game Culture of the West to Create an Ecosystem of Cafes & Communities Back Home," *The Economic Times,* June 30, 2019, https://economictimes.indiatimes.com/news/ politics-and-nation/how-india-caught-on-the-new-age-board-game-culture-of -the-west-to-create-an-ecosystem-of-cafes-communities-back-home/articleshow /70005721.cms.

16 Charlie Hall, "Tabletop Games Dominated Kickstarter in 2018, While Video Games Declined," *Polygon,* January 15, 2019, https://www.polygon.com/2019/1/15/181841 08/kickstarter-2018-stats-tabletop-video-games.

17 Espen Aarseth, "Just Games," *Game Studies* 17, no. 1 (2017): 1, http://gamestudies.o rg/1701/articles/justgames.

18 Booth, *Game Play,* 2.

19 Markku Eskelinen, "Explorations in Game Ecology, Part 1," *Jahrbuch für Computerphilologie* 7 (2005): 93.

20 Greg Costikyan and Drew Davidson, *Tabletop: Analog Game Design* (Pittsburgh, PA: ETC Press, 2011); Salen and Zimmerman, *Rules of Play.*

21 Woods, *Eurogames,* 8; see Mäyrä, *An Introduction,* for an example.

22 Espen Aaresth, "The Game and Its Name: What Is a Game Autuer," in *Visual Authorship,* ed. Torben Grodal, Bente Larsen, and Iben Thorving Laursen (Denmark: Narayana Press, 2004), 261.

23 See Toby Miller and Marwan M. Kraidy, *Global Media Studies* (Cambridge, UK: Polity Press, 2016), 4.

24 Julian McDougall, *Media Studies: The Basics* (London: Routledge, 2012), 5.

25 Miller and Kraidy, *Global Media Studies,* 9.

26 Arnaudo, *Storytelling,* 22.

27 Jaako Stenros and Annika Waern, "Games as Activity: Correcting the Digital Fallacy," in *Videogame Studies*, ed. Monica Evans (Oxford: Interdisciplinary Press, 2011), 1.

28 Stenros and Waern, "Games as Activity," 1, emphasis theirs.

29 Stenros and Waern, "Games as Activity," 5.

30 Stenros and Waern, "Games as Activity," 2.

31 See Tanya Pobuda, "Assessing Gender and Racial Representation in the Board Game Industry," *Analog Game Studies* 5, no. 4 (2018), http://analoggamestudies. org/2018/12/assessing-gender-and-racial-representation-in-top-rated-boardga megeek-games/.

Chapter 1

1 George Skaff Elias, Richard Garfield, and K. Robert Gutschera, *Characteristics of Games* (Cambridge, MA: MIT Press, 2012), 1.

2 Salen and Zimmerman, *Rules of Play*, 255.

3 Petri Lankoski and Staffan Björk, "Formal Analysis of Gameplay," in *Game Research Methods*, ed. Petri Lankoski and Staffan Björk (Philadelphia, PA: ETC Press, 2015), 23.

4 Mattia Thibault, "Notes on the Narratological Approach to Board Game," *KOME— An International Journal of Pure Communication Inquiry* 4, no. 2 (2016): 79.

5 Lankoski and Björk, "Formal Analysis," 23.

6 Alan McKee, *Textual Analysis* (London: Sage, 2003), 4.

7 Lankoski and Björk, "Formal Analysis," 24.

8 Fernándaz-Vara, *Introduction*, 17.

9 Fernándaz-Vara, *Introduction*, 18.

10 McKee, *Textual Analysis*, 18.

11 McKee, *Textual Analysis*, 1.

12 Arnaudo, *Storytelling*, 27.

13 Arnaudo, *Storytelling*, 21.

14 Arnaudo, *Storytelling*, 30.

15 Aki Järvinen, *Games Without Frontiers* (Saarbrücken: Verlag Dr. Müller, 2009); see also Woods, *Eurogames*, 80.

16 McKee, *Textual Analysis*, 100.

17 Ian Bogost, "The Rhetoric of Video Games," in *The Ecology of Games: Connecting Youth, Games, and Learning*, ed. Katie Salen (Cambridge, MA: The MIT Press, 2008), 119.

18 Woods, *Eurogames*, 105.

19 Jonathan Ray Lee, "Capitalism and Unfairness in Catan: Oil Springs," *Analog Game Studies* 4, no. 2 (2017), ¶1, http://analoggamestudies.org/2017/03/capitalism-and-unfairness-in-catan-oil-springs/.

20 Jonathan Walton, "Governmentality and Freedom in Pay Day and 14 Days," *Analog Game Studies* 5, no. 3 (2018), ¶1, http://analoggamestudies.org/2018/09/governmentality-and-freedom-in-pay-day-and-14-days/.

21 Will Robinson, "Orientalism and Abstraction in Eurogames," *Analog Game Studies* 1, no. 5 (2014), http://analoggamestudies.org/2014/12/orientalism-and-abstraction-in-eurogames/; Pobuda, "Assessing."

22 Karen Hellekson, *The Alternate History* (Kent, OH: Kent State University Press, 2001), 2.

23 Hellekson, *Alternate History*, 4–5.

24 Matt Hills, "Time, Possible Worlds, and Counterfactuals," in *The Routledge Companion to Science Fiction*, ed. Mark Bould, Andrew Butler, Adam Roberts, and Sherryl Vint (London: Routledge, 2009), 435–7.

25 Arnaudo, *Storytelling*, 34.

26 Christopher Allen and Shannon Appelcline, *Meeples Together* (US: Amazon Kindle, 2018).

27 Salen and Zimmerman, *Rules of Play*, 255.

28 Allen and Appelcline, *Meeples Together*.

29 Matt Leacock, Foreword to *Meeples Together* by Christopher Allen and Shannon Appelcline (US: Amazon Kindle, 2018), loc. 151.

30 Arnaudo, *Storytelling*, 41.

31 Allen and Appelcline, *Meeples Together*, loc. 1924.

32 Allen and Appelcline, *Meeples Together*, loc. 419.

33 Bogost, "Rhetoric," 119.

34 Matt Leacock, "No Single Player Can Win This Board Game. It's Called Pandemic," *New York Times*, March 25, 2020, https://www.nytimes.com/2020/03/25/opinion/pandemic-game-covid.html.

Chapter 2

1 Bogost, "Rhetoric," 119.

2 Booth, *Game Play*, 179.

3 Frank D'Angelo, "The Rhetoric of Intertextuality," *Rhetoric Review* 29, no. 1 (2009): 32.

4 Clarke Rountree and John Rountree, "Burke's Pentad as a Guide for Symbol-Using Citizens," *Studies in Philosophy and Education* 34, no. 4 (2015): 349–62.

5 Booth, *Game Play*, 179.

6 Kenneth Burke, *A Grammar of Motives* (Berkeley, CA: University of California Press, 1945).

7 Rountree and Rountree, "Burke's Pentad," 349.

8 Bogost, "Rhetoric," 119.

9 Bogost, *Persuasive Games*, 2.

10 Bogost, *Persuasive Games*, 3.

11 Bogost, *Persuasive Games*, 241–2.

12 Bogost, *Persuasive Games*, 10.

13 Burke, *Grammar*, xix.

14 Tom Grimwood, "Procedural Monsters: Rhetoric, Commonplace and 'Heroic Madness' in Video Games," *Journal for Cultural Research* 22, no. 3 (2018): 310–24.

15 Dean Takahashi, "Brenda Romero's Train Board Game Will Make You Ponder," May 11, 2013, *Venture Beat*, https://venturebeat.com/2013/05/11/brenda-romero-train-board-game-holocaust/.

16 See Takahashi, "Brenda Romero."

17 Mary Flanagan, *Critical Play* (Cambridge, MA: MIT Press, 2009), 13.

18 Flanagan, *Critical Play*, 6; Evan Torner, Aaron Trammell, and Emma Waldron, "Reinventing Analog Game Studies," *Analog Game Studies* 1, no. 1 (2014), http://analoggamestudies.org/2014/08/reinventing-analog-game-studies/.

19 Roger Caillois, *Man, Play and Games*, trans. Meye Barash (Urbana, IL: University of Illinois Press, 1961); see also Woods, *Eurogames*, 111–13.

20 Woods, *Eurogames*, 153.

21 Elias, Garfield, and Gutschera, *Characteristics*, 139; Woods, *Eurogames*, 111.

22 Elias, Garfield, and Gutschera, *Characteristics*, 139.

23 Arnaudo, *Storytelling*, 35.

24 Elias, Garfield, and Gutschera, *Characteristics*, 150.

25 Elias, Garfield, and Gutschera, *Characteristics*, 140.

26 See John Kaufeld, "Randomness, Player Choice, and Player Experience," in *Tabletop*, ed. Greg Costikyan and Drew Davidson (Pittsburgh, PA: ETC Press, 2011).

27 Arnaudo, *Storytelling*, 120.

28 Evan Torner, "Uncertainty in Analog Role-Playing Games, Part 1," *Analog Game Studies* 1, no. 1 (2014), http://analoggamestudies.org/2014/08/uncertainty-in-analog-role-playing-games-part-1/.

29 Woods, *Eurogames*, 84.

30 Woods, *Eurogames*, 107–8.

31 Pat Harrigan and Matthew Kirschenbaum, ed., *Zones of Control* (Cambridge, MA: MIT Press, 2016).

32 Greg Loring-Albright, "Can Friendship Be Stronger Than War? Mechanics of Trauma in The Grizzled," *Analog Game Studies* 4, no. 1 (2017), http://analoggamestudies.org/2017/01/mechanics-of-trauma-in-the-grizzled/.

33 Loring-Albright, "Can Friendship."

34 Arnaudo, *Storytelling*, 29.

35 Booth, *Game Play*, 68.

36 Elias, Garfield, and Gutschera, *Characteristics*, 155.

37 Greg Costikyan, *Uncertainty in Games* (Cambridge, MA: MIT Press, 2013), 2.

38 Costikyan, *Uncertainty*, 9–10.

39 Elias, Garfield, and Gutschera, *Characteristics*, 142.

40 Arnaudo, *Storytelling*, 25.

41 Costikyan, *Uncertainty*, 84.

42 Elias, Garfield, and Gutschera, *Characteristics*, 144, emphasis mine.

43 Elias, Garfield, and Gutschera, *Characteristics*, 145.

44 William Benoit, "On Aristotle's Example," *Philosophy and Rhetoric* 20, no. 4 (1987): 264.

45 Barry Atkins and Tanya Krzywinska, "Introduction," in *Videogame, Player, Text*, ed. Barry Atkins and Tanya Krzywinska (Manchester: Manchester University Press 2007), 5, cited in Grimwood, "Procedural," 313.

Chapter 3

1   Arthur Asa Berger, *Applied Discourse Analysis* (London: Palgrave Pivot, 2017), 4.

2   Teun Van Dijk, *Discourse and Communication* (Berlin: Walter de Gruyter, 1985), 2; Berger, *Applied Discourse Analysis*.

3   David Machin and Andrea Mayr, *How to Do Critical Discourse Analysis* (Thousand Oaks, CA: Sage, 2012), 1.

4   James Paul Gee, *An Introduction to Discourse Analysis*, 3rd ed. (New York: Routledge, 2011), 3.

5   Matt Forbeck, "Metaphor vs. Mechanics: Don't Fight the Fusion," in *The Kobold Guide to Board Game Design*, ed. Mike Selinker (Kirkland, WA: Open Design, 2011), 19.

6   Nelson Phillips and Cynthia Hardy, "What Is Discourse Analysis?" in *Discourse Analysis*, ed. Nelson Phillips and Cynthia Hardy (Thousand Oaks, CA: Sage, 2002), 6.

7   Margaret Adolphus, "How to . . . Use Discourse Analysis," Emerald Publishing, n.d., http://www.emeraldgrouppublishing.com/research/guides/methods/discourse_ana lysis.htm.

8   Gee, *An Introduction*, 2.

9   Rodney H. Jones, Alice Chik, and Chrisoph A. Hafner, "Introduction: Discourse Analysis and Digital Practices," in *Discourse and Digital Practices*, ed. Rodney H. Jones, Alice Chik, and Christoph A. Hafner (London: Routledge, 2015), 1.

10 Gee, *An Introduction*, 38.

11 Sonia Fizek, "Pivoting the Player: A Methodological Toolkit for Player Character Research in Offline Role-Playing Games," PhD Bangor University, 2012, https://rk e.abertay.ac.uk/ws/portalfiles/portal/15206754/Pivoting_the_Player_Fizek.pdf, 201.

12 Hans-Joachim Backe, "Within the Mainstream: An Ecocritical Framework for Digital Game History," *Ecozon@* 8, no. 2 (2017), https://core.ac.uk/download/pdf/156888970.pdf.

13 Pieter Wouters, Herre van Oostendorp, Rudy Boonekamp, and Erik van der Spek, "The Role of Game Discourse Analysis and Curiosity in Creating Engaging and Effective Serious Games by Implementing a Back Story and Foreshadowing," *Interacting with Computers* 23, no. 4 (2011): 329–36.

14 James Paul Gee, "Discourse Analysis of Games," in *Discourse and Digital Practices*, ed. Rodney H. Jones, Alice Chik, and Christoph A. Hafner (London: Routledge, 2015), 20.

15 Michel Foucault, *Discipline and Punish*, trans. Alan Sheridan (Harmondsworth: Penguin, 1974), 102.

16 Mel Stanfill, *Exploiting Fandom* (Iowa City, IA: University of Iowa Press, 2019), 7.

17 James Paul Gee, *How to Do Discourse Analysis* (New York: Routledge, 2011), 199.

18 Gee, *How to Do*, 202.

19 Woods, *Eurogames*, 104.

20 Forbeck, "Metaphor," 22.

21 Woods, *Eurogames*, 105.

22 Greg Aleknevicus, "German Games are Fraudulent," *The Games Journal*, 2004, http://www.thegamesjournal.com/articles/Fraudulent.shtml; quoted in Woods, *Eurogames*, 106.

23 Booth, *Game Play*.

24 Elias, Garfield, and Gutschera, *Characteristics*, 212.

25 Elias, Garfield, and Gutschera, *Characteristics*, 213.

26 Elias, Garfield, and Gutschera, *Characteristics*, 215.

27 Salen and Zimmerman, *Rules of Play*, 317.

28 Woods, *Eurogames*, 95.

29 Teun A. Van Dijk, "Principles of Critical Discourse Analysis," *Discourse and Society* 4, no. 2 (1993): 249–50.

30 Elisabeth Zerofsky, "Is Poland Retreating from Democracy?" *The New Yorker*, July 23, 2018, https://www.newyorker.com/magazine/2018/07/30/is-poland-retreating-from-democracy.

31 Forbeck, "Metaphor," 23.

Chapter 4

1 Michel de Certeau, *The Practice of Everyday Life*, trans. Steven Randall (Berkeley, CA: University of California Press, 1984), 169.

2 Colin Burnett, "Hidden Hands at Work: Authorship, the Intentional Flux, and the Dynamics of Collaboration," in *A Companion to Media Authorship*, ed. Jonathan Gray and Derek Johnson (Malden, MA: Wiley & Sons, 2013), 128.

3 Brown and Waterhouse-Watson, "Reconfiguring Narrative," 7.

4 Vicki Mayer, Miranda J. Banks, and John T. Caldwell, "Introduction: Production Studies: Roots and Routes," in *Production Studies*, ed. Vicki Mayer, Miranda J. Banks, and John T. Caldwell (New York: Routledge, 2009), 5.

5 John Thornton Caldwell, *Production Culture* (Durham, NC: Duke University Press, 2008), 345.

6 Jennifer Holt and Alisa Perren, "Introduction: Does the World Really Need One More Field of Study?" in *Media Industries: History, Theory, and Method*, ed. Jennifer Holt and Alisa Perren (Malden, MA: Wiley-Blackwell, 2009), 2.

7 Michele Hilmes, "Nailing Mercury: The Problem of Media Industry Historiography," in *Media Industries*, ed. Jennifer Holt and Alisa Perren (Malden, MA: Wiley-Blackwell, 2009), 22, my emphasis.

8 Holt and Perren, "Introduction," 10, emphasis in original.

9 Mayer, Banks, and Caldwell, "Introduction," 4.

10 Andrew Sarris, "Notes on the Auteur Theory in 1962," *Film Culture* 27 (Winter 1962): 6–17, reprinted in *Theories of Authorship*, ed. John Caughie (London: Routledge, 2013), 61–5.

11 Hilmes, "Nailing Mercury," 26.

12 Caldwell, *Production.*

13 Espen Aarseth, "The Game and Its Name: What Is a Game Auteur," in *Visual Authorship*, ed. Torben Grodal, Bente Larsen, and Iben Thorving Laursen (Denmark: Narayana Press, 2004), 261.

14 Stephanie Jennings, "Co-Creation and the Distributed Authorship of Video Games," in *Examining the Evolution of Gaming and Its Impact on Social, Cultural, and Political Perspectives*, ed. Keri Duncan Valentin and Lucas John Jensen (Hershey, PA: IGI Global, 2016), 124.

15 Stuart Hall, "Encoding and Decoding in the Television Discourse," paper for the Council of Europe Colloquy on "Training in the Critical Heading of Televisual Language," organized by the Council & the Centre for Mass Communication Research, University of Leicester, 1973, September, https://core.ac.uk/download/pdf/81670115.pdf.

16 Janet Murray, *Hamlet on the Holodeck* (Cambridge, MA: MIT Press, 1997), 152–3.

17 Murray, *Hamlet,* 153.

18 Aarseth, "The Game and Its Name," 264, 267.

19 Bogost, *Persuasive Games.*

20 Michael Mateas and Andrew Stern, "Procedural Authorship: A Case-Study of the Interactive Drama Façade," in *Digital Arts and Culture*, Copenhagen, Denmark,

2005, http://citeseerx.ist.psu.edu/viewdoc/download?doi=10.1.1.567.1894&rep= rep1&type=pdf, 1.

21 Souvik Mukherjee, *Video Games and Storytelling* (Houndsmills, UK: Palgrave, 2015), 140.

22 Arnaudo, *Storytelling,* 166–7.

23 Ryan Laukat, interview with author, Skype, 2019.

24 Mark J. P. Wolf, *Building Imaginary Worlds* (New York: Routledge, 2012), 2.

25 Caldwell, *Production,* 199.

26 Jan Švelch, "Regarding Board Game Errata," *Analog Game Studies* 1, no. 5 (2014), http://analoggamestudies.org/2014/12/regarding-board-game-errata/.

27 Adam Arvidsson, *Brands* (London: Routledge, 2006), 3.

28 See Celia Lury, *Brands* (London: Routledge, 2004), 1.

29 See Zoe Fraade-Blanar and Aaron M. Glazer, *Superfandom* (New York: Norton, 2017).

30 Sarah Banet-Weiser, *Authentic TM* (New York: New York University Press, 2012), 3.

31 Emma Pett, "'Stay Disconnected': Eventising *Star Wars* for Transmedia Audiences," *Participations* 13, no. 1 (2016): 165, https://www.participations.org/Volume%2013/ Issue%201/S1/2.pdf.

32 Banet-Weiser, *Authentic TM*, 5.

33 Thomas Schatz, "Film Industry Studies and Hollywood History," in *Media Industries,* ed. Jennifer Holt and Alisa Perren (Malden, MA: Wiley-Blackwell, 2009), 46, my emphasis.

34 Arizton, "Board Games Market—Global Outlook and Forecast 2019–2023," *ReportLinker,* August 2018, https://www.reportlinker.com/p05482343/Board-Games-Market-Global-Outlook-and-Forecast.html.

35 Schatz, "Film Industry."

36 Brian Tinsman, "Understanding the Tabletop Game Industry," *Game Design Workshop,* interview by Tracy Fullerton, 2018, https://www.gamedesignworkshop .com/understanding-the-tabletop-game-industry.

37 Arnaudo, *Storytelling,* 169.

38 See Booth, *Game Play.*

39 Paolo Bertetti, "*Conan the Barbarian*: Transmedia Adventures of a Pulp Hero," in *Transmedia Archeology,* by Carlos A. Scolari, Paolo Bertetti, and Matthew Freeman (Houndsmill, UK: Palgrave, 2014), 16.

40 Nick Bestor, "Playing in Licensed Storyworlds: Games, Franchises, and Fans," PhD Dissertation, University of Texas, Austin, 2019.

41 See Booth, *Game Play.*

42 Paul Booth, "Playing by the Rules: Storium, *Star Wars*, and Ludic Fandom," *Journal of Fandom Studies* 5, no. 3 (2017): 276.

43 Henry Jenkins, *Convergence Culture* (New York: New York University Press, 2006), 18.

44 See Timothy Havens and Amanda D. Lotz, *Understanding Media Industries* (Oxford, UK: Oxford University Press, 2012), 110–11.

Chapter 5

1 Mia Consalvo, "Zelda 64 and Video Game Fans: A Walkthrough of Games, Intertextuality, and Narrative," *Television & New Media* 4, no. 3 (2003): 321–34; Greg Crawford and Jason Rutter, "Playing the Game: Performance in Digital Game Audiences," in *Fandom*, ed. Jonathan Gray, Cornel Sandvoss, and C. Lee Harrington (New York: New York University Press, 2007); Hector Postigo, "Of Mods and Modders Chasing Down the Value of Fan-Based Digital Game Modifications," *Games and Culture* 2, no. 4 (2007): 300–13; Hanna Wirman, "On Productivity and Game Fandom," *Transformative Works and Cultures* 3 (2009), http://journal.trans formativeworks.org/index.php/twc/article/view/145/115.

2 Jenkins, *Convergence*; Jonathan Gray, *Show Sold Separately* (New York: New York University Press, 2010).

3 One exception is Kurt Lancaster's exploration of *Babylon 5* role-players as fans (*Interacting with Babylon 5* (Austin: University of Texas Press, 2001)).

4 Booth, *Game Play*, 3.

5 Jones and Clayton, "Introduction," 2, emphasis added.

6 Henry Jenkins, *Textual Poachers* (New York: Routledge, 1992); Camille Bacon-Smith, *Enterprising Women* (Philadelphia, PA: University of Pennsylvania Press, 1992); see Janice Radway, *Reading the Romance* (North Carolina: The University of North Carolina Press, 1984); bell hooks, "Oppositional Gaze: Black Female Spectators," in *Black Looks* (New York: Routledge, 1992); John Fiske, "Cultural Economy of Fandom," in *The Adoring Audience*, ed. Lisa A. Lewis, 30–49 (New York: Routledge, 1992).

7 Henry Jenkins with Suzanne Scott, "A Conversation," in *Textual Poachers: Television Fans and Participatory Culture*, 2nd ed. (New York: Routledge, 2012), ix.

8 Karen Hellekson, in conversation with Will Brooker and Mark Duffett, "Fannish Identities and Scholarly Responsibilities: A Conversation," in *The Routledge Companion to Media Fandom*, ed. Melissa A. Click and Suzanne Scott (New York: Routledge, 2018), 69, emphasis mine.

9 See Alexandra Edwards, "Literature Fandom and Literary Fans," in *A Companion to Media Fandom and Fan Studies*, ed. Paul Booth (New York: Wiley, 2018).

10 Matt Hills, *Fan Cultures* (London: Routledge, 2002), 72.

11 Hills, *Fan Cultures*, 72.

12 Kristina Busse and Karen Hellekson, "Introduction: Work in Progress," in *Fan Fiction and Fan Communities in the Age of the Internet*, ed. Karen Hellekson and Kristina Busse (Jefferson, NC: McFarland, 2006), 24.

13 See Aaron Trammell, "Analog Games and the Digital Economy," *Analog Game Studies* 6, no. 1 (2019), http://analoggamestudies.org/2019/03/analog-games-and-t he-digital-economy/.

14 Megan Condis, "No Homosexuals in Star Wars? BioWare, 'Gamer' Identity, and the Politics of Privilege in a Convergence Culture," *Convergence* 21, no. 2 (2014): 199.

15 Paul Booth and Peter Kelly, "The Changing Faces of *Doctor Who* Fandom: New Fans, New Technologies, Old Practices?" *Participations* 10, no. 1 (2013), http://www .participations.org/Volume%2010/Issue%201/5%20Booth%20&%20Kelly%2010.1 .pdf; Francesca Coppa, "Fuck Yeah, Fandom Is Beautiful," *The Journal of Fandom Studies* 2, no. 1 (2014): 73–82.

16 Kenneth Burke, "Terministic Screens," in *Language as Symbolic Action* (Berkeley: University of California Press, 1966), 45.

17 Booth, "Board, Game, and Media," 649.

18 Jenkins, *Textual Poachers*, 284.

19 Arnaudo, *Storytelling*, 14.

20 Booth, "Playing by the Rules," 268.

21 Paul Booth, *Playing Fans* (Iowa City: University of Iowa Press, 2015), 16.

22 Booth, *Playing Fans*.

23 Suzanne Scott, *Fake Geek Girls* (New York, NY: New York University Press, 2019), 10.

24 Pierre Bourdieu, *Distinction*, trans. Richard Nice (Cambridge: Harvard University Press, 1984).

25 Gonzalo Frasca, "Ludology Meets Narratology: Similitude and Differences Between (Video) Games and Narrative," *Parnasso* 3 (1999), 365–71; Henry Jenkins, "Game Design as Narrative Architecture," in *First Person*, ed. Noah Wardrip-Fruin and Pat Harrigan (Cambridge: MIT Press, 2004); Celia Pearce, "Theory Wars: An Argument Against Arguments in the So-Called Ludology/Narratology Debate," *DiGRA Conference: Changing Views—Worlds in Play*, 2005, http://lmc.gatech.edu/~cpearce 3/PearcePubs/ PearceDiGRA05.pdf.

26 Jenkins, *Textual Poachers*, 5; Mark Andrejevic, "Watching Television Without Pity: The Productivity of Online Fans," *Television and New Media* 9, no. 1 (2008): 24–46; Lancaster, *Interactive*; Paul Booth, *Digital Fandom 2.0*, 2nd ed. (New York: Peter Lang, 2016).

27 Karra Shimabukuro, "Buffy the Vampire Slayer: The Game as Liminal Space," *Intensities* 7, no. 1 (2014), 77, https://intensitiescultmedia.files.wordpress.com/2 014/08/7-shimabukuro-bufffy-board-game-pp-74-83.pdf.

28 Ruth A. Deller, "The Art of Neighbours Gaming: Facebook, Fan-Crafted Games and Humour," *Intensities* 7, no. 1 (2014), https://intensitiescultmedia.files.wordpress. com/2014/08/10-deller-the-art-of-neighbours-gaming-pp-97-106.pdf.

29 Greg Costikyan, "Games, Storytelling, and Breaking the String," in *Second Person*, ed. Pat Harrigan and Noah Wardrip-Fruin (Cambridge: MIT Press, 2007), 5.

30 Matthew Kirschenbaum, "War Stories: Board Wargames and (Vast) Procedural Narratives," in *Third Person*, ed. Pat Harrigan and Noah Wardrip-Fruin (Cambridge: MIT Press, 2009).

31 Seymour Chatman, *Story and Discourse* (Ithaca: Cornell University Press, 1978).

32 Booth, *Game Play*, 152.

33 Salen and Zimmerman, *Rules of Play*, 60.

34 Jenkins, with Scott, "A Conversation," xxv.

35 See Paul Booth, "*BioShock*: Rapture through Transmedia," in *The Rise of Transtexts*, ed. Benjahim M.L. Derhy Kurtz, and Melanie Bourdaa (London: Routledge, 2016).

36 Lancaster, *Interacting*, xxiv.

37 Hills, *Fan Cultures*, 93.

38 Friedman, "Play Paradigm," 1–3, emphasis mine.

39 Booth, *Game Play*, 3.

40 Friedman, "Play Paradigm," 6.

Chapter 6

1 Floyd J. Fowler, Jr., *Survey Research Methods*, 5th ed. (Thousand Oaks, CA: Sage, 2014), 2.

2 See Richard N. Landers and Kristina N. Bauer, "Quantitative Methods and Analysis for the Study of Players and Their Behaviour," in *Game Research Methods*, ed. Petri Lankoski and Staffan Björk (Pittsburgh, PA: ETC Press, 2015).

3 Fowler, Jr., *Survey Research*, 6.

4 Amany Saleh and Krishna Bista, "Examining Factors Impacting Online Survey Response Rates in Educational Research: Perceptions of Graduate Students," *Journal of MultiDisiplinary Evaluation* 13, no. 29 (2017): 63–74.

5 George Beam, *The Problem with Survey Research* (New Brunswick, NJ: Transaction Publishers, 2012), xv–xvi.

6 Woods, *Eurogames*.

7 Vatvani, "Analysis—Part I."

8 Roger Sapsford, *Survey Research* (Thousand Oaks, CA: Sage, 2011), 10.

9 See Joe Murphy, Craig A. Hill, and Elizabeth Dean, "Social Media, Sociality, and Survey Research," in *Social Media, Sociality, and Survey Research*, ed. Craig A. Hill, Elizabeth Dean, and Joe Murphy (Hoboken, NJ: Wiley, 2014), 1–34.

10 William Smith, "Does Gender Influence Online Survey Participation?: A Record-linkage Analysis of University Faculty Online Survey Response Behavior," *ERIC Document Reproduction Service No. ED 501717*, 2008, 2, https://files.eric.ed.gov/full text/ED501717.pdf.

11 Woods, *Eurogames.*

12 Smith, "Does Gender"; Saleh and Bista, "Examining Factors."

13 Dinish Vatvani, "An Analysis of Board Games: Part II—Complexity Bias in BGG," December 8, 2018, https://dvatvani.github.io/BGG-Analysis-Part-2.html#BGG -Analysis-Part-2.

14 Vatvani, "Analysis—Part I."

15 See Craig A. Hill and Jill Dever, "The Future of Social Media, Sociality, and Survey Research," in *Social Media, Sociality, and Survey Research,* ed. Craig A. Hill, Elizabeth Dean, and Joe Murphy (Hoboken, NJ: Wiley, 2014), 295–318.

16 Fowler, Jr., *Survey Research,* 10.

17 Beam, *The Problem.*

18 Sapsford, *Survey Research,* 7.

Chapter 7

1 Chris Anderson, *The Long Tail* (New York: Hyperion, 2006).

2 David Silverman, "Introducing Qualitative Research," in *Qualitative Research,* ed. David Silverman (Thousand Oaks, CA: Sage, 2016), 3.

3 See Jenny Hockey and Martin Forsey, "Ethnography Is Not Participant Observation: Reflections on the Interview as Participatory Qualitative Research," in *The Interview,* ed. Jonathan Skinner (London: Bloomsbury, 2012); Jenny Hockey, "Interviews as Ethnography? Disembodied Social Interaction in Britain," in *British Subjects,* ed. Nigel Rapport (Oxford: Berg, 2002).

4 Carolyn Ellis, Tony E. Adams, and Arthur P. Bochner, "Autoethnography: An Overview," *Historical Social Research* 36, no. 4, 138 (2011): 275.

5 Jean J. Schensul and Margaret Diane LeCompte, *Essential Ethnographic Methods* (Lanham, MD: AltaMira, 2013), 241.

6 Rafael J. Engel and Russell K. Schutt, *The Practice of Research in Social Work,* 2nd ed. (Thousand Oaks, CA: Sage, 2009), 346.

7 McKee, *Textual Analysis,* 84.

8 Ashley Brown, "Awkward: The Importance of Reflexivity in Using Ethnographic Methods," in *Game Research Methods,* ed. Petri Lankowski and Staffan Björk (Pittsburgh, PA: ETC Press, 2015), 79.

9 Harrie Jansen, "The Logic of Qualitative Survey Research and Its Position in the Field of Social Research Methods," *Forum: Qualitative Social Research* 11, no. 2 (2010): 6, http://www.qualitative-research.net/index.php/fqs/article/view/1450/29 46, emphasis mine.

10 Ellis, Adams, and Bochner, "Autoethnography," 278.

11 Trammell, "Analog Games," 2.

Chapter 8

1 Flanagan, *Critical Play*.
2 Alex Andriesse, "Progress in Play: Board Games and the Meaning of History," *The Public Domain Review*, February 20, 2019, https://publicdomainreview.org/2019 /02/20/progress-in-play-board-games-and-the-meaning-of-history/.
3 Woods, *Eurogames*, 123.
4 Pobuda, "Assessing."
5 Erin Ryan, "Gender Representation in Board Game Cover Art," *The Cardboard Republic*, June 29, 2016, https://www.cardboardrepublic.com/articles/extra-pieces/ gender-representation-in-board-game-cover-art.
6 Gil Hova, "Women in Gaming vs. Invisible Ropes," *Formal Ferret Games*, October 27, 2014, https://gil.hova.net/2014/10/27/women-in-gaming-vs-invisible-ropes/.
7 Adrienne Shaw, "What Is Video Game Culture? Cultural Studies and Game Studies," *Games and Culture* 5, no. 4 (2010): 404.
8 James P. Spradley, *The Ethnographic Interview* (Long Grove, IL: Waveland Press, 1979), 58.
9 Spradley, *Ethnographic*, 3.
10 See Amanda Cote and Julia G. Raz, "In-Depth Interviews for Games Research," in *Game Research Methods*, ed. Petri Lankowski and Staffan Björk (Pittsburgh, PA: ETC Press, 2015), 93.
11 Benjamin Woo, *Getting a Life* (Montreal: McGill-Queen's University Press, 2018), 19.
12 Silverman, "Introducing," 52, emphasis mine.
13 Hills, *Fan Cultures*, 66.
14 McKee, *Textual Analysis*, 87.
15 Booth and Kelly, "Changing Faces."
16 McKee, *Textual Analysis*, 88.
17 See Woods, *Eurogames*.
18 Hova, "Women in Gaming."
19 Ryan, "Gender Representation."
20 Hanna Pitkin, *The Concept of Representation* (Berkeley, CA: University of California Press, 1967), 1.
21 Meaghan Gartner, Lisa Kiang, and Andrew Supple, "Prospective Links Between Ethnic Socialization, Ethnic and American Identity, and Well-Being Among Asian-American Adolescents," *Journal of Youth and Adolescence* 43, no. 10 (2014): 1715–27.
22 Woods, *Eurogames*.
23 Antonnet Johnson, "Positionality and Performance: A Player's Encounter with the Lost Tribes of *Small World*," *Analog Game Studies* 3, no. 5 (2016), http://analogga

mestudies.org/2016/09/positionality-and-performance-a-players-encounter-with-the-lost-tribes-of-small-world/.

24 Dravvin, "Designing to Be Inclusive," *Wren Games*, February 25, 2019, http://wrengames.co.uk/main/designing-to-be-inclusive/.

25 Lila Sadkin, "Wingspan Is Important: A Different Kind of Review," *BeBold*, March 18, 2019, https://www.beboldgames.com/games/wingspan-is-important-a-different-kind-of-review.

26 See Mike Selinker, "Trump's Tariffs Could Ruin the American Board Game Industry," *Polygon*, June 5, 2019, https://www.polygon.com/2019/6/5/18652411/trump-china-tariff-board-games.

27 Sophie Williams, interview with author, Skype, 2019.

28 Siobhan Roberts, "She Invented a Board Game with Scientific Integrity. It's Taking Off," *New York Times*, March 11, 2019, https://www.nytimes.com/2019/03/11/science/wingspan-board-game-elizabeth-hargrave.html.

29 Roberts, "She Invented."

30 Jon Bolding, "A Cancelled Board Game Revealed How Colonialism Inspires and Haunts Games," *Vice*, April 12, 2019, https://www.vice.com/en_us/article/vb9gd9/a-cancelled-board-game-revealed-how-colonialism-inspires-and-haunts-games.

31 Bolding, "A Cancelled Board Game."

32 Kevin Draper, "Should Board Gamers Play the Roles of Racists, Slavers and Nazis?" *New York Times*, August 1, 2019, https://www.nytimes.com/2019/08/01/style/board-games-cancel-culture.html.

33 Johnson, "Positionality."

34 Jeffrey Hinebaugh, *A Board Game Education* (Lanham, MD: Rowman and Littlefield, 2009).

Chapter 9

1 Arnaudo, *Storytelling*, 32.

2 Tony E. Adams, Stacy Holman Jones, and Carolyn Ellis, *Autoethnography* (Oxford: University Press, 2014), 46.

3 Jeanette Monaco, "Memory Work, Autoethnography and the Construction of a Fan-Ethnography," *Participations* 7, no. 1 (2010), http://www.participations.org/Volume%207/Issue%201/monaco.pdf, 103.

4 Heewon Chang, Faith Wambura Ngunjiri, and Kathy-Ann C. Hernandez, *Collaborative Autoethnography* (New York: Routledge, 2012), 19.

5 Dale Leorke, "Solo Board Gaming: An Analysis of Player Motivations," *Analog Game Studies* 5, no. 4 (2018), http://analoggamestudies.org/2018/12/solo-board-gaming-an-analysis-of-player-motivations/.

6 Sarah Wall, "An Autoethnography on Learning About Autoethnography," *International Journal of Qualitative Methods* 5, no. 2 (2006): 146–60.

7 Ellis, Adams, and Bochner, "Autoethnography," 275.

8 Katherine Larsen and Lynn Zubernis, *Fandom at the Crossroads* (Newcastle, UK: Cambridge Scholars Press, 2012).

9 Hills, *Fan Cultures*, 72.

10 Hills, *Fan Cultures*, 72.

11 Ross Garner, "Not My Lifeblood: Autoethnography, Affective Fluctuations and Popular Music Antifandom," in *A Companion to Media Fandom and Fan Studies*, ed. Paul Booth (New York, NY: Wiley-Blackwell, 2019), 94.

12 Grace A. Giorgio, "Reflections on Writing through Memory in Autoethnography," in *The Handbook to Autoethnography*, ed. Stacy Holman Jones, Tony Adams, and Carolyn Ellis (Walnut Creek, CA: Left Coast Press, 2013), 406.

13 See Elias, Garfield, and Gutschera, *Characteristics*, 26.

14 Booth, *Playing Fans*, 107.

15 Hills, *Fan Cultures*, 81.

16 Ellis, Adams, and Bochner, "Autoethnography," 273–4.

17 See Elaine Campbell, "'Apparently Being a Self-Obsessed C**t Is Now Academically Lauded': Experiencing Twitter Trolling of Autoethnographers," *Forum: Qualitative Social Research* 18, no. 3 (2017), http://www.qualitative-research.net/index.php/fqs/article/view/2819/415.

18 Stacy Holman Jones, Tony Adams, and Carolyn Ellis, "Coming to Know Autoethnography as More than a Method," in *The Handbook to Autoethnography*, ed. Stacy Holman Jones, Tony Adams, and Carolyn Ellis (Walnut Creek, CA: Left Coast Press, 2013), 35.

19 Ellis, Adams, and Bochner, "Autoethnography," 274.

20 Campbell, "Apparently Being," 30.

21 Jimmie Manning and Tony E. Adams, "Popular Culture Studies and Autoethnography: An Essay on Method," *The Popular Culture Studies Journal* 3, nos. 1 and 2 (2015): 192.

22 Clifford Geertz, *The Interpretation of Cultures* (New York: Basic Books, 1973), 10.

23 Norman K. Denzin, *Interpretive Interactionism* (Newbury Park, CA: Sage, 1989), 83.

24 See Michael Foith, "Virtually Witness Augmentation Now: Video Games and the Future of Human Enhancement," *M/C Journal* 16, no. 6 (2013), http://journal.media-culture.org.au/index.php/mcjournal/article/view/729; Kurt Borchard, "Super Columbine Massacre RPG! and Grand Theft Autoethnography," *Cultural Studies Critical Methodologies* 15, no. 6 (2015): 446–54; Renee Chia-Lei Chen, "Autoethnographic Research through Storytelling in Animation and Video Games," Master's Thesis, The Ohio State University, 2016; Sapach, "Let's Play."

25 Graeme Lachance, "Living Pedagogies of a Game-Master: An Autoethnographic Education of Liminal Moments," Master's Thesis, University of Ottawa, 2016; Moyra Turkington, "A Look Back from The Future: Play and Performance in Biosphere 2013," *Analog Game Studies* 2, no. 6 (2015), http://analoggamestudies.org/2015/09/a-look-back-from-the-future-play-and-performance-in-biosphere-2013/.

26 Manning and Adams, "Popular Culture Studies," 188.

27 Giorgia, "Reflections," 407.

28 Svetlana Boym, *The Future of Nostalgia* (New York: Basic Books, 2001), 52.

29 Adrienne Shaw, "Rethinking Game Studies: A Case Study Approach to Video Game Play and Identification," *Critical Studies in Media Communication* 30, no. 5 (2013): 348.

30 Elias, Garfield, and Gutschera, *Characteristics*, 25–6.

31 Nick Yee, "Solo Board Gamers: Who Are the 1%," *Quantric Foundry*, 2017, https://quanticfoundry.com/2017/07/12/solo-board-gamers/.

32 Elias, Garfield, and Gutschera, *Characteristics*.

33 *Gloomhaven* Inox Brute card 2016.

34 *Gloomhaven* Quatryl Tinkerer card 2016.

35 Dimitra Fimi, "Was Tolkien Really Racist?" *The Conversation*, December 6, 2018, 12, https://theconversation.com/was-tolkien-really-racist-108227.

36 Aaron Trammell, "Representation and Discrimination in Role-Playing Games," in *Role-Playing Game Studies*, ed. Sebastian Deterding and José Zagal (New York: Routledge, 2018), 440–7.

37 Arnaudo, *Storytelling*, 132.

38 *Gloomhaven* Scenario Book, "Barrow Lair," 2016.

39 See Sebastian Deterding and José P. Zagal, "The Many Faces of Role-Playing Game Studies," in *Role-Playing Game Studies*, ed. José P. Zagal and Sebastian Deterding (London: Routledge, 2018), 4.

40 Isaac Childres, interview with author, Skype, 2019.

41 Arnaudo, *Storytelling*, 21.

42 Jenny Sundén, "Desires at Play: On Closeness and Epistemological Uncertainty," *Games and Culture* 7, no. 2 (2012): 164–84.

43 Arnaudo, *Storytelling*, 41.

44 Keith Berry, "Spinning Autoethnographic Reflexivity, Cultural Critique, and Negotiating Selves," in *The Handbook to Autoethnography*, ed. Stacy Holman Jones, Tony Adams, and Carolyn Ellis (Walnut Creek, CA: Left Coast Press, 2013), 212–13.

45 Ellis, Adams, and Bochner, "Autoethnography," 283.

46 Ellis, Adams, and Bochner, "Autoethnography," 283.

47 See Campbell, "'Apparently Being.'"

Conclusion

1 Booth, *Digital Fandom 2.0.*

2 Richard Maxwell and Toby Miller, "Ecological Ethics and Media Technology," *International Journal of Communication* 2 (2008): 331.

3 See Maxwell and Miller, "Ecological Ethics."

4 My thanks to Rachel Fernandez for this perceptive thought.

5 Richard Maxwell and Toby Miller, *Greening the Media* (Oxford, UK: Oxford University Press, 2012), 4.

6 Maxwell and Miller, *Greening*, 6.

7 Trammell, "Analog Games."

8 Climate Home News, "'Tsunami of Data' Could Consume One Fifth of Global Electricity by 2025," *The Guardian*, December 11, 2017, https://www.theguardian.com/environment/2017/dec/11/tsunami-of-data-could-consume-fifth-global-electricity-by-2025.

9 Fred Pearce, "Energy Hogs: Can World's Huge Data Centers Be Made More Efficient?" *Yale Environment 360*, April 3, 2018, https://e360.yale.edu/features/energy-hogs-can-huge-data-centers-be-made-more-efficient.

10 Maxwell and Miller, *Greening*, 16.

11 See Eleanor Albert and Beina Xu, "China's Environmental Crisis," *Council on Foreign Relations*, January 18, 2016, https://www.cfr.org/backgrounder/chinas-environmental-crisis.

12 Joshua King, "Plastic Fantastic: Is There an Eco-Friendly Solution to Gaming's Fatal Attraction?" *Tabletop Gaming Magazine*, June 26, 2018, https://www.tabletopgaming.co.uk/board-games/articles/plastic-fantastic-is-there-an-eco-friendly-solution-to-gamings-fatal.

13 King, "Plastic Fantastic."

14 King, "Plastic Fantastic."

15 Of course, people have to be willing to play games focused on climate change and environmentalism in the first place; it is possible that the gamers playing these games are already predisposed to care about the environment.

16 Johnson, "Positionality"; Bruce Whitehill, "American Games: A Historical Perspective," *International Journal for the Study of Board Games* 2 (1999): 116–44.

17 Sam Illingworth and Paul Wake, "Developing Science Tabletop Games: Catan® and Global Warming," *Journal of Science Communication* 18, no. 4 (2019): 1–23.

18 Illingworth and Wake, "Developing."

19 Illingworth and Wake, "Developing," 6.

20 Sean Cubitt, *Eco Media* (Amsterdam: Rodopi B.V., 2005), 1.

21 Anthony A. Leiserowitz, "Day After Tomorrow: Study of Climate Change Risk Perception," *Environment: Science and Policy for Sustainable Development* 49, no. 9 (2004): 34.

22 Leiserowitz, "Day After Tomorrow," 34.

23 King, "Plastic Fantastic."

24 Max Boykoff and Michael K. Goodman, "Conspicuous Redemption? Reflections on the Promises and Perils of the Celebritization of Climate Change," *Geoforum* 40 (2009): 395–406.

References

Aarseth, Espen. "Just Games." *Game Studies* 17, no. 1 (2017). http://gamestudies.org/17
01/articles/justgames.

Aarseth, Espen. "The Game and Its Name: What Is a Game Auteur." In *Visual
Authorship: Creativity and Intentionality in Media*, edited by Torben Grodal, Bente
Larsen, and Iben Thorving Laursen, 261–9. Denmark: Narayana Press, 2004.

Adams, Tony E., Stacy Holman Jones, and Carolyn Ellis. *Autoethnography*. Oxford:
University Press, 2014.

Adolphus, Margaret. "How to...Use Discourse Analysis." *Emerald Publishing*. N.d. http:
//www.emeraldgrouppublishing.com/research/guides/methods/discourse_ana
lysis.htm.

Albert, Eleanor, and Beina Xu. "China's Environmental Crisis." *Council on Foreign
Relations*, January 18, 2016. https://www.cfr.org/backgrounder/chinas-environmen
tal-crisis.

Aleknevicus, Greg. "German Games are Fraudulent." *The Games Journal* (2004). http://
www.thegamesjournal.com/articles/Fraudulent.shtml.

Allen, Christopher, and Shannon Appelcline. *Meeples Together: How and Why
Cooperative Board Games Work*. US: Amazon Kindle, 2019.

Anderson, Chris. *The Long Tail*. New York: Hyperion, 2006.

Andrejevic, Mark. "Watching Television Without Pity: The Productivity of Online
Fans." *Television and New Media* 9, no. 1 (2008): 24–6.

Andriesse, Alex. "Progress in Play: Board Games and the Meaning of History." *The
Public Domain Review*, February 20, 2019. https://publicdomainreview.org/2019
/02/20/progress-in-play-board-games-and-the-meaning-of-history/.

Arizton. "Board Games Market – Global Outlook and Forecast 2019–2023."
ReportLinker, August 2018. https://www.reportlinker.com/p05482343/Board-Games
-Market-Global-Outlook-and-Forecast.html.

Arnaudo, Marco. *Storytelling in the Modern Board Game: Narrative Trends from the Late
1960s to Today*. Jefferson, NC: McFarland, 2018.

Arvidsson, Adam. *Brands: Meaning and Value in Media Culture*. London:
Routledge, 2006.

Atkins, Barry, and Tanya Krzywinska. "Introduction." In *Videogame, Player, Text*, edited
by Barry Atkins and Tanya Krzywinska, 1–7. Manchester: Manchester University
Press, 2007.

Backe, Hans-Joachim. "Within the Mainstream: An Ecocritical Framework for Digital
Game History." *Ecozon@* 8, no. 2 (2017). https://core.ac.uk/download/pdf/15688897
0.pdf.

Bacon-Smith, Camille. *Enterprising Women*. Philadelphia, PA: University of Pennsylvania Press, 1992.

Banet-Weiser, Sarah. *Authentic TM: Politics and Ambivalence in a Brand Culture*. New York: New York University Press, 2012.

Beam, George. *The Problem with Survey Research*. New Brunswick, NJ: Transaction Publishers, 2012.

Benoit, William. "On Aristotle's Example." *Philosophy and Rhetoric* 20, no. 4 (1987): 261–7.

Berger, Arthur Asa. *Applied Discourse Analysis: Popular Culture, Media, and Everyday Life*. London: Palgrave Pivot, 2017.

Berry, Keith. "Spinning Autoethnographic Reflexivity, Cultural Critique, and Negotiating Selves." In *The Handbook to Autoethnography*, edited by Stacy Holman Jones, Tony Adams, and Carolyn Ellis, 209–27. Walnut Creek, CA: Left Coast Press, 2013.

Bertetti, Paolo. "Conan the Barbarian: Transmedia Adventures of a Pulp Hero." In *Transmedia Archeology: Storytelling in the Borderlines of Science Fiction, Comics, and Pulp Magazines*, by Carlos A. Scolari, Paolo Bertetti, and Matthew Freeman, 15–38. Houndsmill, UK: Palgrave, 2014.

Bestor, Nick. "Playing in Licensed Storyworlds: Games, Franchises, and Fans." PhD Dissertation, University of Texas, Austin. 2019.

Bhatt, Shephali. "How India Caught on the New-Age Board Game Culture of the West to Create an Ecosystem of Cafes & Communities Back Home." *The Economic Times*, June 30, 2019. https://economictimes.indiatimes.com/news/politics-and-nation/how-india-caught-on-the-new-age-board-game-culture-of-the-west-to-create-an-ecosystem-of-cafes-communities-back-home/articleshow/70005721.cms.

Bogost, Ian. *Persuasive Games*. Cambridge: MIT Press, 2007.

Bogost, Ian. "The Rhetoric of Video Games." In *The Ecology of Games: Connecting Youth, Games, and Learning*, edited by Katie Salen, 117–40. Cambridge, MA: The MIT Press, 2008.

Bolding, Jon. "A Cancelled Board Game Revealed How Colonialism Inspires and Haunts Games." *Vice*, April 12, 2019. https://www.vice.com/en_us/article/vb9gd9/a-cancelled-board-game-revealed-how-colonialism-inspires-and-haunts-games.

Booth, Paul. "*BioShock*: Rapture through Transmedia." In *The Rise of Transtexts*, edited by Benjahim M. L. Derhy Kurtz and Melanie Bourdaa, 153–68. London: Routledge, 2016.

Booth, Paul. "Board, Game, and Media: Interactive Board Games as Multimedia Convergence." *Convergence: The International Journal of Research into New Media Technologies* 22, no. 6 (2016): 647–60.

Booth, Paul. *Digital Fandom 2.0: New Media Studies*, 2nd ed. New York: Peter Lang, 2016.

Booth, Paul. *Game Play: Paratextuality in Contemporary Board Games*. New York: Bloomsbury, 2015.

Booth, Paul. "Playing by the Rules: Storium, *Star Wars*, and Ludic Fandom." *Journal of Fandom Studies* 5, no. 3 (2017): 267–84.

Booth, Paul. *Playing Fans: Negotiating Fandom and Media in the Digital Age*. Iowa City: University of Iowa Press, 2015.

Booth, Paul, and Peter Kelly. "The Changing Faces of *Doctor Who* Fandom: New Fans, New Technologies, Old Practices?" *Participations* 10, no. 1 (2013). http://www.part icipations.org/Volume%2010/Issue%201/5%20Booth%20&%20Kelly%2010.1.pdf.

Borchard, Kurt. "Super Columbine Massacre RPG! and Grand Theft Autoethnography." *Cultural Studies/Critical Methodologies* 15, no. 6 (2015): 446–54.

Bourdieu, Pierre. *Distinction: A Social Critique of the Judgment of Taste*. Translated by Richard Nice. Cambridge: Harvard University Press, 1984.

Boykoff, Max, and Michael K. Goodman. "Conspicuous Redemption? Reflections on the Promises and Perils of the Celebritization of Climate Change." *Geoforum* 40 (2009): 395–406.

Boym, Svetlana. *The Future of Nostalgia*. New York: Basic Books, 2001.

Brown, Adam, and Deb Waterhouse-Watson. "Reconfiguring Narrative in Contemporary Board Games: Story-Making Across the Competitive-Cooperative Spectrum." *Intensities: The Journal of Cult Media* 7, no. 1 (2014): 5–19. https://intensi tiescultmedia.files.wordpress.com/2014/08/2-brown-and-waterhouse-watson-rec onfiguring-narrative-pp-5-19.pdf.

Brown, Ashley. "Awkward: The Importance of Reflexivity in Using Ethnographic Methods." In *Game Research Methods*, edited by Petri Lankowski and Staffan Björk, 77–92. Pittsburgh, PA: ETC Press, 2015.

Burke, Kenneth. *A Grammar of Motives*. Berkeley, CA: University of California Press, 1945.

Burke, Kenneth. "Terministic Screens." In *Language as Symbolic Action: Essays on Life, Literature, and Method*, 44–62. Berkeley: University of California Press, 1966.

Burnett, Colin. "Hidden Hands at Work: Authorship, the Intentional Flux, and the Dynamics of Collaboration." In *A Companion to Media Authorship*, edited by Jonathan Gray and Derek Johnson, 112–32. Malden, MA: Wiley & Sons, 2013.

Busse, Kristina, and Karen Hellekson. "Introduction: Work in Progress." In *Fan Fiction and Fan Communities in the Age of the Internet*, edited by Karen Hellekson and Kristina Busse, 261–32. Jefferson, NC: McFarland, 2006.

Caillois, Roger. *Man, Play and Games*. Translated by Meye Barash. Urbana, IL: University of Illinois Press, 1961.

Caldwell, John Thornton. *Production Culture*. Durham, NC: Duke University Press, 2008.

Campbell, Elaine. "'Apparently Being a Self-Obsessed C**t Is Now Academically Lauded': Experiencing Twitter Trolling of Autoethnographers." *Forum: Qualitative*

Social Research 18, no. 3 (2017). http://www.qualitative-research.net/index.php/fqs/article/view/2819/4151.

Caña, Victora. Interview with author. Skype, 2019.

Cassano, Maria. "The 10 Best Strategy Board Games for Adults." *Bustle*, January 2019. https://www.bustle.com/p/the-10-best-strategy-board-games-for-adults-15561360.

Chang, Heewon, Faith Wambura Ngunjiri, and Kathy-Ann C. Hernandez. *Collaborative Autoethnography*. New York: Routledge, 2012.

Chatman, Seymour. *Story and Discourse: Narrative Structure in Fiction and Film*. Ithaca: Cornell University Press, 1978.

Chen, Renee Chia-Lei. "Autoethnographic Research through Storytelling in Animation and Video Games." Master's Thesis, The Ohio State University, 2016.

Childres, Isaac. Interview with author. Skype, 2019.

Childres, Isaac. "My Top 10 Board Game Loves." *Cephalofair*, May 10, 2014. www.cephalofair.com/2014/05/top-10-board-game-loves.html.

Climate Home News. "'Tsunami of Data' Could Consume One Fifth of Global Electricity by 2025." *The Guardian*, December 11, 2017. https://www.theguardian.com/environment/2017/dec/11/tsunami-of-data-could-consume-fifth-global-electricity-by-2025.

Condis, Megan. "No Homosexuals in *Star Wars*? BioWare, 'Gamer' Identity, and the Politics of Privilege in a Convergence Culture." *Convergence* 21, no. 2 (2014): 198–212.

Consalvo, Mia. "Zelda 64 and Video Game Fans: A Walkthrough of Games, Intertextuality, and Narrative." *Television & New Media* 4, no. 3 (2003): 321–34.

Coppa, Francesca. "Fuck Yeah, Fandom Is Beautiful." *The Journal of Fandom Studies* 2, no. 1 (2014): 73–82.

Costikyan, Greg. "Games, Storytelling, and Breaking the String." In *Second Person: Role-Playing and Story in Games and Playable Media*, edited by Pat Harrigan and Noah Wardrip-Fruin, 5–14. Cambridge: MIT Press, 2007.

Costikyan, Greg. *Uncertainty in Games*. Cambridge, MA: MIT Press, 2013.

Costikyan, Greg, and Drew Davidson. *Tabletop: Analog Game Design*. Pittsburgh, PA: ETC Press, 2011.

Cote, Amanda, and Julia G. Raz. "In-Depth Interviews for Games Research." In *Game Research Methods*, edited by Petri Lankowski and Staffan Björk, 93–116. Pittsburgh, PA: ETC Press, 2015.

Crawford, Greg, and Jason Rutter. "Playing the Game: Performance in Digital Game Audiences." In *Fandom: Identities and Communities in a Mediated World*, edited by Jonathan Gray, Cornel Sandvoss, and C. Lee Harrington, 271–84. New York: New York University Press, 2007.

Cubitt, Sean. *Eco Media*. Amsterdam: Rodopi B.V., 2005.

D'Angelo, Frank. "The Rhetoric of Intertextuality." *Rhetoric Review* 29, no. 1 (2009): 31–47.

de Certeau, Michel. *The Practice of Everyday Life*. Translated by Steven Randall. Berkeley, CA: University of California Press, 1984.

Deller, Ruth A. "The Art of *Neighbours* Gaming: Facebook, Fan-Crafted Games and Humour." *Intensities: The Journal of Cult Media* 7, no. 1 (2014): 97–106. https://in tensitiescultmedia.files.wordpress.com/2014/08/10-deller-the-art-of-neighbours-g aming-pp-97-106.pdf.

Denzin, Norman K. *Interpretive Interactionism*. Newbury Park, CA: Sage, 1989.

Deterding, Sebastian, and José P. Zagal. "The Many Faces of Role-Playing Game Studies." *Role-Playing Game Studies: Transmedia Foundations*, edited by José P. Zagal and Sebastian Deterding, 1–16. London: Routledge, 2018.

Draper, Kevin. "Should Board Gamers Play the Roles of Racists, Slavers and Nazis?" *New York Times*, August 1, 2019. https://www.nytimes.com/2019/08/01/style/board-games-cancel-culture.html.

Dravvin. "Designing to Be Inclusive." *Wren Games*, February 25, 2019. wrengames. co.uk/main/designing-to-be-inclusive/.

Edwards, Alexandra. "Literature Fandom and Literary Fans." In *A Companion to Media Fandom and Fan Studies*, edited by Paul Booth, 47–64. New York: Wiley, 2018.

Eisenack, Klaus. "A Climate Change Board Game for Interdisciplinary Communication and Education." *Simulation and Gaming* 44, no. 2–3 (2013): 328–48.

Elias, George Skaff, Richard Garfield, and K. Robert Gutschera. *Characteristics of Games*. Cambridge, MA: MIT Press, 2012.

Ellis, Carolyn, Tony E. Adams, and Arthur P. Bochner. "Autoethnography: An Overview." *Historical Social Research* 36, no. 4, 138 (2011): 273–90.

Engel, Rafael J., and Russell K. Schutt. *The Practice of Research in Social Work*, 2nd ed. Thousand Oaks, CA: Sage, 2009.

Eskelinen, Markku. "Explorations in Game Ecology, Part 1." *Jahrbuch für Computerphilologie* 7 (2005): 93–110.

Fatsis, Stefen. *Word Freak: Heartbreak, Triumph, Genius, and Obsession in the World of Competitive Scrabble Players*. New York, Penguin, 2002.

Fernándaz-Vara, Clara. *Introduction to Game Analysis*, 2nd ed. New York: Routledge, 2019.

Fimi, Dimitra. "Was Tolkien Really Racist?" *The Conversation*, December 6, 2018. https://theconversation.com/was-tolkien-really-racist-108227.

Finkel, Irving. *Ancient Board Games in Perspective: Papers from the 1990 British Museum Colloquium, with Additional Contributions*. London: British Museum Press, 2007.

Fiske, John. "The Cultural Economy of Fandom." In *The Adoring Audience*, edited by Lisa A. Lewis, 30–49. New York: Routledge, 1992.

Fizek, Sonia. "Pivoting the Player: A Methodological Toolkit for Player Character Research in Offline Role-Playing Games." PhD Bangor University, 2012. https://rk e.abertay.ac.uk/ws/portalfiles/portal/15206754/Pivoting_the_Player_Fizek.pdf

Flanagan, Mary. *Critical Play: Radical Game Design*. Cambridge, MA: MIT Press, 2009.

Foith, Michael. "Virtually Witness Augmentation Now: Video Games and the Future of Human Enhancement." *M/C Journal* 16, no. 6 (2013). http://journal.media-culture.o rg.au/index.php/mcjournal/article/view/729.

Forbeck, Matt. "Metaphor vs. Mechanics: Don't Fight the Fusion." In *The Kobold Guide to Board Game Design*, edited by Mike Selinker, 19–24. Kirkland, WA: Open Design, 2011.

Foucault, Michel. *Discipline and Punish*. Translated by Alan Sheridan. Harmondsworth: Penguin, 1974.

Fowler, Floyd J., Jr. *Survey Research Methods*, 5th ed. Thousand Oaks, CA: Sage, 2014.

Fraade-Blanar, Zoe, and Aaron M. Glazer. *Superfandom: How Our Obsessions Are Changing What We Buy and Who We Are*. New York: Norton, 2017.

Frasca, Gonzalo. "Ludology Meets Narratology: Similitude and Differences Between (Video) Games and Narrative." *Parnasso* 3 (1999): 365–71.

Friedman, Ted. "The Play Paradigm: What Media Studies Can Learn from Game Studies." *Flow TV*, 2008. http://www.flowjournal.org/2008/12/the-play-paradigm-wh at-media-studies-can-learn-from-game-studies-ted-friedman-georgia-state-uni versity/.

Garner, Ross. "Not My Lifeblood: Autoethnography, Affective Fluctuations and Popular Music Antifandom." In *A Companion to Media Fandom and Fan Studies*, edited by Paul Booth, 91–106. New York, NY: Wiley-Blackwell, 2019.

Gartner, Meaghan, Lisa Kiang, and Andrew Supple. "Prospective Links Between Ethnic Socialization, Ethnic and American Identity, and Well-Being Among Asian-American Adolescents." *Journal of Youth and Adolescence* 43, no. 10 (2014): 1715–27.

Gee, James Paul. *An Introduction to Discourse Analysis: Theory and Method*, 3rd ed. New York: Routledge, 2011.

Gee, James Paul. "Discourse Analysis of Games." In *Discourse and Digital Practices: Doing Discourse Analysis in the Digital Age*, edited by Rodney H. Jones, Alice Chik, and Christoph A. Hafner, 18–27. London: Routledge, 2015.

Gee, James Paul. *How to Do Discourse Analysis*. New York: Routledge, 2011.

Geertz, Clifford. *The Interpretation of Cultures*. New York: Basic Books, 1973.

Giorgio, Grace A. "Reflections on Writing through Memory in Autoethnography." In *The Handbook to Autoethnography*, edited by Stacy Holman Jones, Tony Adams, and Carolyn Ellis, 406–24. Walnut Creek, CA: Left Coast Press, 2013.

Gray, Jonathan. *Show Sold Separately: Promos, Spoilers, and Other Media Paratexts*. New York: New York University Press, 2010.

Grimwood, Tom. "Procedural Monsters: Rhetoric, Commonplace and 'Heroic Madness' in Video Games." *Journal for Cultural Research* 22, no. 3 (2018): 310–24.

Hall, Charlie. "Tabletop Games Dominated Kickstarter in 2018, While Video Games Declined." *Polygon*, January 15, 2019. https://www.polygon.com/2019/1/15/181841 08/kickstarter-2018-stats-tabletop-video-games.

Hall, Stuart. "Encoding and Decoding in the Television Discourse." Paper for the Council of Europe Colloquy on "Training in the Critical Heading of Televisual Language." Organized by the Council & the Centre for Mass Communication Research, University of Leicester, September, 1973. https://core.ac.uk/download/pd f/81670115.pdf.

Harrigan, Pat, and Matthew Kirschenbaum, eds. *Zones of Control: Perspectives on Wargaming.* Cambridge, MA: MIT Press, 2016.

Havens, Timothy, and Amanda D. Lotz. *Understanding Media Industries.* Oxford, UK: Oxford University Press, 2012.

Hellekson, Karen. *The Alternate History: Refiguring Historical Time.* Kent, OH: Kent State University Press, 2001.

Hellekson, Karen, in conversation with Will Brooker and Mark Duffett. "Fannish Identities and Scholarly Responsibilities: A Conversation." In *The Routledge Companion to Media Fandom*, edited by Melissa A. Click and Suzanne Scott, 63–74. New York: Routledge, 2018.

Hill, Craig A., and Jill Dever. "The Future of Social Media, Sociality, and Survey Research." In *Social Media, Sociality, and Survey Research*, edited by Craig A. Hill, Elizabeth Dean, and Joe Murphy, 295–318. Hoboken, NJ: Wiley, 2014.

Hills, Matt. *Fan Cultures.* London: Routledge, 2002.

Hills, Matt. "Time, Possible Worlds, and Counterfactuals." In *The Routledge Companion to Science Fiction*, edited by Mark Bould, Andrew Butler, Adam Roberts, and Sherryl Vint, 433–41. London: Routledge, 2009.

Hilmes, Michele. "Nailing Mercury: The Problem of Media Industry Historiography." In *Media Industries: History, Theory, and Method*, edited by Jennifer Holt and Alisa Perren, 21–33. Malden, MA: Wiley-Blackwell, 2009.

Hinebaugh, Jeffrey. *A Board Game Education.* Lanham, MD: Rowman and Littlefield, 2009.

Hockey, Jenny. "Interviews as Ethnography? Disembodied Social Interaction in Britain." In *British Subjects: An Anthropology of Britain*, edited by Nigel Rapport, 209–22. Oxford: Berg, 2002.

Hockey, Jenny, and Martin Forsey. "Ethnography Is Not Participant Observation: Reflections on the Interview as Participatory Qualitative Research." In *The Interview: An Ethnographic Approach*, edited by Jonathan Skinner, 69–88. London: Bloomsbury, 2012.

Holt, Jennifer, and Alisa Perren. "Introduction: Does the World Really Need One More Field of Study?" In *Media Industries: History, Theory, and Method*, edited by Jennifer Holt and Alisa Perren, 1–16. Malden, MA: Wiley-Blackwell, 2009.

hooks, bell. "Oppositional Gaze: Black Female Spectators." In *Black Looks: Race and Representation.* New York: Routledge, 1992.

Hova, Gil. "Women in Gaming vs. Invisible Ropes." *Formal Ferret Games*, October 27, 2014. https://gil.hova.net/2014/10/27/women-in-gaming-vs-invisible-ropes/.

Illingworth, Sam, and Paul Wake. "Developing Science Tabletop Games: *Catan®* and Global Warming." *Journal of Science Communication* 18, no. 4 (2019): 1–23.

Jansen, Harrie. "The Logic of Qualitative Survey Research and Its Position in the Field of Social Research Methods." *Forum: Qualitative Social Research* 11, no. 2 (2010). http://www.qualitative-research.net/index.php/fqs/article/view/14 50/2946.

Järvinen, Aki. *Games Without Frontiers: Theories and Methods for Game Studies and Design.* Saarbrücken: Verlag Dr. Müller, 2009.

Jenkins, Henry. *Textual Poachers: Television Fans and Participatory Culture.* New York: Routledge, 1992.

Jenkins, Henry. "Game Design as Narrative Architecture." In *First Person: New Media as Story, Performance and Game*, edited by Noah Wardrip-Fruin and Pat Harrigan, 118–30. Cambridge: MIT Press, 2004.

Jenkins, Henry. *Convergence Culture: Where Old and New Media Collide.* New York: New York University Press, 2006.

Jenkins, Henry, with Suzanne Scott. "A Conversation." *Textual Poachers: Television Fans and Participatory Culture*, 2nd ed., vii–l. New York: Routledge, 2012.

Jennings, Stephanie C. "Co-creation and the Distributed Authorship of Video Games." In *Examining the Evolution of Gaming and Its Impact on Social, Cultural, and Political Perspectives*, edited by Keri Duncan Valentin and Lucas John Jensen, 123–46. Hershey, PA: IGI Global, 2016.

Johnson, Antonnet. "Positionality and Performance: A Player's Encounter with the Lost Tribes of Small World." *Analog Game Studies* 3, no 5 (2016). http://analoggamestu dies.org/2016/09/positionality-and-performance-a-players-encounter-with-the-lost -tribes-of-small-world/.

Jones, Bethan, and Wickham Clayton. "Introduction to the Special Issue: The Transmedia Relationship Between Film/TV Texts and Board Games." *Intensities: The Journal of Cult Media* 7, no. 1 (2014): 1–4. https://intensitiescultmedia.files.wordp ress.com/2014/08/1-jones-and-clayton-editors-introduction-pp-1-41.pdf.

Jones, Robert. "From Shooting Monsters to Shooting Movies: Machinima and the Transformative Play of Video Game Fan Culture." In *Fan Fiction and Fan Communities in the Age of the Internet*, edited by Karen Hellekson and Kristina Busse, 261–81. Jefferson, NC: McFarland, 2006.

Jones, Rodney H., Alice Chik, and Chrisoph A. Hafner. "Introduction: Discourse Analysis and Digital Practices." In *Discourse and Digital Practices: Doing Discourse Analysis in the Digital Age*, edited by Rodney H. Jones, Alice Chik, and Christoph A. Hafner, 1–17. London: Routledge, 2015.

Jones, Stacy Holman, Tony Adams, and Carolyn Ellis. "Coming to Know Autoethnography as More than a Method." In *The Handbook to Autoethnography*, edited by Stacy Holman Jones, Tony Adams, and Carolyn Ellis, 17–48. Walnut Creek, CA: Left Coast Press, 2013.

Kaufeld, John. "Randomness, Player Choice, and Player Experience." In *Tabletop: Analog Game Design*, edited by Greg Costikyan and Drew Davidson, 33–38. Pittsburgh, PA: ETC Press, 2011.

King, Joshua. "Plastic Fantastic: Is There an Eco-Friendly Solution to Gaming's Fatal Attraction?" *Tabletop Gaming Magazine*, June 26, 2018. https://www.tabletopgamin g.co.uk/board-games/articles/plastic-fantastic-is-there-an-eco-friendly-solution -to-gamings-fatal.

Kirschenbaum, Matthew. "War Stories: Board Wargames and (Vast) Procedural Narratives." In *Third Person: Authoring and Exploring Vast Narratives*, edited by Pat Harrigan and Noah Wardrip-Fruin, 357–71. Cambridge: MIT Press, 2009.

Lachance, Graeme. "Living Pedagogies of a Game-Master: An Autoethnographic Education of Liminal Moments." Master's thesis, University of Ottawa, 2016.

Lancaster, Kurt. *Interacting with Babylon 5*. Austin: University of Texas Press, 2001.

Landers, Richard N., and Kristina N. Bauer. "Quantitative Methods and Analysis for the Study of Players and Their Behaviour." In *Game Research Methods*, edited by Petri Lankoski and Staffan Björk, 151–74. Pittsburgh, PA: ETC Press, 2015.

Lankoski, Petri, and Staffan Björk. "Formal Analysis of Gameplay." In *Game Research Methods*, edited by Petri Lankoski and Staffan Björk, 23–36. Pittsburgh, PA: ETC Press, 2015.

Larsen, Katherine, and Lynn Zubernis. *Fandom at the Crossroads: Celebration, Shame and Fan/producer Relationships*. Newcastle, UK: Cambridge Scholars Press, 2012.

Laukat, Ryan. Interview with author. Skype, 2019.

Leacock, Matt. Foreword to *Meeples Together: How and Why Cooperative Board Games Work* by Christopher Allen and Shannon Appelcline. US: Amazon Kindle, 2018.

Leacock, Matt. "No Single Player Can Win This Board Game. It's Called Pandemic." *New York Times*, March 25, 2020. https://www.nytimes.com/2020/03/25/opinion/pa ndemic-game-covid.html.

Lee, Jonathan Rey. "Capitalism and Unfairness in Catan: Oil Springs." *Analog Game Studies* 4, no. 2 (2017). http://analoggamestudies.org/2017/03/capitalism-and-unf airness-in-catan-oil-springs/.

Leiserowitz, Anthony A. "Day After Tomorrow: Study of Climate Change Risk Perception." *Environment: Science and Policy for Sustainable Development* 49, no. 9 (2004): 22–39.

Leorke, Dale. "Solo Board Gaming: An Analysis of Player Motivations." *Analog Game Studies* 5, no. 4 (2018). http://analoggamestudies.org/2018/12/solo-board-gaming- an-analysis-of-player-motivations/.

Loring-Albright, Greg. "Can Friendship Be Stronger Than War? Mechanics of Trauma in The Grizzled." *Analog Game Studies* 4, no. 1 (2017). http://analoggamestudies. org/2017/01/mechanics-of-trauma-in-the-grizzled/.

Lury, Celia. *Brands: The Logos of the Global Economy*. London: Routledge, 2004.

Manning, Jimmie, and Tony E. Adams. "Popular Culture Studies and Autoethnography: An Essay on Method." *The Popular Culture Studies Journal* 3, no. 1 and 2 (2015): 187–221.

Mateas, Michael, and Andrew Stern. "Procedural Authorship: A Case-Study of the Interactive Drama *Façade*." In *Digital Arts and Culture: Digital Experience: Design, Aesthetics, Practice (DAC 2005)*, Copenhagen, Denmark, 2005. http://citeseerx.ist .psu.edu/viewdoc/download? doi=10.1.1.567.1894&rep=rep1&type=pdf.

Machin, David, and Andrea Mayr. *How to Do Critical Discourse Analysis*. Thousand Oaks, CA: Sage, 2012.

Maxwell, Richard, and Toby Miller. "Ecological Ethics and Media Technology." *International Journal of Communication* 2 (2008): 331–53.

Maxwell, Richard, and Toby Miller. *Greening the Media*. Oxford, UK: Oxford University Press, 2012.

Mayer, Vicki, Miranda J. Banks, and John T. Caldwell. "Introduction: Production Studies: Roots and Routes." In *Production Studies: Cultural Studies of Media Industries*, edited by Vicki Mayer, Miranda J. Banks, and John T. Caldwell, 1–12. New York: Routledge, 2009.

Mäyrä, Frans. *An Introduction to Game Studies*. London, UK: Sage, 2008.

McDougall, Julian. *Media Studies: The Basics*. London: Routledge, 2012.

McKee, Alan. *Textual Analysis: A Beginner's Guide*. London: Sage, 2003.

Miller, Toby, and Marwan M. Kraidy. *Global Media Studies*. Cambridge, UK: Polity Press, 2016.

Monaco, Jeanette. "Memory Work, Autoethnography and the Construction of a Fan-Ethnography." *Participations* 7, no. 1 (2010). http://www.participations.org/Volum e%207/Issue%201/monaco.pdf.

Mukherjee, Souvik. *Video Games and Storytelling: Reading Games and Playing Books*. Houndsmills, UK: Palgrave, 2015.

Murphy, Joe, Craig A. Hill, and Elizabeth Dean. "Social Media, Sociality, and Survey Research." In *Social Media, Sociality, and Survey Research*, edited by Craig A. Hill, Elizabeth Dean, and Joe Murphy, 1–34. Hoboken, NJ: Wiley, 2014.

Murray, Janet. *Hamlet on the Holodeck: The Future of Narrative in Cyberspace*. Cambridge, MA: MIT Press, 1997.

Orbanes, Philip. *Monopoly: The World's Most Famous Game-And How It Got That Way*. Philadelphia: DeCapo Press, 2007.

Pearce, Celia. "Theory Wars: An Argument Against Arguments in the So-Called Ludology/ Narratology Debate." DiGRA Conference: Changing Views—Worlds in Play, 2005. http://lmc.gatech.edu/~cpearce3/PearcePubs/ PearceDiGRA05.pdf.

Pearce, Fred. "Energy Hogs: Can World's Huge Data Centers Be Made More Efficient?" *Yale Environment 360*, April 3, 2018. https://e360.yale.edu/features/energy-hogs-ca n-huge-data-centers-be-made-more-efficient.

Pett, Emma. "'Stay Disconnected': Eventising *Star Wars* for Transmedia Audiences." *Participations* 13, no. 1 (2016): 152–69.

Phillips, Nelson, and Cynthia Hardy. "What Is Discourse Analysis?" In *Discourse Analysis*, edited by Nelson Phillips and Cynthia Hardy, 1–17. Thousand Oaks, CA: Sage, 2002.

Pilon, Mary. *The Monopolists: Obsession, Fury, and the Scandal Behind the World's Favorite Board Game*. New York: Bloomsbury, 2015.

Pitkin, Hanna. *The Concept of Representation*. Berkeley, CA: University of California Press, 1967.

Pobuda, Tanya. "Assessing Gender and Racial Representation in the Board Game Industry." *Analog Game Studies* 5, no. 4 (2018). http://analoggamestudies.org/2018/1 2/assessing-gender-and-racial-representation-in-top-rated-boardgamegeek-games/.

Postigo, Hector. "Of Mods and Modders Chasing Down the Value of Fan-Based Digital Game Modifications." *Games and Culture* 2, no. 4 (2007): 300–13.

Radway, Janice. *Reading the Romance*. North Carolina: The University of North Carolina Press, 1984.

Reinhard, Andrew. *Archaeogaming: An Introduction to Archaeology in and of Video Games*. New York: Berghahn, 2018.

Roberts, Siobhan. "She Invented a Board Game with Scientific Integrity. It's Taking Off." *New York Times*, March 11, 2019. https://www.nytimes.com/2019/03/11/science/wi ngspan-board-game-elizabeth-hargrave.html.

Robinson, Will. "Orientalism and Abstraction in Eurogames." *Analog Game Studies* 1, no. 5 (2014). http://analoggamestudies.org/2014/12/orientalism-and-abstraction-in-eurogames/.

Rountree, Clarke, and John Rountree. "Burke's Pentad as a Guide for Symbol-Using Citizens." *Studies in Philosophy and Education* 34, no. 4 (2015): 349–62.

Russell, Jeanne V. "Using Games to Teach Chemistry: An Annotated Bibliography." *Journal of Chemical Education* 76, no. 4 (1999): 481–8.

Ryan, Erin. "Gender Representation in Board Game Cover Art." *The Cardboard Republic*, June 29, 2016. https://www.cardboardrepublic.com/articles/extra-pieces/gender-representation-in-board-game-cover-art.

Sadkin, Lila. "*Wingspan* Is Important: A Different Kind of Review." *BeBold*, March 18, 2019. https://www.beboldgames.com/games/wingspan-is-important-a-different-ki nd-of-review.

Saleh, Amany, and Krishna Bista. "Examining Factors Impacting Online Survey Response Rates in Educational Research: Perceptions of Graduate Students." *Journal of MultiDisiplinary Evaluation* 13, no. 29 (2017): 63–74.

Salen, Katie, and Eric Zimmerman. *Rules of Play: Game Design Fundamentals*. Cambridge, MA: MIT Press, 2004.

Sapach, Sonja. "Let's Play with Research Methodologies." *First Person Scholar*, January 3, 2018. http://www.firstpersonscholar.com/lets-play-with-research-methodo logies/.

Sapsford, Roger. *Survey Research*. Thousand Oaks, CA: Sage, 2011.

Sarris, Andrew. "Notes on the Auteur Theory in 1962." *Film Culture* 27 (Winter 1962): 6–17. Reprinted in *Theories of Authorship*, edited by John Caughie, 61–5. London: Routledge, 2013.

Schatz, Thomas. "Film Industry Studies and Hollywood History." In *Media Industries: History, Theory, and Method*, edited by Jennifer Holt and Alisa Perren, 45–56. Malden, MA: Wiley-Blackwell, 2009.

Schensul, Jean J., and Margaret Diane LeCompte. *Essential Ethnographic Methods: A Mixed Methods Approach.* Lanham, MD: AltaMira, 2013.

Scott, Suzanne. *Fake Geek Girls.* New York, NY: New York University Press, 2019.

Selinker, Mike. "Trump's Tariffs Could Ruin the American Board Game Industry." *Polygon*, June 5, 2019. https://www.polygon.com/2019/6/5/18652411/trump-china-tariff-board-games.

Shaw, Adrienne. "Rethinking Game Studies: A Case Study Approach to Video Game Play and Identification." *Critical Studies in Media Communication* 30, no. 5 (2013): 347–61.

Shaw, Adrienne. "What Is Video Game Culture? Cultural Studies and Game Studies." *Games and Culture* 5, no. 4 (2010): 403–24.

Shimabukuro, Karra. "*Buffy the Vampire Slayer*: The Game as Liminal Space." *Intensities: The Journal of Cult Media* 7, no. 1 (2014): 74–83. https://intensitiescultmedia.files.wordpress.com/2014/08/7-shimabukuro-bufffy-board-game-pp-74-83.pdf.

Silverman, David. "Introducing Qualitative Research." In *Qualitative Research*, edited by David Silverman, 3–14. Thousand Oaks, CA: Sage, 2016.

Smith, William. "Does Gender Influence Online Survey Participation?: A Record-linkage Analysis of University Faculty Online Survey Response Behavior." *ERIC Document Reproduction Service* No. ED 501717. 2008. https://files.eric.ed.gov/fulltext/ED501717.pdf.

Spradley, James P. *The Ethnographic Interview.* Long Grove, IL: Waveland Press, 1979.

Stanfill, Mel. *Exploiting Fandom: How the Media Industry Seeks to Manipulate Fans.* Iowa City, IA: University of Iowa Press, 2019.

Stenros, Jaako, and Annika Waern. "Games as Activity: Correcting the Digital Fallacy." In *Videogame Studies: Concepts, Cultures and Communication*, edited by Monica Evans, 11–22. Oxford: Interdisciplinary Press, 2011.

Sundén, Jenny. "Desires at Play: On Closeness and Epistemological Uncertainty." *Games and Culture* 7, no. 2 (2012): 164–84.

Švelch, Jan. "Regarding Board Game Errata." *Analog Game Studies* 1, no. 5 (2014). http://analoggamestudies.org/2014/12/regarding-board-game-errata/.

Takahashi, Dean. "Brenda Romero's Train Board Game Will Make You Ponder." *Venture Beat*, May 11, 2013. https://venturebeat.com/2013/05/11/brenda-romero-train-board-game-holocaust/.

Thibault, Mattia. "Notes on the Narratological Approach to Board Game." *KOME – An International Journal of Pure Communication Inquiry* 4, no. 2 (2016): 74–81.

Tinsman, Brian. "Understanding the Tabletop Game Industry." Game Design Workshop, interview by Tracy Fullerton, 2018. https://www.gamedesignworkshop .com/understanding-the-tabletop-game-industry.

Torner, Evan. "Uncertainty in Analog Role-Playing Games, Part 1." *Analog Game Studies* 1, no. 1 (2014). http://analoggamestudies.org/2014/08/uncertainty-in-ana log-role-playing-games-part-1/.

Torner, Evan, Aaron Trammell, and Emma Waldron. "Reinventing Analog Game Studies." *Analog Game Studies* 1, no. 1 (2014). http://analoggamestudies.org/2014/0 8/reinventing-analog-game-studies/.

Trammell, Aaron. "Analog Games and the Digital Economy." *Analog Game Studies* 6, no. 1 (2019). http://analoggamestudies.org/2019/03/analog-games-and-the-digital-economy/.

Trammell, Aaron. "Representation and Discrimination in Role-Playing Games." In *Role-Playing Game Studies: Transmedia Foundations*, edited by Sebastian Deterding and José Zagal, 440–7. New York: Routledge, 2018.

Turkington, Moyra. "A Look Back from the Future: Play and Performance in Biosphere 2013." *Analog Game Studies* 2, no. 6 (2015). http://analoggamestudies.org/2015/0 9/a-look-back-from-the-future-play-and-performance-in-biosphere-2013/.

Van Dijk, Teun A. *Discourse and Communication: New Approaches to the Analysis of Mass Media Discourse and Communication*. Berlin: Walter de Gruyter, 1985.

Van Dijk, Teun A. "Principles of Critical Discourse Analysis." *Discourse and Society* 4, no. 2 (1993): 249–83.

Vatvani, Dinish. "An Analysis of Board Games: Part I - Introduction and General Trends." March 5, 2018. https://dvatvani.github.io/BGG-Analysis-Part-1.html#BGG -Analysis-Part-1.

Vatvani, Dinish. "An Analysis of Board Games: Part II - Complexity Bias in BGG." December 8, 2018. https://dvatvani.github.io/BGG-Analysis-Part-2.html#BGG -Analysis-Part-2.

Wall, Sarah. "An Autoethnography on Learning About Autoethnography." *International Journal of Qualitative Methods* 5, no. 2 (2006): 146–60.

Walton, Jonathan. "Governmentality and Freedom in *Pay Day* and *14 Days*." *Analog Game Studies* 5, no. 3 (2018). http://analoggamestudies.org/2018/09/governmentali ty-and-freedom-in-pay-day-and-14-days/.

Whalen, Tara. "Playing Well with Others: Applying Board Game Design to Tabletop Display Interfaces." In *ACM Symposium on User Interface Software and Technology*, vol. 5. New York: ACM Press, 2003.

Whitehill, Bruce. "American Games: A Historical Perspective." *International Journal for the Study of Board Games* 2 (1999): 116–44.

Williams, Sophie. Interview with author. Skype, 2019.

Wirman, Hanna. "On Productivity and Game Fandom." *Transformative Works and Cultures* 3 (2019). http://journal.transformativeworks.org/index.php/twc/article/ view/145/115.

Wolf, Mark J. P. *Building Imaginary Worlds: The History and Theory of Subcreation*. New York: Routledge, 2012.

Woo, Benjamin. *Getting a Life: The Social Worlds of Geek Culture*. Montreal: McGill-Queen's University Press, 2018.

Woods, Stewart. *Eurogames: The Design, Culture, and Play of Modern European Board Games*. Jefferson, NC: McFarland, 2012.

Wouters, Pieter, Herre van Oostendorp, Rudy Boonekamp, and Erik van der Spek. "The Role of Game Discourse Analysis and Curiosity in Creating Engaging and Effective Serious Games by Implementing a Back Story and Foreshadowing." *Interacting with Computers* 23, no. 4 (2011): 329–36.

Yee, Nick. "Solo Board Gamers: Who Are the 1%." *Quantric Foundry*, 2017. https://quanticfoundry.com/2017/07/12/solo-board-gamers/.

Zerofsky, Elisabeth. "Is Poland Retreating from Democracy?" *The New Yorker*, July 23, 2018. https://www.newyorker.com/magazine/2018/07/30/is-poland-retreating-from-democracy.

Index

Index of Games